GOOD PROGRAMMING PRACTICE
IN ADA

COMPUTER SCIENCE TEXTS

Good Programming Practice in Ada ®

PAUL A. LUKER

BSc, MSc, PhD

California State University, Chico

BLACKWELL SCIENTIFIC PUBLICATIONS

OXFORD LONDON EDINBURGH

BOSTON PALO ALTO MELBOURNE

© 1987 by
Blackwell Scientific Publications
Editorial offices:
Osney Mead, Oxford OX2 0EL
    (*Orders*: Tel. 0865 240201)
8 John Street, London WC1N 2ES
23 Ainslie Place, Edinburgh EH3 6AJ
52 Beacon Street, Boston
    Massachusetts 02108, USA
667 Lytton Avenue, Palo Alto
    California 94301, USA
107 Barry Street, Carlton
    Victoria 3053, Australia

First published 1987

Set by Setrite Typesetters Ltd
Hong Kong
Printed and bound
in Great Britain

Ada® is a registered trademark of the
US Government, Ada Joint Program Office

DISTRIBUTORS

USA and Canada
    Blackwell Scientific Publications Inc
    PO Box 50009, Palo Alto
    California 94303
    (*Orders*: Tel. (415) 965-4081)

Australia
    Blackwell Scientific Publications
    (Australia) Pty Ltd
    107 Barry Street
    Carlton, Victoria 3053
    (*Orders*: Tel. (03) 347-0300)

British Library
Cataloguing in Publication Data

Luker, Paul A.
    Good programming practice in Ada.
    —(Computer science texts).
    1. Ada (Computer program language)
    I. Title   II. Series
    005.13'3   QA76.73.A15

    ISBN 0−632−01746−5
    ISBN 0−632−01507−1

Library of Congress
Cataloging-in-Publication Data

Luker, Paul A.
    Good programming practice in Ada.

    (Computer science texts)
    1. Ada (Computer program
    language) I. Title.
    II. Series
    QA76.73.A35L85 1987   995.13'3
    87−13189
    ISBN 0−632−01746−5
    ISBN 0−632−01507−1 (pbk.)

DEDICATION

I dedicate this book to certain ladies of:

The past DORA ARABELLA

The present CHRISTINE

The future ELLEN, BETH AND ANNA

Contents

Preface

Ada is a large, relatively new high level programming language, which, for various reasons, will almost certainly be used extensively for some years to come. In writing this book, I have not assumed any specific background of the reader, although some previous programming experience is desirable. A number of references have been made to Pascal, not so much because a knowledge of Pascal is necessary but rather as a means of contrasting some of Ada's features with those of Pascal, for the benefit of Pascal programmers who might not otherwise appreciate the differences.

There are already many books about Ada, some on Ada programming in general and others on more specific subjects, such as tasking. My intention in writing this book was to provide a text that not only introduces most of the features of the language but also gives advice on how those features should (and should not) be used. The main criterion for assessing how to write programs is a rather elusive one, called style. Another factor which is often important (and equally elusive) is portability, i.e. what aspects of a program make it difficult to move from one system, on which it works correctly, to another. It is frustrating and annoying to find that programs cannot easily be transported. Style and portability considerations are discussed throughout the book. Whole books, such as [6], are devoted to these aspects of Ada programming.

Programming style is a very subjective issue. Nevertheless, there are certain habits that are widely recognized as good, while there are others which are generally regarded as bad. In assessing style, two terms consistently recur: readability and applicability. These attributes do not relate to any particular language, they belong to the discipline of programming methodology called software engineering, which had a profound influence on the design of Ada. Software engineering and the development of Ada form the basis of Chapter 1.

There are varying degrees of failure of the portability test. On the face of it, the least acceptable outcome is for a program to fail to compile on a new target system. This frequently occurs, owing to 'slight' differences in the language as it has been implemented on the different systems. With this outcome, however, you know exactly where you stand! In practice, it is far worse to have a program that *seems* to work in exactly the same way as it did before, but which, in fact does not, leaving you blissfully unaware of the actual situation. Ada has been carefully specified and control is exercised over implementations to prevent the spawning of dialects. Also, certain features of the language make any implementation dependent characteristics more obvious. This is not sufficient safeguard to guarantee portability, for as long as there are different machines with different hardware characteristics, there will be implementation dependence. Any such dependencies are highlighted throughout the book. So, if you are careful, it is possible to obtain a high degree of portability using Ada.

It is important to get an overall feel for the language before you rush into the details. Chapter 2 provides this overview. All program units in this book (identified as a Unit) have been compiled and run under one or more Ada compilers.

I have assumed that the material will be read in the given sequence, with each chapter relying on material introduced by its predecessors. Any exceptions to this treatment are mentioned in the text. Chapter 10 is one that you might consult from time to time, if your input and output requirements cannot be satisfied by what has already been introduced. Treat 10.3, in particular, as a reference section.

Chapter 11, despite its length, barely scratches the surface of tasking. It does, however, provide sufficient information to give a solid foundation for more specialized study.

In Chapter 12, I have attempted to put Ada in context, by (superficially) comparing it with some other languages and pointing out some of its strengths and weaknesses.

It is true of all programming languages that learning is achieved by using the language, rather than by just reading about it. Ada is no exception. In fact, because there is so much to it, it is essential that you become familiar with *using* the simpler features of the language before attempting to learn the more advanced ones. The practical work suggested at the end of most chapters is intended to be a guide to the type of assignment that will reinforce the learning process; I prefer this to a rigid set of exercises.

Another consequence of its size is that learning Ada is a time-consuming process. I have never known a programming language about which there is something new to learn each time I teach a course! The language is not without its faults, but I hope that you will learn to enjoy its many strengths and, in so doing, become an Ada programmer with excellent style.

Inevitably, many debts have been incurred during the writing of this book. I would like to acknowledge some of them.

First, a thank you goes to Alan Burns, a former colleague at the University of Bradford. Alan had been asked to write this book, while I had been asked to write one on another subject. By various twists of fate, with my emigration (a test of portability) as a catalyst, our roles reversed. Although the original plan for this book was based on course material that Alan had produced, the final product has evolved as a result of a number of Ada courses that I have taught in Britain and the United States. So, to all my students goes another thank you, for all their feedback.

Most of the examples in the book were developed (or adapted) for my courses at Chico and run using local facilities. However, some of the programs located 'features' of the (unvalidated) Ada compiler that we have on campus. Consequently, I am indebted to the Computer Science Department of the University of Calgary for their generosity in allowing me to use their facilities. In particular, I would like to thank Graham Birtwistle, another former colleague from Bradford, who is not a member of the Ada fan club, and Dave Mason, who allocates accounts and (large) disk quotas. Ralph Huntsinger, who, appropriately, holds a joint appointment at Chico and Calgary, made it possible to use the Calgary facilities from the discomfort of my own office.

Frank Wales, Ada consultant for The Instruction Set, has weeded out a number of errors and inconsistencies. Thanks Frank. I cannot thank the anonymous reviewer personally, however I would like to record my appreciation for the many perceptive comments and suggestions he or she made, helping this text to boldly go where no other has been. (I hope that's the last split infinitive!) Any remaining errors in this book are my own.

Dominic Vaughan of Blackwell Scientific Publications has been very helpful and extremely patient during the gestation period of this book.

I am grateful to the Ada Joint Programming Office for permission to reproduce the specification of the package STANDARD in Appendix B and listings of the pre-defined i/o packages.

My biggest debt, as always, is to those who suffered most during the writing of this book. Christine not only made it all possible, she proofread most of the material, and even managed to provide encouragement besides meeting the needs of a family. Ellie, Beth and Anna have also suffered at the hands of an absent, or absent-minded, or irascible father.

Chapter 1

Introduction

It is hard to believe that computer science is still a very young discipline, when we are so aware of the staggering technological progress that has been made over the last forty years. Today, we have computers that have tremendous processing power and yet are sufficiently small and cheap that they can be purchased for use in the home. Unfortunately, the developments that have taken place in hardware have not been matched by the software that is available. Consequently, our ability to utilize the hardware effectively is lacking in several respects — this phenomenon is known as the software crisis. Various aspects of this crisis have played an important role in the design and development of Ada.

1.1 The software crisis

In the early 1960s, when computing was becoming well established, the total cost of a computer system was dominated by the price of the hardware. However, a decade later, the cost of hardware has fallen significantly, while the complexity of the software required has increased. This software complexity translates directly into much higher costs for software development, to the extent that the software component of many computer systems has become more expensive than the hardware. Indeed, today, the cost of the hardware may be negligible compared to the expense of the software that is required to run on it.

Much of the software produced today is deficient for one reason or another. A large price tag is only one area of dissatisfaction. The worst indictment against software is that it often does not meet the user's requirements. Sometimes, this is the user's fault, for issuing an inadequate or ambiguous specification. More usually, though, it results from the programming task being more complex than originally perceived, with a concomitant propensity for the software to be delivered late. It may seem strange that experienced system analysts should continue to underestimate the time and resources required for a particular project, but it is a fact. Programmers at all levels frequently experience this for themselves (don't you?). Intuitively, we might not feel that a task is a complex one and yet its implementation could prove to be far from straightforward. This

1

reflects the wide gulf between the natural language with which we communicate in everyday life, together with the concepts in which we normally think and, on the other hand, the programming language with which we have to work. Software tools are still largely machine orientated rather than problem orientated.

Another problem with software is that it often fails. This may result from inadequate design or inadequate testing. Whatever the reason, the software should have some capacity for recovery. In an educational environment, if the operating system of the central computer deadlocks, this will cause little more than annoyance to the current users. Even so, an orderly recovery from the deadlock would not inconvenience users as much as a re-boot would. In the real world, however, things may be more critical. The pilot of a high performance aircraft, totally dependent on a flight control computer, does not want to be told that there is an error on line 1807 of the control program or that it has deadlocked. As a matter of routine, the program should be able to recognize and recover from errors without any need for human intervention.

Software maintenance is not the easiest of programming activities and it is made much more difficult and costly, owing to the nature of the software itself. Very frequently, the implementors of a system are retained to maintain it, as they are the only people who understand it. This is clearly unsatisfactory. The code should be sufficiently easy to understand that any competent programming team can maintain it.

One of the most sought after goals for software products is portability, which requires that software be transferred from one computer system to another without need for modification and with no differences in behaviour. This remains a goal which is far too elusive. It is clearly a waste of time, effort and money having to convert a program which runs on one machine, to run on another. The conversion process can also introduce errors into the code.

An important factor in addressing the problems associated with the software crisis is the implementation language. Even for very large problems, which are too complex for any single human brain to master, the total implementation can be made more successful if the language used enables these large problems to be developed as a number of more manageable, mutually consistent modules.

1.2 The programming language

The first high level language, FORTRAN, dates back to 1957, with ALGOL 58 (revised to become ALGOL 60) not far behind. ALGOL 60 is a language which has more of the attributes required for software development than FORTRAN. These characteristics include additional types, good control instructions and readability. Like FORTRAN, ALGOL 60 also has subprograms. Unfortunately, ALGOL remained a largely European and Scandinavian language, being totally dominated by FORTRAN in North America. During the 1960s, COBOL (1960) was introduced for commercial applications, and PL/1 (1965) was launched for both general purpose and commercial use.

By this time, ALGOL 60 had been found to be deficient in certain areas. In SIMULA 67, some of the features of ALGOL 60 were enhanced, others were cleaned up, and the **class** was added, to produce a language far superior to those which had gone before. Sadly, SIMULA has been widely misunderstood and misrepresented. It is a general purpose programming language which was, perhaps, launched ahead of its time. If SIMULA has not been a heavily used language, it has certainly influenced the design of more modern languages, including Ada and Smalltalk. See [8] for an interesting summary of the origins of the features of Ada.

Other developments on the ALGOL front included ALGOL W, from whose roots came Pascal. Intended as a language for teaching systematic programming, that is to say, the science of logically constructing (large) programs, Pascal has become widely used in universities and colleges for just that purpose. Niklaus Wirth deliberately kept Pascal a small language. Nevertheless, it has considerable expressive power and admirable qualities as a vehicle for software development. This has led to widespread interest in Pascal as a 'serious' programming language, for commercial software packages and general systems programs. It has also had considerable success in replacing BASIC on personal computers. BASIC, which was first released in 1967, has commanded widespread appeal owing to its highly interactive nature. Many Pascal systems for micro computers are also highly interactive, giving the user the advantage of interactive program development coupled with the better readability and security of Pascal. Pascal played an influential role in the design of Ada, as we shall see.

One common feature of all the languages cited is that they were designed for computers with a von Neumann architecture, where there is a single processor which sequentially executes instructions held in memory. Another common attribute is that all the above languages are procedural, as they require that programs explicitly state the sequence of instructions to be followed. Special purpose languages have been developed for other architectures and for different classes of problems. Some of these developments are very important and will be referred to in Chapter 12.

Ada could be viewed as a product of the evolution of ALGOL-based general purpose programming languages. Its designers have taken many of the good features of the earlier languages, extended or improved them, where necessary, and added other elements to produce a language, which is specifically intended to support software engineering.

1.3 A language for software engineering

Software engineering is a subject now firmly established in the computer science curriculum. It embraces several design techniques which provide a methodology for a disciplined approach to software design. This discipline must be continued during the implementation phase to ensure that the design criteria are not compromised. The implementation language must have characteristics which encourage and even enforce that discipline.

Before discussing the required attributes, consider the main goals that software engineering tries to achieve. It is a fact that large software systems usually have a considerably long life (at least ten years). However, few systems remain static throughout their existence, as the user's requirements may change, or the environment may change. The software will almost certainly change. In this light, the main goals are:

Readability. The code must be readable and relate to the real world problem, rather than its computer implementation. If the price of readability is less concise code, then it is a price worth paying.

Reliability. The software should not include errors of design or implementation. At the same time, however, it should be able to successfully handle any fault conditions from within its own working, or from its environment.

Maintainability. It should be possible to modify software, either to correct it or upgrade it, without undue effort and without side-effects.

Although not a primary goal, portability is a major concern in software development. It obviously makes sense to have software which may be easily transferred from one system to another in order to avoid costly redesign or extensive modification.

How can the programming language help? Some of the language characteristics necessary to make these goals attainable are now introduced. Each feature contributes to a lesser or greater extent to all of the above goals.

Data abstraction

This enables information to be treated at a level appropriate to the needs in question. At the highest level, we are only concerned with the logical description of the data, which should be readable and should relate to the problem. There might also be some lower level considerations, such as precisely how some data is mapped into memory. Take a collection of records as an example. At the higher level, we need only be concerned about the logical structure of each record to define the processing operations required. However, this high level processing may call routines to transfer records between memory and disk. At this level (and only this) the *implementation* details of the record are pertinent.

Information hiding

Any details which are only relevant to a particular part of a program should be hidden from all other parts. For example, we might want a routine to sort an array of integers. As a user, our only concern will be that we can call the required routine, specify the array of integers to be sorted and know how to access the corresponding sorted array of integers. The sorting mechanism itself is (usually) of no concern, and should therefore be hidden.

Modularity

This is the key to handling the development of complex software systems. It must be possible to represent each functional component of the system with a module, which has well-defined interfaces with other modules. By collecting related entities into one module, a coherent unit is created, which serves to localize the effects of any changes to those entities, especially when local information can be hidden.

Strong typing

By forcing all objects to be designated as being of a specific type, a language gives its translator the ability to weed out all inconsistent and incorrect usage. Many of the errors detected at compile-time might otherwise become obscure and infrequent errors at run-time, which makes the software unreliable and difficult to debug.

High level structure

A range of control structures should be provided to allow the natural, readable and concise expression of algorithms.

Error handling

It must be possible to trap all fault conditions within the software, without the software itself failing and exiting to the run-time system for a post mortem dump. This is just as desirable for a customer at a cash dispenser as it is for the pilot of the high performance aircraft, although the pilot may disagree.

Templates

If modules can be written in general terms, as templates for more specific units, this will avoid unnecessary duplication, as well as provide a consistent solution to some general problem.

Consistency

All language features should be consistent, to aid comprehension and learnability. It is also important that these features be *used* consistently. This is one of the reasons that consideration of style is an essential component of this book.

Language control

The only way that portability can be achieved is by having *one* language standard, which is monitored and maintained by a single body. This body should have the sole authority to approve implementations of the language.

1.4 The evolution of Ada

The story of Ada goes back to the early 1970s, when the US Department of Defense (DoD) became aware of the escalating costs of software for defence systems along with other manifestations of the software crisis. Over half these software costs arose in the area of embedded systems, in which the computer is an integral part of some larger system, such as a flight control system for an aircraft. Other, more peaceful examples of embedded systems are a controller of an industrial process, or a micro-processor controlling a domestic washing machine.

One of the main reasons for the very high cost of software for embedded systems was the number of implementation languages in use. It has been estimated that there were about 400 of them, both low and high level. An important consequence of this was that programmer training would inevitably be specific to a particular project. Also, there was much duplication of effort, owing to the extremely low portability of software and techniques.

In 1975, a working group was set up under the aegis of the DoD to identify the requirements for a high level language for the DoD, and to make recommendations regarding its implementation. A requirements document, STRAWMAN, was issued in April 1975, which, after evaluation of feedback, led to WOODENMAN in August of the same year. This, in turn, led to a complete set of requirements (TINMAN), which was released in 1976.

The requirements were quite varied and, not surprisingly, included characteristics necessary for programming embedded systems, such as concurrency, fault handling and low level specification capability. Twenty-three existing languages were evaluated against the TINMAN requirements, and none was found to be suitable. It was concluded that a single new language was both desirable and feasible. Three languages, Pascal, ALGOL 68 and PL/1, were identified as being appropriate as base languages.

Further minor revisions of the requirements were made to produce IRONMAN in 1977. Having established that considerable economic savings would be made if a new language were to be developed, the design of the language was put out to tender. From 17 responses, four were selected for further development. (It is interesting to note that all four were based on Pascal.) To avoid identification of the design teams during evaluation, the languages were given code names (Blue, Green, Red and Yellow). The first design phase was completed in early 1978 and, after further evaluation, Green and Red were selected for the next phase of the competition, to meet the final requirements specification, STEELMAN. This was completed by March 1979. Ada had been chosen as the name for the language, in honour of Ada Lovelace, regarded as the world's first programmer (of Charles Babbage's analytical engine of the 1840s). Despite this, the language name is often treated as an acronym, ADA. The Association for Computing Machinery is guilty of this error.

In May 1979, it was announced that 'Green is Ada'. The successful design team was an international consortium, largely European, led by

Jean Ichbiah from France. Testing and evaluation of Ada then began
in earnest. Thoughts were also turning to implementation control and
validation of Ada compilers. Refinements were made to the language,
and a draft ANSI standard was published in 1982. The standard itself
(incorporating further minor amendments) was approved in 1983, and
serves as the Language Reference Manual (LRM).

In 1980, the Ada Joint Program Office (AJPO) was established to
manage all matters relating to Ada. Dialects of the language are not
recognized, which is effectively enforced by Ada being registered as
a trademark of the DoD. AJPO also oversees the validation of Ada
compilers.

1.5 The language reference manual

The LRM [4] is the definitive document on the syntax and semantics of
Ada. It comprises some 250 pages and, as would be expected, does not
make light reading. As a reference work, it is not intended that it be read
like a book but consulted when required. There is a comprehensive index
and extensive cross-referencing. Any serious Ada programmer should
have the LRM close at hand. Like many manuals, the LRM is not always
easy to understand. Some of the descriptions are not particularly clear
and may have to be read several times, often in conjunction with cross-
referenced passages. The LRM is, nonetheless, the ultimate arbiter, so
learn your way around it as soon as you can.

Throughout this book, references to the (major) relevant sections of
the LRM are given, wherever appropriate, as new features are introduced.

1.6 Applications of Ada

Ada is a general purpose language, which includes features for programming embedded systems. Owing to the strong influence of software
engineering practice on the design of the language, Ada is particularly
suitable for the development of large software systems.

Ada is used for the implementation of embedded systems, and not
just those in the military environment. The concurrency and low level
features make it suitable as a systems language, for operating systems, for
example. However, where speed is important, Ada may not be suitable
for these applications, as will be explained at the appropriate time.

Compilers and software tools, such as an interactive dialogue development system can be implemented and maintained more easily in Ada

than in other languages. Ada is equally suited to data processing applications, such as financial packages, and scientific applications, such as providing a library of numerical analysis routines or providing a system for the simulation of queuing systems.

An interesting use of Ada is as a software design language. The original functional specification of a product can be written in Ada. This can be extended into a prototype of the eventual implementation, the behaviour of which is essentially simulated, using the concurrency of Ada to represent the concurrency in the actual problem. If the implementation language is itself Ada, then the final step, the implementation, is straightforward.

Chapter 2

Overview of the language

In view of the many functional requirements that had to be met by the language designers, it is not surprising that Ada is a large language compared with some of its antecedents. Consequently, it will take longer to learn Ada thoroughly than it would Pascal. As with all things, learning is best achieved by gaining plenty of first hand experience. You cannot possibly hope to learn and understand all the features of Ada in a crash course. It will take time.

This book introduces many of the simpler (Pascal-like) features of Ada before going on to the more specialized facets, such as packages and tasks. Tasking is very complex and is a subject in its own right, which cannot be adequately covered in a book of this nature. The package, however, is the most important construct in Ada. The ability to use packages correctly is the hallmark of a good Ada programmer. So, as soon as you can, think in terms of packages and don't constrain your perspective to that of any other language. Think in Ada.

This chapter is intended to impart an impression of the language as a whole, before its elements are studied in more detail. It is only necessary at this stage to get a feel for the more advanced features. All will be revealed in good time. In this chapter, references to the LRM are only given for features that are not specifically discussed in detail in later chapters.

2.1 Elements of Ada Programs

Unit 2.1 shows a simple but complete Ada program, although, as you will notice, it does not produce any output! Input and output will be introduced a little later, after the program has been explained.

```
procedure MAIN is
  -- Adds two numbers together
  FIRST, SECOND, RESULT:INTEGER;
begin
  FIRST:=1;
  SECOND:=2;
  RESULT:=FIRST + SECOND;
end MAIN;
```

Unit 2.1   The first program.

10

The main program [LRM 10.1]

Perhaps the first thing that you will notice is the fact that the program begins with the word **procedure** and not **program**. In Ada, the main program is written as a parameterless procedure, which does not have to be called explicitly, as it is automatically executed by the run-time system. Here, the identifier MAIN has been used for the procedure. Some implementations recognize this as indicating the main program in a multiple compilation (to which we will return in a later chapter).

Statement termination

Each statement in an Ada program is *terminated* by a semicolon. This differs from ALGOL and Pascal, where the semicolon is used as a statement separator, which can, unfortunately, lead to confusion.

Lexical conventions [LRM 2.1, 2.2, 2.10]

Ada uses the ASCII character set, which includes both upper and lower case letters. Older terminals (such as teletypes) do not support such a rich character set, therefore any Ada program may be expressed using a basic character set comprising the upper case letters, digits, space and nineteen 'special characters'. One consequence of this is that no distinction is made between upper and lower case letters in an Ada program, unless they are character literals or part of a string literal.

The full character set should be used wherever possible. It is usual to distinguish between reserved words and identifiers, in order to enhance readability. There are several conventions which are used. The most important consideration is to be consistent in the application of whichever convention you (or your employer) decide upon. Throughout this book, the reserved words are presented in lower case, while all identifiers, whether pre-defined or user-defined, appear in upper case. It is possible to make further distinctions. For example, some programmers like to differentiate between global and local identifiers. In Ada, other means should be used to make the program clear.

The space and new line are separators between the lexical units of an Ada program. Multiple spaces and new lines may be used where desired, in order to enhance readability. The tab is also treated as a separator but should be avoided, as it may have different effects on different implementations. As most displays support a line of 80 characters, this should be regarded as the maximum length of a program line.

Only one statement or declaration should appear on a line. Violation of this rule has a more detrimental effect on program legibility than is commonly realized. (Any teacher of programming, who has to read and understand many students' programs, will verify this.) The importance of a clear program layout should be self-evident. There is no specific layout imposed on the Ada programmer, but blank lines and indentation should be used to highlight the program structure. Indentation should always be applied in multiples of some fixed constant (I always use two). Again, whichever format you choose, apply it consistently.

Three characters that have a special meaning in Ada may be replaced by an alternative. This may be important where there might be local character set differences, or where a peripheral device does not support the special character. Different national implementations of the ISO code are permitted to provide different symbols for '#'. This is, in fact, one of the symbols that may be replaced in Ada; a colon may be used instead. (Also, '!' may be used for the vertical bar '|', and '%' may be used for quotation '"'.)

Reserved words [LRM 2.9]

In common with other languages, Ada has a number of reserved words, which cannot be used for any purpose other than that defined by the language. (A few reserved words may have different meanings in different contexts — not always a commendable feature — and three are also used as identifiers for pre-defined attributes.) In the program of Unit 2.1, there were four reserved words: **procedure**, **is**, **begin**, **end**. For reasons already explained, the last of these *could* have been written as:

> end END End EnD ENd enD eND eNd

All of these are lexically equivalent, but few are desirable.

Identifiers [LRM 2.3]

Identifiers should always be meaningful in the context of the problem domain. In Ada, identifiers must begin with a letter, which may be followed by any number of letters, digits or underscores. Underscores are only permitted between letters and/or digits. In other words, they cannot be used to terminate an identifier, nor can two underscores be adjacent. No restriction is imposed on the length of identifiers, although the maximum advisable line length of characters should be the absolute limit. Remember that upper and lower case letters are equivalent in identifiers.

The main consideration with identifiers is that they should convey sufficient meaning without leading to confusion. Distinct identifiers should not differ by only one character, and certainly not by the presence or absence of underscores. This is bound to confuse the programmer as well as the program reader. It is always helpful to have identifiers with pronounceable names. Do not invent acronyms, however clever. In time, which may be a very short period, the meaning is lost or becomes blurred.

Strong typing

Ada enforces the philosophy of strong typing, by making operations specific to a particular type and preventing the assignment of values inappropriate to the type of an object. Many breaches of the typing rules will be reported at compile-time, a very useful and desirable aid to program development. Violations at run-time will be detected and can be handled within the program, if required, otherwise program execution will fail.

Comments [LRM 2.7]

Comments are introduced by two adjacent hyphens and continue to the end of the line on which they occur. They have no effect on program compilation or execution, being provided solely to aid program understanding. As with all programming languages, comments should be used judiciously, conveying the required additional meaning without being too verbose or misleading. Comments should not state the obvious. Consider the following:

```
BUFF_MAX:=80;      -- sets BUFF_MAX to 80
BUFF_MAX:=80;      -- initializes buffer size
```

The second of these is preferable for obvious reasons.

The use of comments should not obscure the structure and layout of the code. Comments should be aligned and not extend to the left of the current level of indentation.

2.2 Input/Output

It may come as a surprise to learn that the Ada language does not itself include any facilities for input and output. Instead, input/output (i/o) is realized via pre-defined packages. The rationale behind this is clear; i/o operations are implementation dependent and, as such, should not form part of a language for which portability is a concern. This is one reason why the package is so important; it enables the facilities offered by the raw language to be enhanced, while enabling implementation dependences to be separated from the language itself.

The pre-defined standard package TEXT_IO must be available in all implementations of Ada. The LRM specifies exactly the facilities that the package must provide. TEXT_IO is used for all human readable (i.e. character based) i/o and is therefore used for all i/o other than file processing and special purpose applications. Briefly, TEXT_IO provides GET and PUT procedures for input and output respectively, of characters and character strings. Unit 2.2. is a complete Ada program, which illustrates the use of some of the facilities provided by TEXT_IO.

```
with TEXT_IO;      -- for the compiler
use  TEXT_IO;      -- for shorthand reference

procedure MAIN is
  ANSWER:CHARACTER;
begin
  PUT("Type any character: ");   -- output procedure
  GET(ANSWER);                   -- input procedure
  NEW_LINE;                      -- gives a new line
  PUT("You typed: ");            -- strings are quoted
  PUT(ANSWER);
  NEW_LINE;                      -- gives a new line
end MAIN;
```

Unit 2.2 A program with input and output.

Because the program depends on the things defined in the TEXT_IO package, it is necessary to convey this information to the compiler. This is the purpose of the with statement at the head of the program. The use statement allows the programmer to be lazy, by removing the need to prefix all the names of TEXT_IO procedures by the package name. So PUT in the above example is used as an abbreviation for TEXT_IO.PUT.

Note that the same procedure name, PUT, is used for the input of characters *and* strings. This is an example of *overloading*, a process which allows more than one subprogram (procedure or function) to have the same name, as long as the context of use enables the correct subprogram to be applied. In this example, a call of PUT with a CHARACTER parameter, will cause the PUT for CHARACTER to be called. Overloading is an important feature of Ada (which does not only apply to subprograms).

Each PUT and GET may only be used for i/o of *one* value of a particular type. It is not possible, using TEXT_IO, to output a line comprising, say, a string and a character with only one call of PUT. Two separate calls are required (to two different procedures).

TEXT_IO does *not* provide procedures for i/o of any other type. Instead, it provides templates (called generics) from which the relevant procedures can be created. When programming in Ada, many programs will require the input and/or output of numeric data. Rather than having to create the required i/o facilities in every program, it is better to assume their provision by some other package. In this book, the existence of a package called SIMPLE_IO will be assumed. (*Note.* This will not be provided by your Ada system, although you may find something similar. If you want to use SIMPLE_IO, you will have to type it in from the listing given in Chapter 10.) SIMPLE_IO provides GET and PUT procedures for the types: BOOLEAN, CHARACTER, FLOAT, INTEGER and STRING. For many programs, SIMPLE_IO will satisfy most of your needs, and there is no need to use TEXT_IO. The use of SIMPLE_IO is similar to the use of TEXT_IO.

Unit 2.3 incorporates i/o into Unit 2.1, using SIMPLE_IO. A GET procedure for integers will expect to find an integer literal (with no decimal point), terminated by a blank or line terminator.

```
with SIMPLE_IO;  -- a non-standard package
use  SIMPLE_IO;

procedure MAIN is
   FIRST, SECOND:INTEGER;
begin
   PUT("Type 2 integers: ");
   GET(FIRST);
   GET(SECOND);
   NEW_LINE;
   PUT("Their sum is : ");
   PUT(FIRST + SECOND);
   NEW_LINE;
end MAIN;
```

Unit 2.3 Modified Unit 2.1 with output.

To understand exactly how TEXT_IO works, relies on a knowledge of more advanced features of Ada, hence the delay of a detailed treatment of i/o until Chapter 10. However, you will find many of the facilities of TEXT_IO quite useful to you in programs you write before that chapter is reached. So, dip into Chapter 10 as and when you need to, for an explanation of what TEXT_IO provides. More specialized i/o, such as file i/o, will also be discussed in Chapter 10.

2.3 Exceptions

Ada has a number of pre-defined *exceptions*, error indications which may be *raised* during the execution of Ada programs. The programmer can also define further exceptions for some specific purpose. For example, if an attempt is made to assign a value, which is outside the valid range associated with the recipient variable, the pre-defined exception CONSTRAINT_ERROR will automatically be raised.

Exceptions provide the programmer with an opportunity to make the program take some remedial action, if some error occurs at run-time. This is an important requirement for robust software. If an exception is raised that is not handled, then program execution will terminate (as would happen with *any* run-time error in Pascal).

2.4 Blocks

One important legacy of Ada's ancestry is its block structure. The block structure of Ada reflects the more general approach to blocks of ALGOL 60, rather than the more restricted view of Pascal, in which only the main program and subprograms are regarded as blocks. Therefore, in Ada, any sequence of statements may contain a block. Blocks support the concepts of localization and internal modularity, by providing a means for grouping related entities within a module and associating declarations and error handling locally within that module.

The structure of a block is:

```
declare
        -- declaration part, if any
begin
        -- sequence of statements
exception
        -- exception handler(s), if any
end;
```

The declaration part is optional. When present, this section defines identifiers which only exist throughout the life time of the block. The exception handler, which is used for handling exceptions raised during execution of the *sequence of statements* of the block, is also optional. Blocks with neither declarations nor exception handlers are not of much use. It is possible to name blocks, as we shall see. This does allow blocks to be used to provide named sections of code; however, for many such uses, subprograms are more appropriate.

Unit 2.4 illustrates the use of a block. Note the initialization of

TEMP at its declaration at the top of the block. When declarations are encountered during program execution, these declarations are said to be *elaborated*. Upon elaboration, memory for variables is allocated, and any initializations are performed.

```
with SIMPLE_IO;   -- a non-standard package
use  SIMPLE_IO;

procedure SWITCH is
  FIRST, SECOND:INTEGER;
begin
  PUT("Type two integers: ");
  GET(FIRST);
  GET(SECOND);
  declare                 -- a block
    TEMP:INTEGER:=FIRST;  -- an intialised local
  begin                   -- execution of the block
    FIRST:=SECOND;
    SECOND:=TEMP;
  end;
  NEW_LINE;
  PUT("Integers reversed: ");
  PUT(FIRST);
  PUT(SECOND);
  NEW_LINE;
end SWITCH;
```

Unit 2.4 Example of a block.

2.5 Program units

In addition to blocks, there are four other, more important, constructs for providing modularity in Ada. Collectively, they are called program units, as they form the major components from which programs are constructed. Blocks, on the other hand, must be contained within some program unit. Each of the program units is introduced in turn.

Subprograms

The term 'subprogram' is used extensively in the LRM to mean both procedures and functions. Structurally, the two are very similar, comprising a heading, followed by a declaration part (optional), then a statement part, which may include an exception handler. In outline, then, subprograms have the structure:

```
-- subprogram heading
        -- declaration part, if any
begin
        -- sequence of statements
exception
        -- exception handler(s), if any
end;
```

Note the similarity with the structure of blocks. Unlike blocks, however, subprograms are only executed when called during program execution. Procedures are called via a procedure statement, while functions are called from expressions to which the function returns a single value. Functions may return a value of any type, which includes structured types. The value returned by a function is specified in a return statement with the function body. All subprograms may have parameters. A small program, which contains a procedure and a function is shown in Unit 2.5.

```
with SIMPLE_IO;   -- a non-standard package
use  SIMPLE_IO;

procedure MAIN is
  NUMBER:INTEGER;

  procedure PUT(MESS:in STRING; NUM:in INTEGER) is
    -- no local declarations
  begin
    NEW_LINE;
    PUT(MESS);
    PUT(NUM);
    NEW_LINE;
  end PUT;

  function FOURTH(N:in INTEGER) return INTEGER is
    SQUARE:INTEGER:=N * N;     -- expressions allowed here
  begin
    return SQUARE * SQUARE;    -- value to be returned
  exception
    when NUMERIC_ERROR =>      -- if number too large
      PUT("Number too large.");
      return INTEGER'LAST;     -- the largest positive integer
  end FOURTH;

begin       -- MAIN
  PUT("Type integer: ");
  GET(NUMBER);
  PUT("Number       : ",NUMBER);-- calls the PUT above
  PUT("Fourth power: ",FOURTH(NUMBER));
end MAIN;
```

Unit 2.5 Example of subprograms.

The procedure, PUT, has no local declarations, consisting only of a statement part, which, in turn, calls three procedures defined in SIMPLE_IO. Note that this procedure further overloads PUT, by adding another meaning. The function has a local variable, SQUARE, which is initialized to the square of the value of the function argument, N. Note that expressions involving variables may be used in declaration initializations. These expressions are evaluated at *run-time*, when the relevant declarative part is elaborated; in this case, that will be at each call of the function. If, during a call to this function, the result becomes too large to be represented, the exception handler provided will trap the error, print a warning message and return the largest INTEGER value on the particular implementation to the point of call. (This exception handler will not trap a similar error invoked when initializing SQUARE; the reason for this will be explained in 5.8.)

Packages

The package is the main building block for constructing Ada programs. A package is, generally, a collection of related items, which forms a self-contained unit. Packages have already been used in all but one of the program examples presented so far. TEXT_IO is just one of a number of standard packages available in Ada. Using the facilities provided by TEXT_IO, it was possible to produce our very own, custom built, package, SIMPLE_IO. Now is not the time, however, to look at SIMPLE_IO as an example of a package; a simpler example will be used to illustrate the main points.

A package comprises two parts, a specification and a body. The specification is the interface between the package and its users. It contains a list of those features, such as types and subprograms, that are accessible from outside. The package body may include declarations, which are hidden from the view of package users. Any actions, such as subprogram bodies, are also contained within the package body. If there are no actions, then the package need not have a body, as will be illustrated in Chapter 7.

```
package HIDDEN_INTEGER is          -- specification
   procedure INCREMENT;
   function FIND return NATURAL;
      -- NATURAL is a pre-defined subtype for non-negative integers
end HIDDEN_INTEGER;

package body HIDDEN_INTEGER is
   COUNT:NATURAL;                  -- hidden from view

   procedure INCREMENT is
   begin
     COUNT:=COUNT + 1;
   end INCREMENT;

   function FIND return NATURAL is
   begin
     return COUNT;
   end FIND;

begin                              -- package body statements
   COUNT:=0;                       -- obeyed once on elaboration
end HIDDEN_INTEGER;
```

Unit 2.6   Example of a package.

Most elements of the structure of a package are illustrated in the example of Unit 2.6. The package has a variable, COUNT, which is hidden from view, being accessible only from within the package body. The package specification states that two subprograms are visible and therefore callable by package users. The bodies of the subprograms are within the package body, so they may access COUNT. So, while direct access to COUNT is denied package users, they are allowed to INCREMENT and FIND the value of COUNT via subprogram calls.

Tasks

The task is the program unit that allows concurrent programs to be constructed. A concurrent program is one in which there is more than one thread of control, so that two or more elements are *apparently* executing simultaneously. Of course, if there is only one processor, the concurrency will remain apparent, rather than be real. Even on a single processor system, there are many applications, particularly in embedded systems, where it is necessary to express concurrency. Typically, there will be a number of modules, each of which has a distinct function to perform. Each such module (a *task* in Ada) will lead an independent existence; independent, that is, until there is a need for tasks to synchronize or communicate with each other. Ada provides the means of defining, executing, controlling and synchronizing tasks. The example provided here is only a sketch, to give an idea of the structure and use of tasks.

Assume that we have a number of tasks, each of which, at some point in its life cycle, requires the use of some resource which cannot be simultaneously shared by any other task. Access to the resource may be controlled by a single task which has no other purpose. Code for such a resource controller task is given below.

```
-- A resource controller task.

task CONTROLLER is
   entry ACQUIRE;
   entry RELEASE;
end CONTROLLER;

task body CONTROLLER is
begin
   loop
      accept ACQUIRE;
      accept RELEASE;
   end loop;
end CONTROLLER;
```

Any task wishing to use the resource would have to follow the protocol:

```
-- previous actions
CONTROLLER.ACQUIRE;
-- This task now has mutually exclusive
-- access to the unshareable resource.
CONTROLLER.RELEASE;
-- remaining actions
```

Like packages, tasks have a specification and body. The specification defines the *entries* which may be called by other tasks that wish to synchronize or, in Ada parlance, *rendezvous* with the owner. The called task is able to control when and how it accedes to requests for rendezvous. CONTROLLER will only accept a call of ACQUIRE if the resource is available. Any unsuccessful caller of ACQUIRE will wait in a queue. On allocating the resource, the CONTROLLER will wait until the user signals its relinquishing of the resource by calling RELEASE.

The similarity between packages and tasks ends with their syntactic structure. Packages are passive objects, which cannot control the *way* in which they are used. Tasks, on the other hand, are active and can exercise dynamic control.

Generics

Subprograms and packages may be made *generic*, which transforms them into templates for constructing actual subprograms and packages (res-pectively). In structure, they are similar to the subprograms and packages already illustrated. An example will not be given here. It is sufficient to introduce the idea of generics.

Consider the block used to exchange two integers in Unit 2.4. That could easily be made into a procedure for interchanging the values of two integers. Owing to the strong typing of Ada, it would not be possible to use this procedure on any type other than INTEGER, although the sequence of actions only involves assignment, which is not an operation unique to the INTEGER type. By making the procedure a generic, it is then possible to create procedures for interchanging values of (just about) any type; one procedure would be required for each type to be interchanged.

2.6 Separate compilation

The desirability of being able to develop large programs using a collection of small, coherent, well-tested modules, was mentioned in Chapter 1. Ada encourages programs to be developed in this way by offering separate

compilation. Once a module has been compiled, it does not have to be re-
compiled unless it, or another module on which it depends, is changed. In
the examples we have seen so far, SIMPLE_IO would be compiled once
only. Any changes to SIMPLE_IO itself would obviously necessitate its
re-compilation and, in this event, all programs that use the package
would also have to be re-compiled before execution.

The modules that may be compiled separately are called *compilation
units*, which are not the same as program units! Briefly, compilation units
include subprograms, packages and generics, or certain parts of them. It
is possible, for example, to separately compile package specifications and
bodies. Consequently, top-down design is easily achievable at the implementation level in Ada.

2.7 Pragmas [LRM 2.8, Annex B]

Pragmas provide a means of conveying information to the compiler.
There are fourteen pragmas defined in the LRM, all of which must be
supported by Ada implementations, but this support should not be taken
to imply that the pragmas will have any effect other than just being
recognized. In addition, implementations may provide other pragmas, but
the use of these should be avoided, as they impair portability.

The nature of pragmas is wide-ranging; they may simply control compilation listing or may relate to various aspects of memory management
and control. By the very nature of most pragmas, their effects are governed
by the characteristics of the implementation, which includes hardware
aspects. Consequently, it should always be remembered that the language-
defined pragmas may have different effects (which includes no effect!) on
different implementations.

If pragmas are used, their presence should be made obvious, at the
beginning of a declarative section, unless the pragma has to be placed
more specifically. Comments should be used to make the purpose of the
pragma obvious. Care must be taken to position and name pragmas
correctly, otherwise they may be ignored (possibly without a murmur
from the compiler).

Some of the pragmas will be mentioned in later chapters, when they
are relevant to the topic under discussion. This section concludes with
some examples of pragmas, taken out of context. For their full meanings,
consult the LRM.

```
pragma LIST(ON);          -- switches compilation listing on
pragma LIST(OFF);         -- switches it off
pragma OPTIMIZE(SPACE);   -- denotes that memory is the main
                          -- optimizing criterion in the block
                          -- for an optimizing compiler.
                          -- TIME is the alternative to SPACE.
```

2.8 Getting started on your system

However standard a language, the interface with its compiler and other software utilities varies from system to system. This book cannot tell you how to access and use the Ada compiler on your system. Nevertheless, a few general guidelines may be useful.

First, it helps if you know the operating system and its utilities. It doesn't assist the language learning process if you are struggling to master the system editor.

Once you have surmounted local difficulties, either find the documentation on your local Ada system or, better still, locate the resident expert. Each implementation will have its own version of the LRM, with any implementation specific features highlighted. Ignore that for now. You need to know how to use the system.

Discover what the file naming conventions are; in particular, find out if a filename extension is required for Ada source programs. When you use an Ada system for the first time, you will need to create a library for all your compiled units. This will also establish links to the pre-defined package library.

The processes of compilation, linking, loading and execution will normally be separate. If you have a program that begins:

```
procedure MAIN is....
```

in source file "myprog.a", then a typical sequence might be:

```
ada_compile myprog.a
ada_load MAIN
run MAIN
```

Note that the name of the unit (here it is MAIN) is used for specifying the unit to be loaded and executed.

It is always worth finding out if there is a source-orientated debugger with the system. Such utilities can be very useful. If you are using an optimizing compiler, you should decline the optimization with the appropriate flag or parameter to the compiler. Object code that does not correspond to the source code can be disheartening to the beginner.

Also track down the information on the packages that are provided by the system (in addition to the mandatory ones like TEXT_IO) and find out what they do. They may be very useful. As has already been mentioned, if no equivalent of SIMPLE_IO is available, you might like to type it in yourself, not forgetting to compile it (before any compilation units that need to use it!).

Don't be too surprised if you discover the occasional feature (a euphemism for bug) in your compiler. The validation of a compiler does not guarantee perfection.

Practising Ada 2

Your aim should be to familiarize yourself with the use of your local Ada system. The following suggestions are a guide.
1 Find out how to access and use Ada on your system, using section 2.8 as a guide.
2 Type in Unit 2.2, compile it and run it on your system.
3 See if there is an equivalent of SIMPLE_IO on your system. If not, type it in from the listing of Unit 10.3. Compile the package into your library (but don't attempt to run it!).
4 After you have compiled SIMPLE_IO, type in Unit 2.3 (or modify the unit to use a local i/o package), compile it and run it.
5 Assess each of the following identifiers for syntactic and stylistic acceptability:
   (i) TRNSDC
  (ii) P_R_G
 (iii) social_security_number
 (iv) PROCEDURE
  (v) INCOME_tax
 (vi) INPUT_FILE_
 (vii) A_1
(viii) ROLL_RATE_GYRO_LANE_1
 (ix) INTEGER1

  (x) 1_LANE_AILERON
 (xi) rrgl1
(xii) cum_en_cons

Chapter 3

Declarations, scalar types and operations

In a strongly typed language, each type has its own set of values and an associated set of operations that may be applied. Ada provides a number of pre-defined types, as well as the means for creating new types. For all types, *objects*, which may be *variables* or *constants*, can (and must) be declared. The values of variables may be changed during program execution, whereas the value of a constant is fixed. There are several classes of type in Ada. The subject of this chapter is the class of scalar types, objects of which have a single value [LRM 3.5].

There are five pre-defined scalar types: characters, Boolean and three numeric types. A porgrammer may also define an *enumeration type* by listing the set of values that it can take. From all of these types, it is possible to create *subtypes*, the values for which form a contiguous subrange of the values of the *base* or parent type. Ada also allows new types to be *derived* from existing types. Derived types will be discussed in detail in Chapter 8; suffice it to say now that they inherit the values and operations of the original type but are nevertheless distinct types.

The three numeric types in Ada are the integer and two forms of real numbers. In addition to floating point numbers, the most common real number representation in general purpose programming languages, Ada supports fixed point real numbers. All numeric types are implementation dependent. Consideration of portability will be given as the types are discussed in detail.

Those scalar types which possess an ordered succession of values are called *discrete types*. Discrete types, which include all scalar types except real numbers of either form, may be used in certain contexts from which all other types (including reals) are excluded.

Implicit type conversions only occur in a few special cases in Ada, which is as it should be in a strongly typed language. If you really want to convert a value of one type to a value of another type, then you have to state the conversion explicitly, so that the compiler does not accuse you of being inconsistent.

Before looking at the scalar types in detail, it is necessary to consider some general aspects of declarations in Ada.

3.1 Declarations [LRM 3.1, 3.2, 3.3, 3.9]

Declaration Order

Ada does not impose a fixed declaration sequence for types and objects (variables and constants). This provides much greater flexibility, allowing, for example, constants to be defined for a type introduced earlier in the same declarative part. This is not possible in Pascal. There are many examples of this flexibility in this chapter (and those that follow). The major constraint on the order of declarations is that an item must be declared before it is used. (There is a further rule regarding the order in declaration sequence that contain the bodies of program units; this will be covered at the appropriate time.)

Elaboration of declarations

Declarations must be made in some declarative part. As you would expect, the compiler makes full use of this declarative part during the compilation process. However, in Ada, the declarative part may have some significance during program execution. At some time during the execution of a program, a declarative part will be *elaborated*. This means that the items in the declaration are brought into effect in the sequence in which they are declared. This process may involve some computation, validity checking and assignment, as we shall see. For simple programs with only one program unit, the declarative part will be elaborated once only, immediately before execution of the program statements.

Object declarations

An object declaration associates one or more identifiers with a particular type, and may be used to initialize the objects that the identifiers represent. A multiple declaration such as:

      A, B:INTEGER;

is equivalent to the sequence:

      A:INTEGER;
      B:INTEGER;

Variables are not normally initialized automatically in Ada, therefore initialization must be explicitly performed before use. This can be done during elaboration of the declaration, if the initial value is specified as part of the declaration as in

> A, B:INTEGER:=0;

which initializes both A and B to zero. Initialization on declaration should *always* be done, where it is not easy to show that a variable is otherwise initialized before use. If the initial value is known at the point of declaration, then it is more concise, and more *readable* to incorporate the initialization into the declaration. Some practitioners advocate initializing variables as late as possible, for safety. However, with good modularization, initialization on declaration does not necessarily conflict with this advice. Initialization values can, in fact, be expressions, as we shall see.

Declarations may include a *constraint*, which restricts the range of values that an object may take, as in:

> SMALL:INTEGER range −128..127;

Here, SMALL is of type INTEGER, but any attempt to assign a value to it which is outside the specified range will cause the pre-defined exception CONSTRAINT_ERROR to be raised. Further examples of constraints will be given as each type is introduced.

Until now, all the examples have illustrated the declaration of *variable* objects. Objects of almost any type in Ada may be declared as *constant* objects, which are initialized to some value that cannot subsequently be changed. The syntax for constant declarations is the same as that for variable declarations, with the reserved word **constant** preceding the type identifier. There must, of course, be an assignment of a value to a constant. Consider the following constant and variable declarations in the given sequence.

> PLAYER_LIMIT:constant INTEGER:=4;
> MINIMUM:constant INTEGER:=0;
> VARIABLE:INTEGER:=10;
> INIT_VAR:constant INTEGER:=VARIABLE;
> ANOTHER_VARIABLE:INTEGER:=MINIMUM;

VARIABLE is, indeed, a variable, which is initialized to ten, whereas INIT_VAR is a constant, which has the same value as that to which VARIABLE has been initialized. The value of VARIABLE may be altered during program execution, but INIT_VAR will keep the value ten throughout its existence. The final declaration shows the use of a constant, the declaration of which has already been elaborated. The value of the constant is assigned as the initial value of the variable ANOTHER _VARIABLE. This small example illustrates that declarations are ela- borated in the given sequence, analogously to the execution of program statements.

Constants should be used wherever possible as they provide an addi- tional safety factor — they cannot be altered — and they help software maintainability. They should not be used simply as synonyms for literal values. So, don't bother with:

    ZERO:constant INTEGER:=0;
    VARIABLE:INTEGER:=ZERO;

The literal 0 is perfectly understandable (and constant).

3.2 Type INTEGER

Integer literals [LRM 2.4]

Decimal integer literals may contain decimal digits, underscores and an optional exponent. Underscores should be used to make long integer literals more readable; they have no effect on the value of the integer. An underscore can only be used between two digits. Do not use commas in your numeric literals. Integer literals may have a *non-negative integer* exponent (which includes zero). A decimal integer literal must, therefore, begin and end with a decimal digit. The following are all decimal integer literals:

               123
                 0
           123_456
        12_345_678
               1E6 -- one million
              15E0 -- fifteen
          12_345e3 -- either case for exponent
                   -- but be consistent

Integer literals may be expressed in any base up to sixteen (hexadecimal). However, a base other than ten should only be used if it is appropriate to the problem. For bases higher than ten, the letters A through F are used for the digits corresponding to the decimal numbers 10 through 15 respectively. It is good practice to comment the use of based literals, so that the meaning is clear. The syntax for forming based literals is illustrated in the examples which follow. The base must come first. The decimal value of each literal is given as a comment. With based literals, it is usual to group them in fours, with underscores between, as in the first literal. The exponent of a based literal is a decimal number which represents the power of the base to which the literal is raised.

```
2#1111_1111# -- 255
   16#00FF# -- 255
  2#1111#E1 -- 30      (15 * 2)
   16#1#E2 -- 256      (1 * 16*16)
```

You would have to have an extremely good reason for using based literals with exponents!

Integer implementation [LRM 3.5.4]

The range of values for integers is machine dependent. It may be assumed that all implementations will allocate at least 16 bits for the pre-defined type INTEGER (although 32 bits are commonly used), thus integers in the range −32768 (or −32767) to +32767 (depending on whether one's or two's complement representation is used) should be assumable by objects of type INTEGER. It is possible to find the first and last values for all scalar types. For the discrete types, of which integers are a subset, the pre-defined attributes FIRST and LAST are used. We could use these for INTEGER thus:

```
BIGGEST:constant INTEGER:=INTEGER'LAST;
A_VARIABLE:INTEGER:=INTEGER'FIRST;
```

BIGGEST is a constant with the largest INTEGER value *for this implementation* while A_VARIABLE is a variable, which is initialized to the smallest value of INTEGER (on this implementation). FIRST and LAST are *attributes*, which will be covered in more detail in Chapter 8.

An implementation may also provide other pre-defined integer types, such as LONG_INTEGER and SHORT_INTEGER with, respectively, larger and smaller ranges than INTEGER. Any implementation only *has* to provide a type INTEGER; different implementations may allocate different ranges to INTEGER, but at least INTEGER has to be recognized and supported. All other integer types, like LONG_INTEGER, are *not* standard, and are therefore not portable. Their use should be avoided. To understand these points, look at the table below, which shows the pre-defined integer types of two different Ada implementations.

NAME	System 1	System 2
LONG_INTEGER	32 bits	UNDEFINED
INTEGER	16 bits	32 bits
SHORT_INTEGER	8 bits	16 bits
SHORT_SHORT_INTEGER	UNDEFINED	8 bits

Constants defined in the standard package SYSTEM, which is always available to your program, make the absolute implementation limits accessible. SYSTEM.MIN_INT is the smallest integer (of any type) that the implementation can support, and SYSTEM.MAX_INT is the largest such integer. It is not essential to know all this, in order to write correct Ada programs. However, such details are crucial where portability is concerned. The only way to ensure that you get the integers you want is to declare your own types. More will be said about this in Chapter 8.

Integer declarations [LRM 3.2]

After the general introduction to declarations in 3.1, it will suffice to add a few more examples.

```
FULL_BYTE:constant INTEGER:=255;
BYTE:INTEGER   range  0..FULL_BYTE;
                        -- a constrained variable
BIGGEST_YET:INTEGER:=INTEGER'FIRST;
READING_1, READING_2:INTEGER
        range_FULL_BYTE..FULL_BYTE:=0;
                        -- both are initialized to 0
```

Note that objects may be used for the specification of ranges as well as for the initialization of other objects. In fact, any expression of the correct type may be used for the lower and upper bounds of a constraint. Examples will be given later.

Integer operators [LRM 4.5]

Ada provides a number of operators for use with integers. Associated with these operators are several levels of precedence, which are used to determine the evaluation sequence of expressions. Highest precedence operators are evaluated first; operators of equal precedence are evaluated from left to right. No two operators may be adjacent. As is customary in high-level programming languages, parentheses may be used to force an earlier evaluation. These evaluation rules apply over operators of all types in Ada. The construction of more general expressions will be covered later in this chapter. For now, we concentrate on integers.

When discussing the operators, A and B will be used to denote the operands. No type mixing is allowed, therefore A and B must both be integer expressions.

Two integer operations enjoy the highest precedence:

A**B	-- exponentiation, A to power B
abs A	-- absolute value of A

For exponentiation, B must be a non-negative integer; if B is zero, the result will, correctly, be 1. "abs", which is a standard function in many languages, is an operator in Ada.

At the next (lower) level of precedence are the four integer multiplying operators (three of which involve division!):

A*B	-- multiplication
A/B	-- integer division of A by B
A rem B	-- remainder of integer division
A mod B	-- modulus of A with respect to B

In contrast to Pascal, the division operators of Ada are all well-defined for positive and negative operands and will work in the same way over all implementations. Their effects are best illustrated by a table.

A	B	A/B	A rem B	A mod B
21	8	2	5	5
21	-8	-2	5	-3
-21	8	-2	-5	3
-21	-8	2	-5	-5

Integer division always yields the integer part of the result, without any rounding, and "rem" gives the remainder of that division, which will have the same sign as A. The relation: $A=(A/B)*B+(A \text{ rem } B)$ will always be true.

The result of applying "mod", the modulus operator, is not as easily explained for negative operands. If both operands have the same sign, then "mod" yields the same result as "rem". The sign of (A and B) will be the same as the sign of B and the result will obviously have an absolute value lower than that of B. The result must also satisfy the relation: $A=B**N+(A \text{ mod } B)$ in which N is some positive or negative integer. It may be more useful to remember that if A and B have different signs, then the relation: $A \text{ mod } B = B\text{-abs}(A \text{ rem } B)$ is always true.

After that diversion into the meanings of operators, we move down to the next precedence, which contains the two *unary* adding operators:

    +A   -- has no effect
    −B   -- negates B

At the lowest precedence level (for integers), are the two *binary* adding operators:

    A+B   -- addition
    A−B   -- subtraction of B from A

Note that the unary minus operator does not have the high precedence that it is accorded in some other languages. Some examples of simple integer expressions will illustrate some of the points concerning evaluation order.

    A+B*C   -- evaluates B*C first
    (A+B)*C   -- evaluates A+B first
    A/B*C   -- evaluates A/B first
    A*B**C   -- evaluates B**C first
    −A**B   -- evaluates A**B first
    A*(−B)   -- parentheses required (no operator adjacency)

The syntax rules of Ada do not permit an exponentiation operator to follow another one immediately, unless parentheses are used. So, for example, A**2**B would be rejected by the compiler (its meaning is not clear), and would have to be written as either (A**2)**B or A**(2**B).

A complete program, which illustrates the declaration and use of integers is given in Unit 3.1. (The program has no deeper significance.)

```
with SIMPLE_IO;  -- a non-standard package
use  SIMPLE_IO;

procedure MAIN is
  BIG_1:INTEGER:=-100;
  BIG_2:INTEGER:=50;
  POWER:constant INTEGER:=2;
  INT_1:INTEGER range 0..9:=3;
  ANOTHER_1:INTEGER;
begin
  ANOTHER_1:=abs BIG_1 - INT_1 * BIG_2;                -- -50
  INT_1:=BIG_1 / ANOTHER_1;                            --   2
  -- The above elements are assignment compatible.
  -- If the result is not in the range 0..9 then
  -- the exception CONSTRAINT_ERROR will be raised.
  BIG_1:=BIG_2 mod (INT_1 + 1);                        --   2
  BIG_2:=-BIG_1 ** POWER + BIG_2 rem (BIG_1 + INT_1); --  -2
```

```
      ANOTHER_1:=(BIG_2 ** INT_1) ** (BIG_1 + 1);        -- 64
      PUT(BIG_1);                                        --  2
      PUT(BIG_2);                                        -- -2
      PUT(INT_1);                                        --  2
      PUT(ANOTHER_1);                                    -- 64
      NEW_LINE;
   end MAIN;
```

Unit 3.1   Integer operators.

3.3 Type BOOLEAN [LRM 3.5.3, 4.5]

There are only two literals associated with this type, FALSE and TRUE (or their lower case equivalents).

Boolean declarations [LRM 3.2]

The following examples show how Boolean objects are declared and initialized.

> OK:BOOLEAN;
> FLAG_1, FLAG_2:BOOLEAN:=FALSE;
> -- both initialized to FALSE
> POWER_ON:BOOLEAN:=TRUE;
> DOWN:constant BOOLEAN:=FALSE;

Although it is possible to define Boolean constants, where there are only two possible values, there is little point. You will often find that a temptation to use a Boolean constant implies that an enumeration type would be more appropriate (see 3.8).

Boolean operators [LRM 4.5]

There are four logical operators for use with Boolean operands, together with two operator-like elements referred to by the unwieldy name of *short-circuit control forms*.

In the examples, P, Q and R represent operand expressions of type BOOLEAN. The highest precedence logical operator, "not", is for finding the logical complement of its operand. The remaining operators have the same precedence level, below that of "not". These operators are "and", "or" and "xor". The last is provided for computing the exclusive or operation. The actions of the logical operators are best summarized by a truth table.

P	Q	not P	P and Q	P or Q	P xor Q
FALSE	FALSE	TRUE	FALSE	FALSE	FALSE
FALSE	TRUE	TRUE	FALSE	TRUE	TRUE
TRUE	FALSE	FALSE	FALSE	TRUE	TRUE
TRUE	TRUE	FALSE	TRUE	TRUE	FALSE

Restrictions on certain uses of the logical operators are imposed by the syntax rules of the language, with the result that Boolean expressions may not contain a mixture of the logical binary operators, "and", "or" and "xor", unless parentheses are used. (This restriction extends to the use of the short-circuit control forms.)

```
P and Q and not R     -- no parentheses required
P and Q or R          -- ILLEGAL: parentheses required
(P and Q) or R        -- valid
P and (Q or R)        -- valid (but different)
```

This enforced use of parentheses does aid the understanding of expressions; however, it is not good practice to construct very complex Boolean expressions, as they can easily lead to confusion.

In the implementation of most programming languages, *both* operands of a binary or dyadic operator will be evaluated before the operation is applied. There are, however, situations where it is not desirable to evaluate the second operand of an "and" or "or" operation, when the result of the operation can be established from the first operand alone. It is for these occasions that Ada provides the short-circuit control forms, which have the same precedence as "and" and "or" (and "xor"):

```
P and then Q     -- if P is FALSE, then result is FALSE
                 -- and Q is not evaluated
                 -- otherwise, Q is evaluated, and the
                 -- result is the same as (P and Q)

P or else Q      -- if P is TRUE, then result is TRUE
                 -- and Q is not evaluated
                 -- otherwise, Q is evaluated and
                 -- is the result
```

The short-circuit control forms should only be used where necessary, perhaps in the interests of efficiency (where evaluation of a complex second operand might be time consuming), or to avoid excessive nesting of certain if statement constructions (see 4.1) and especially to avoid erroneous execution. If, for example, the first operand is testing for the presence or absence of a component in some structure, and the second operand involves the component itself, then, clearly, the second operand must not be evaluated if the first indicates that the component does not exist. To illustrate this, consider an array, LIST, with ten elements, accessed by subscripts 1 to 10. INDEX may take values in the range 0 through 10. To avoid testing a non-existent array element, we could say:

INDEX /= 0 and then LIST(INDEX) > MAX .....

where /= is the inequality operator, soon to be met, or, we might write:

INDEX = 0 or else LIST(INDEX) < = MAX .....

Relational operators [LRM 4.5.2]

The relational operators may be used in conjunction with scalar and non-scalar types (with certain restrictions), but to whatever type of expression they are applied, they always yield a BOOLEAN result. Consequently, they are frequently used in association with the logical operators.

The six relational operators all have the same precedence. In the examples, L and R represent operand expressions of the same type.

L=R	-- equality
L/=R	-- inequality
L<R	-- less than
L<=R	-- less than or equal to
L>R	-- greater than
L>=R	-- greater than or equal to

There are also two operator-like membership tests, **in** and **not in** which behave like, and have the same precedence as, the relational operators. These are used for testing whether or not a value belongs to the range of values of a given type or range. Examples will be given later. The operators "=" and "/=" can be applied to most types in Ada, while the other four relational operators are only pre-defined for scalar types and one-dimensional arrays.

Before giving examples of the use of relational and logical operators in a program, the *relative* precedence of the different classes of operator must be taken into account.

3.4 Expressions [LRM 4.4, 4.5]

The rules for constructing expressions apply to the types that have already been introduced as well as others to come. Only one operator, "&", has yet to be mentioned. This operator is specific to one-dimensional arrays and will be described in Chapter 6. Any additional applications of the operators discussed so far will be analogous to the usage illustrated here. For example, the "+" operator may be applied to *any* numeric type (not only the ones already encountered). Not only that, but, as we shall see, "+" (along with all other operators) can be given further meanings by overloadings defined by the programmer. However, whatever new meanings are given to an operator, its precedence in the hierarchy cannot be altered.

The Ada operators are now listed in precedence order, starting with the highest ranking:

** abs not	-- highest precedence operators
* / mod rem	-- multiplying operators
+ −	-- unary adding operators
+ − &	-- binary adding operators
= /= < <= > >=	-- relational operators
and or xor	-- logical operators

Construction of simple expressions (i.e. arithmetic ones) and Boolean expressions has already been illustrated. It now remains to highlight the important facets of constructing general expressions, which involve the relational operators.

With arithmetic operators having a higher precedence than the relational ones, additional parentheses are not required around simple expressions, which form part of relational expressions, such as

A+3 > B/2

in which the arithmetic expressions will (correctly) be evaluated first. The assignment of a higher precedence to the relational operators over the logical ones also means that extra parentheses are not required around relational expressions that are connected by logical operators. So, in:

A>=0 and A<=9

the relational operators will be evaluated first, yielding BOOLEAN results for the "and". In this expression:

A**3 > B+1   xor   A*A < B−1

all arithmetic expressions are evaluated, then the relational ones, and finally the logical operation. Note the use of spacing here, which reflects the evaluation order. The judicious use of spacing like this can greatly enhance the readability of complex expressions. It is also possible to use additional parentheses to make the meaning clearer, as in

A*(B**2)*3

However, the use of spacing is preferable as it does not introduce more symbols.

A corollary of the relative precedences of relational and logical operators, is that Boolean expressions, which occur in relational expressions, *do* require parentheses, as in

(P and Q) = (P xor R)

The program in Unit 3.2 illustrates many of the features described in this chapter.

```
with SIMPLE_IO;   -- a non-standard package
use  SIMPLE_IO;

procedure MAIN is
   INT_1, INT_2, REM_2:INTEGER;
   ODD, ODD_DIG, EVEN_BIG,
   INT_1_BY_TEN, SAME_ODDNESS:BOOLEAN;
   DIVISOR:constant INTEGER:=2;
begin
   PUT("Type 2 integers: ");
   GET(INT_1);
   GET(INT_2);
   ODD:=abs(INT_1 rem DIVISOR) = 1;
          -- ODD is TRUE if INT_1 is odd
          -- regardless of sign. Note the
          -- need for parentheses.
   ODD_DIG:=ODD and INT_1>=0 and INT_1<=9;
          -- ODD_DIG is TRUE if INT_1 is
          -- a positive, odd digit.
   EVEN_BIG:=not ODD and abs INT_1 >= 10;
          -- EVEN_BIG is TRUE if INT_1 is
          -- even and its magnitude is
          -- greater than 10. Note the
          -- order of evaluation
   INT_1_BY_TEN:=INT_2/=0 and then abs (INT_1 / INT_2) >= 10;
          -- TRUE if the magnitude of
          -- INT_1/INT_2 is ten or more.
          -- The use of and then prevents
          -- the division from being
          -- performed if INT_2 is zero.
   REM_2:=abs (INT_2 rem DIVISOR);
          -- remainder of the (integer)
          -- division by 2.
   SAME_ODDNESS:=(ODD and REM_2=1) or (not ODD and REM_2=0);
          -- TRUE if INT_1 and INT_2
          -- are BOTH even, or are
          -- BOTH odd.
   PUT("First integer is odd        : ");
   PUT(ODD);                                     -- writes TRUE or FALSE
   NEW_LINE;
   PUT("First integer is positive & odd: ");
```

```
    PUT(ODD_DIG);
    NEW_LINE;
    PUT("First integer is even and >=10 : ");
    PUT(EVEN_BIG);
    NEW_LINE;
    PUT("First / Second >= 10            : ");
    PUT(INT_1_BY_TEN);
    NEW_LINE;
    PUT("Both have the same oddness      : ");
    PUT(SAME_ODDNESS);
    NEW_LINE;
  end MAIN;
```

Unit 3.2 Illustration of expressions.

Note the use of a PUT procedure, defined in SIMPLE_IO, for outputting BOOLEAN values. (The package also contains a corresponding GET for BOOLEAN input.) The GET procedure for INTEGERs will raise the exception DATA_ERROR, if it does not find a valid integer literal, as defined in 3.2 (with or without a preceding sign).

3.5 Type CHARACTER [LRM 2.1, 2.5, 2.10, 3.5.2,C]

CHARACTER is a pre-defined type, which comprises the 128 characters of the ASCII character set, the ANSI graphical representation of the ISO character code. Of these characters, 95 are graphical symbols, or printing characters, which include the space character. The remainder are non-printing, or control characters.

Character literals are written by enclosing the required character within apostrophes (single quotes). This can only be done for the printing characters. However, reference may still be made to characters that are not printing characters (and characters not in the basic character set — see 2.1) using constants that are defined in the package ASCII, which is part of the pre-defined package STANDARD. (See Appendix B.) Unit 3.3 shows some declarations and assignments with variables of type CHARACTER.

```
with TEXT_IO;
use  TEXT_IO;

procedure MAIN is
  CH:CHARACTER:=ASCII.QUERY;          -- same as '?'
  LETTER:CHARACTER range 'A'..'Z':='A';
  APOSTROPHE:constant CHARACTER:='''; -- apostrophe literal
begin
  PUT(APOSTROPHE);
  PUT(CH);
  PUT(LETTER);
  CH:=ASCII.LC_A;                     -- assign 'a'
  PUT(CH);
```

```
    LETTER:='B';
    PUT(LETTER);
    PUT(ASCII.LC_B);
    PUT(APOSTROPHE);
    NEW_LINE;
  end MAIN;
```

Unit 3.3 Using type CHARACTER.

Note the use of constants defined in ASCII, and the application of a range constraint to LETTER.

3.6 Type FLOAT [LRM 3.5.7]

Our excursion into the realm of real numbers in this chapter is restricted to the pre-defined type FLOAT, which, as the name implies, is a floating point representation intended for general purpose use. Other floating point types, and fixed point types, will be discussed in Chapter 8 and Appendix A.

Real literals [LRM 2.4]

Real literals (for both floating and fixed point types) are distinguished from integer literals by the presence of a point, which must be preceded by and followed by at least one digit. In common with integers, real literals may have an integer exponent, but for reals, this exponent may be negative. Some examples of valid real literals:

```
    −123.0
12_345.67                   -- underscores may be used
    2.71828_18284_59        -- group fractional part in fives
    1.0E6                   -- one million
    0.5E−8                  -- 0.000000005
```

It is also possible to express real literals in any base up to and including hexadecimal. The comment about relevance to the problem that was made regarding based integer literals is equally applicable to real literals. The following based real literals all represent the same number (decimal 0.06225_58593_75).

```
    2#0.0000_1111_1111#
  16#0.00FF#
    2#1111.1111#E-8
    8#3.77#E-2
  16#FF.0#E-3
```

Floating point implementation [LRM 3.5.7]

There is much to be said about the way that floating (and fixed) point numbers are represented in Ada, especially with regard to the attendant effect on portability. At this point in the book, it is sufficient to note that it may be assumed that an implementation will support at least six decimal digits of precision for FLOAT. The intricate, but nevertheless important, details will appear in Chapter 8. You should note here, though, that FLOAT should not generally be used — it is always better to create your own numeric types.

Floating point declarations [LRM 3.2]

Objects of type FLOAT can be declared and initialized like objects of the other types we have seen, and as with integers and characters, a floating point object may have a constraining range applied at its declaration.

```
X:FLOAT;
ORIGIN:constant FLOAT:=0.0;      -- decimal point must be
                                 -- present
Y:FLOAT:=ORIGIN;
SMALL_REAL:FLOAT range 0.0..1000.0:=500.0;
```

Floating point operators [LRM 4.5]

The floating point operators are analogous to those provided for integers, but there are no floating point equivalents of "mod" and "rem". The precedence of the floating point operators is the same as that of their integer counterparts. (It is important to realize that the operators provided for FLOAT, although similar to those provided for INTEGER, are nevertheless different operators; this is no different from the situation in ALGOL and Pascal.)

In the list of operators, X and Y represent floating point operands and I is an integer operand.

```
X**I       -- exponentiation, I may be negative
           -- I must be an integer
abs X      -- absolute value of X
X*Y        -- multiplication
X/Y        -- division
+X         -- unary addition, no effect
-Y         -- negation of Y
X+Y        -- addition
X-Y        -- subtraction of Y from X
```

Most of the floating point operators are shown in use in the program of Unit 3.4. Note that our assumed package, SIMPLE_IO, provides i/o procedures for type FLOAT. The GET procedure will cause DATA_ERROR to be raised, if a real literal (with or without sign) is not found.

```
with SIMPLE_IO; -- a non-standard package
use  SIMPLE_IO;

procedure MAIN is
  PI:constant FLOAT:=3.14159_265;
  RADIUS_1, RADIUS_2,
  AREA_1, AREA_2:FLOAT;
begin
  PUT("Type first radius : ");
  GET(RADIUS_1);
  PUT("Type second radius: ");
  GET(RADIUS_2);
  AREA_1:=PI * RADIUS_1**2;
  AREA_2:=PI * RADIUS_2**2;
  PUT("   Area 1            Area 2            Difference");
  NEW_LINE;
  PUT(AREA_1);
  PUT("        ");
  PUT(AREA_2);
  PUT("        ");
  PUT(abs (AREA_1 - AREA_2));
  NEW_LINE;
  PUT("Ratio with respect to 1: ");
  PUT(AREA_2 / AREA_1);
  NEW_LINE;
end MAIN;
```

Unit 3.4 Floating point operators.

Example of type conversion

The subject of type conversion is treated more fully in Chapter 8. However, you may well need to use it before then. Remember that there is no *implicit* or automatic type conversion between INTEGER and FLOAT. If you wish to use a floating point object in an integer expression, then you have to convert it to an integer explicitly. (You also have to convert explicitly in the other direction.) Assume that we have the declarations:

        I, J:INTEGER:=2;
        X, Y:FLOAT:=4.0;

Then the following sequence of assignments is valid:

        I:=INTEGER(X);   -- 4
        X:=FLOAT(J);   -- 2.0
        Y:=X/FLOAT(I);   -- 0.5
        X:=FLOAT(I*J);   -- 8.0
        J:=INTEGER(X)/I;   -- 2

3.7 Standard functions

No mention has so far been made of standard functions in Ada. There are none! This may seem very strange, if you are used to having them available in a high level language. The reason for the omission is consistent with the overall philosophy of the design of the language. Considerable care has been taken by the language designers to define the *effects* of all the operators provided in Ada, even though the types upon which they operate may be implementation dependent. This is why the exponentiation operator, "**", may only have an integer exponent, so that the operation is realized by repeated multiplication.

In other high level languages, a commonly used standard function is that which finds the square root of its argument. Evaluation of a square root involves some computation, which will use one of several possible algorithms. Herein lies a problem. Consider Pascal, the specification for which states that a square root function must be provided. That specification does not, however, specify the algorithm to be employed. Consequently, it is up to the implementors to decide, which means that various implementations may well use different methods for computing standard functions. Therefore, programs that use the square root function cannot be assumed to be portable across all implementations, for there is likely to be variation in accuracy and computation time of the function.

Of course, designation of particular algorithms for standard functions could have been made part of the language specification. The imposition of specific methods would not, though, suit all users. In an embedded system, for example, accuracy is commonly sacrificed for the sake of speed, whereas in engineering design, accuracy is the more important attribute. A single routine for a given function could not satisfy both requirements.

Functions, such as that for finding a square root, will still be required by Ada programmers who would not normally wish to provide code of their own. Each implementation normally supports one or more packages which contain commonly used functions. Such packages are not defined by the language, so the names of the packages provided, the functions they make available and the algorithms used are *all* implementation dependent. Of course, to accommodate different user profiles on the same system, an implementation (or group of users) may provide alternative packages with the required characteristics.

The program in Unit 3.5 shows the use of a package for commonly used functions. Although there is variation in package names and package contents, the mode of use of the package on your system will be similar to that illustrated here. Do *not* expect it to be the same.

```
-- Note that function library packages
-- are not standard.

with SIMPLE_IO, FLOAT_MATH_LIB; -- non-standard packages
use  SIMPLE_IO, FLOAT_MATH_LIB;
-- This program uses the functions EXP, LOG and SQRT,
-- in order to raise X to a positive FLOAT power, and
-- to find the square root of X.

procedure MAIN is
  X, POWER:FLOAT;
  X_TO_POWER:FLOAT;
begin
  PUT("Type number and power (both positive reals): ");
  GET(X);
  GET(POWER);
  X_TO_POWER:=EXP(POWER * LOG(X)); -- EXP and LOG in FLOAT_MATH_LIB
  PUT("Result is: ");
  PUT(X_TO_POWER);
  NEW_LINE;
  PUT("square root is: ");
  PUT(SQRT(X));                       -- SQRT in FLOAT_MATH_LIB
  NEW_LINE;
end MAIN;
```

Unit 3.5   Using a function library.

The first thing to check is whether or not any package of functions is already available on your system. You will usually find that a generic package is provided for this purpose. There is often an instantiation for the pre-defined type FLOAT already available in the library supplied, which is the case in Unit 3.5. If you are not so fortunate, and all you have is the generic package MATH_LIB, all you need to do is create your own instantiation and compile it (separately) into your library:

> -- Your own library of functions for FLOAT.
> package FLOAT_MATH_LIB is new MATH_LIB(FLOAT);

You need to compile this before compiling a program that uses it. Once compiled, this package is used just like any other library package, so that the program of Unit 3.5 would be unchanged.

You may find that an implementation groups functions into packages within a library package, differentiating, for example, between arithmetic functions and trigonometric ones. So, the moral is clear. You have to find out *exactly* what is already available.

3.8 Enumeration types [LRM 3.5.1]

An enumeration type is introduced by the programmer's defining all the values that objects of that type may take. These values are specified as enumeration literals, which may either be identifiers or character literals. For any one type the values must be distinct. Unlike Pascal, however, the same literal may appear in more than one enumeration type specification, which is another example of overloading in Ada. Case is only significant for character literals. To conform with the lexical convention adhered to in this book, enumeration literal identifiers will be printed in upper case.

It is possible for an enumeration type to comprise a mixture of identifiers and character literals. If at least one value of an enumeration type is a character literal, then the type is said to be a character type (but not of type CHARACTER). The main significance of this is that string literals of values of a character type may be constructed. Some valid declarations and assignments:

```
    -- some declarative part
        type COLOUR is (RED, BLUE, GREEN, PINK, YELLOW);
        type DAY is (MON, TUE, WED, THU, FRI, SAT, SUN);
        PAINT:COLOUR;
        A_DAY:DAY;
        NICE_DAYS:DAY range SAT..SUN;
        PAY_DAY:constant DAY:=FRI;
        type ANSWERS is ('N', 'n', 'Y', 'y');
        type ODD_ONE is (ONE, 'A', TWO, A, 'Y');
        RESPONSE:ANSWERS;
        STRANGE:ODD_ONE;
    begin                   -- example assignments
        PAINT:=BLUE;
        A_DAY:=THU;
        STRANGE:=A;
        STRANGE:='A';   -- not the same as the last assignment
        RESPONSE:='Y';
        STRANGE:='Y';
        -- and so on
    end;
```

In the declarations above, four enumeration types were declared, together with at least one object of each type. Note that the only constraint on the order of these declarations is that something must be declared before it is used. Therefore, it is not necessary to list all type declarations before all variable declarations, as it is in Pascal. This provides greater flexibility for the Ada programmer, who can define types in terms of objects already declared.

The types COLOUR and DAY both comprise values which are identifiers, whereas type ANSWERS only includes character literals. This exemplifies this particular aspect of overloading in Ada, where four character literals of the pre-defined type CHARACTER are endowed with an additional meaning. In the assignment

> RESPONSE:='Y';

it is clear from the context that the literal 'Y' must be that of type ANSWERS, which is the declared type of the variable RESPONSE. It is not always possible, however, to resolve overloading ambiguities from the context, so it is then necessary to be explicit. As a simple, if contrived, example, consider the relational expression

> 'Y' > 'n'

As it stands, this is ambiguous, as both literals could be of the pre-defined type CHARACTER, or of the user-defined type ANSWERS. (They must both be of the same type, otherwise the expression is invalid.) To resolve the ambiguity, a *type qualification* must be added to at least one of the operands, as in

> ANSWERS'('Y') > ANSWERS'('n')

Because both operands must be of the same type, it is sufficient to say

> ANSWERS'('Y') > 'n'

Situations do occur in Ada, where *qualified expressions* like these are required.

Owing to the possibility of confusion, overloading of enumeration literals should be avoided wherever possible, but not to the extent that unnatural or obscure names have to be used.

The type ODD_ONE contains a mixture of identifier and character literals, and introduces a new meaning for 'A' as well as further overloading 'Y'. Note that the values A and 'A' are quite distinct, the first being an identifier, the second a character literal.

Although enumeration types are provided in Pascal, their usefulness in that language is diluted by the fact that input/output of enumeration values is not possible. This restriction does not apply to Ada. TEXT_IO obviously cannot provide input/output routines specifically for user-defined enumeration types, however, it does provide a generic (template) from which the requisite subprograms can be created. See Chapter 10 for

details. Here, without explanation, is how you would create an i/o package
for type COLOUR:

```
-- assuming: with TEXT_IO;
--    and   : use TEXT_IO;
package COLOUR_IO is new ENUMERATION_IO(COLOUR);
```

An alternative means of performing i/o on enumeration values is to
use some of the attributes of discrete types discussed in Chapter 8. The
main reason for performing enumeration i/o using attributes would be if
you do not have a full implementation of Ada at your disposal.

Enumeration types significantly enhance program readability, by
allowing identifiers to be used for values. It is far better to let a variable
SWITCH have values such as OFF and ON, or DOWN and UP rather
than TRUE or FALSE, or worse still, 0 and 1. The value conveys
meaning via its name, always assuming, of course, that the name is apt. If
there is any natural ordering in the values of an enumeration type, then
the definition should reflect it, such as in

```
type HEAT_OUTPUT is (LOW, MEDIUM, HIGH);
type SIZE is (SMALL, MEDIUM, LARGE);
type SWITCH_STATE is (OFF, ON);
```

The relational operators may then be applied with a clear meaning, for
the specification order of enumeration values defines the underlying
ordering used for comparisons. So, in type SIZE, LARGE is greater than
MEDIUM and SMALL, and MEDIUM is greater than SMALL. This
ordering is also important in the application of the attributes mentioned
in 8.

Finally, it is worth noting that the pre-defined type BOOLEAN is
effectively defined as:

```
type BOOLEAN is (FALSE, TRUE);
```

3.9 Creating types and subtypes [LRM 3.3]

Ada provides a number of pre-defined types, together with facilities for
introducing further, distinct types, such as enumeration types and structured
types, namely arrays and records. There are three aspects concerning the
general use of types, which are important in the writing of Ada programs.

First, the type used for an object must be appropriate to the application in question. Therefore, if we have to represent the days of the week, we create a type like DAY, and do *not* use the integers 1 to 7.

Secondly, separate types should be used for objects that are structurally equivalent but conceptually distinct. To illustrate this, consider writing an operating system, in which processes may have one of three priorities, and peripheral devices fall into one of three groups. We could have

> type STATE is (LOW, MEDIUM, HIGH);
> PROCESS_PRIORITY, PERIPHERAL_SPEED:STATE;

Although this adequately represents the data, it is not a satisfactory solution, as it does not enforce a distinction between process priorities and peripheral speeds, by allowing the assignment

> PROCESS_PRIORITY:=PERIPHERAL_SPEED;

It is highly unlikely that this would be a valid assignment, therefore the two entities should be made distinct:

> type URGENCY is (LOW, MEDIUM, HIGH);
> type SPEED is (LOW, MEDIUM, HIGH);
> PROCESS_PRIORITY:URGENCY;
> PERIPHERAL_SPEED:SPEED;

In this solution, the two types are distinct, although they look the same. This enables the Ada compiler to reject an assignment like the one above at compile-time. *Defensive programming* such as this should be applied over all types used within a program. For maximum security, objects with different dimensions, such as mass, length and time, should be given different types, but in such a way that they *can* be mixed when a clear indication is made that this is what is intended.

Finally, another facet of defensive programming is the use of range constraints to guard against the assignment of wrong values to an object, and to provide a faithful representation of the real-world object.

Subtypes

A subtype is created by applying some constraint to an existing type, known as the *base type*, and associating the constrained type with a type identifier, which can then be used in object declarations, or in the creation of further types and subtypes. It is very important to note that subtypes are not distinct types, but are completely compatible with their base type. Any operation which is applicable to the base type is also applicable to the subtype. The only difference is that the subtype constraint must not be violated, otherwise, for a range constraint, the exception CONSTRAINT_ERROR will be raised. The following declarations illustrate the creation and use of subtypes.

```
-- some declarative part
  -- base type INTEGER
  subtype BYTE_SIZE is INTEGER range −128..127;
  SMALL:BYTE_SIZE:=0;
  LO_BYTE, HI_BYTE:BYTE_SIZE;

  -- base type CHARACTER
  subtype U_CASE is CHARACTER range 'A'..'Z';
  LETTER, ANSWER:U_CASE;
  subtype HEX_LET is U_CASE range 'A'..'F';
  HEX:HEX_LET;

  -- base type DAY
  subtype WEEKEND is DAY range SAT..SUN;
  BLISS:WEEKEND;
  PLAY_DAY:constant WEEKEND:=SAT;
```

All the examples above involve the application of a (contiguous) range constraint on some base type. For certain base types, other kinds of constraint may be applied to create subtypes. For example, there are two types of constraint that may be applied to floating point types, as we shall subsequently see. Ada has two pre-defined INTEGER subtypes, which are defined as:

```
subtype NATURAL is INTEGER range 0..INTEGER'LAST;
subtype POSITIVE is INTEGER range 1..INTEGER'LAST;
```

It is not strictly necessary that a subtype impose a constraint, which makes it possible to declare:

```
subtype SUB_INT is INTEGER;
```

Unconstrained subtypes do not, however, serve any real purpose.

Range constraints may involve simple (i.e. arithmetic) expressions.

```
-- some declarative part
  A:constant INTEGER:=10;
  B:constant INTEGER:=20;
  subtype A_RANGE is INTEGER range −A..A;
  subtype AB_RANGE is INTEGER range −(A+B)..A+B;
```

All the subtypes declared so far have been static: their ranges have only involved constants, which enables them to be determined at compile-time. The range expressions may contain variables, which must, of course, have values when the range expression is elaborated. Subtypes created in this manner are not static:

```
-- some declarative part
-- LIM_VAR is an INTEGER variable
   subtype NON_STATIC is INTEGER
           range -LIM_VAR..LIM_VAR;
```

If there is a subtype declaration:

```
   subtype GENERAL is INTEGER range E1..E2;
```

where E1 and E2 are INTEGER expressions, then if, on elaboration, E1 is greater than E2, the range will be null, with the result that objects of type GENERAL will not be capable of being assigned any values!

Now consider the possibility of range violation. Given the declarations:

```
   subtype BYTE_SIZE is INTEGER range -128..127;
   BIG:INTEGER;
   SMALL:BYTE_SIZE;
```

then both of the assignments below are allowed:

```
   BIG:=SMALL;
   SMALL:=BIG;
```

With the second of these, however, although the construction is legal, there is the possibility that a range violation could occur at run-time.

Any operation that a subtype inherits from its base type, will relate to the base type. Consider the code:

```
-- some declarative part
   subtype TINY is INTEGER range 0..9;
   T1, T2, T3:TINY;
begin
  T1:=8;
  T2:=7;
  T3:=T1*T1/T2;
  -- ......
end;
```

During evaluation of the expression in the last assignment, the sub-expression T1*T1 will be evaluated first, yielding an intermediate value outside the range of the constraint, before the division produces a result that is within the range of the subtype. This will *not* cause an exception to be raised *provided that* the intermediate result is constrained within the limits of the *base* type, otherwise the exception NUMERIC_ERROR will be raised. (The exact point at which this is raised is, of course, implementation dependent.)

Although subtypes may be used to guard against the assignment of values outside the range constraint, this should not be used as a method of input validation. So, rather than have

GET(SMALL);

which would cause CONSTRAINT_ERROR to be raised, if the entered value is not in the range −128..127, it is better to test the value explicitly and take the appropriate corrective action:

```
GET(BIG);
-- check BIG against constraints
-- take appropriate action if the
-- value is not acceptable (such
-- as repeat the GET)
SMALL:=BIG;              -- no range violation
```

Membership testing [LRM 4.5.2]

Two operator-like membership tests are provided by Ada, they are **in** and its complement **not in**. These can be used to determine whether or not an expression is in a given range, or if it is a member of a given subtype. The membership tests have the same precedence as the relational operators and, like them, return a BOOLEAN result. However, they are not operators and cannot therefore be overloaded.

When used as a range test, **in** is not unlike its namesake in Pascal, which is used for set membership testing. Although the Ada membership test can be used in a similar way to the Pascal operator, remember that there are no pre-defined sets in Ada.

The types of the expression and the range definition must be compatible, so that in:

if I + J in 0..99 then .....

I and J must both be of an integer type. Other examples of valid range membership tests are:

FAILED:=OUTPUT not in −10..10;
ALPHANUM:=CH in '0'..'9' or CH in 'A'..'Z' or CH in 'a'..'z';

where FAILED and ALPHANUM are BOOLEAN variables, OUTPUT is an integer and CH is a character.

For the subtype test, the expression must be of the same base type as the type mark, as shown in the examples, which use subtypes recently defined:

if CH in U_CASE then ...
          -- better than: if CH in 'A'..'Z' ...
if I+J in POSITIVE then ...
          -- alternative to: if I+J > 0 then ...
if TODAY in WEEKEND then ...
FAILED:=LO_BYTE * HI_BYTE not in BYTE_SIZE;

3.10 Yet to come

This has not been an exhaustive account of the scalar types. We need to return to some implementation details, particularly for real numbers. Indeed, fixed point types have yet to be introduced. Also, there are some very important general points about types and type creation that must be understood. However, rather than postpone the introduction of control statements any longer, the remaining material concerning scalar types is presented separately, in Chapter 8. That chapter may be read at any time, being independent of the material in the intervening chapters; it would be better, though, to develop confidence in writing simple Ada programs before broaching it.

Practising Ada 3

So far, there have been a lot of details about the scalar types and not much about program statements other than assignment. Before proceeding, however, write small programs which will test your understanding of the material in this chapter. You will need to use SIMPLE_IO, or an equivalent, or instantiate your own i/o packages when required.

Some specific ideas are listed below.

1 Write a program to read two INTEGERs and write the results of applying the arithmetic operators to them.
(What happens if the input data is not an integer?)
2 Do the same for FLOATs.
(What happens if the input data is not real?)
(What happens if you mix types?)
3 Find the equivalent of FLOAT_MATH_LIB on your system and run Unit 3.5. Don't forget that you may have to instantiate a generic library for FLOAT.
4 Look at the descriptions of FLOAT_IO and INTEGER_IO in 10.3 to see how numbers can be formatted. Experiment with your programs for INTEGERs and FLOATs.
5 Define an enumeration type (experiment with character and identifier literals); instantiate an i/o package for the type and then write a program around these to input and output values of the type.
6 Write a program which will read a length in feet and inches and output the equivalent length in metres and centimetres.
7 What are the largest and smallest values of INTEGER and FLOAT on your system?
8 Write a program to read:
(i)   a departure time in the form HH : MM
(ii) a distance in kilometres
(iii) an average speed (km/hour)
The program should calculate the journey time and write out the arrival time, stating on which day relative to the day of departure.
9 Write a program that will read a day of the week and the number of days from that day to some future event. It should write the day of the week on which the event will occur.

Chapter 4

Control statements

Now it is time to give some consideration to the statements that Ada provides for controlling the flow of execution of programs. First, the if statement caters for the execution of code, which is conditional upon the result of the evaluation of some Boolean expression. There is also the loop statement, for repetitive execution of a section of code. Finally, the case statement provides for the selection of one course of action from a number of possibilities.

Each of these statements has its own (unique) terminator, which comprises **end** followed by the reserved word for the particular statement. With the range of statements so clearly delineated, there is no requirement for the compound statement found in other block structured languages, which requires a begin/end pair to be used. Whenever SEQUENCE_OF _STATEMENTS is encountered in the syntactic descriptions in this book, it simply stands for one or more valid Ada statements. Angled brackets are used to denote certain elements of the syntax in informal outlines. For example, ⟨CONDITION⟩ is used to represent a valid condition (generally a Boolean expression). The names of these syntactic features will correspond to the terms used in the LRM, save for a few simplifications.

In all the examples used to illustrate the control statements, note the use of indentation to make the structure of the code clear. It was stated earlier that there is no single convention for program layout; the one presented here reflects the preference of the author.

4.1 The if statement [LRM 5.3]

The simplest form of the if statement is:

```
if ⟨CONDITION⟩ then
   ⟨SEQUENCE_OF_STATEMENTS⟩
end if;
```

⟨CONDITION⟩ must be a BOOLEAN expression, which is evaluated on execution of the if statement. If, and only if, the result of this evaluation is TRUE, then the sequence of statements is executed, as in the simple example:

```
if VARIABLE mod 2 = 0 then
   PUT("Number is even");
end if;
```

Very often, we also want to execute some sequence of statements when the condition evaluates to FALSE. For this, an else clause is used within the if statement:

```
if ⟨CONDITION⟩ then
   ⟨SEQUENCE_OF_STATEMENTS⟩      -- S1
else
   ⟨SEQUENCE_OF_STATEMENTS⟩      -- S2
end if;
```

When the if statement is executed, the condition will be evaluated. If it is TRUE, the sequence S1 will be executed, otherwise (if it is FALSE) the sequence S2 will be executed. So, we can extend the previous example to report the full story:

```
if VARIABLE mod 2 = 0 then
   PUT("Number is even");
else
   PUT("Number is odd");
end if;
```

Pascal programmers should note the requirement for a semi-colon before the **else** and **end**, given that Ada requires one after every statement.

As has been pointed out, **then** and **else** may be followed by any number of statements, without any need for **begin** and **end**. Here, each sequence comprises two statements:

```
if X > Y then
   LARGER:=X;
   SMALLER:=Y;
else
   LARGER:=Y;
   SMALLER:=X;
end if;
```

In this example, the else clause will be executed if Y is greater than or equal to X but what if we want to treat equality as a special case? Clearly, we must then explicitly test for that condition, which leads into the nesting of if statements. The sequence of statements following **then** or

else may include any valid Ada statement, which includes, of course, another if statement. The last example might now become:

```
if X = Y then
  PUT("Numbers are equal");
else
  if X > Y then
    LARGER:=X;
    SMALLER:=Y;
  else              -- Y > X
    LARGER:=Y;
    SMALLER:=X;
  end if;
end if;
```

It is not uncommon for if statements to be nested like this. Consequently, it would be rather tedious to have to repeat the **end if** on a number of consecutive lines. Nesting in this manner does not help clarify the meaning of the construction. For such situations, Ada provides **elsif** as an alternative to **else** followed by **if**. The example can now be rewritten:

```
if X = Y then
  PUT("Numbers are equal");
elsif X > Y then
  LARGER:=X;
  SMALLER:=Y;
else              -- Y > X
  LARGER:=Y;
  SMALLER:=X;
end if;
```

Now, the code is clearer — each condition appears at the same level of indentation, which helps to emphasize their equal status. There is no limit to the number of **elsif**s that may be used. If we represent conditions by C and sequences of statements by S, the general form of an if statement is:

```
if ⟨C1⟩ then
  ⟨S1⟩
elsif ⟨C2⟩ then
  ⟨S2⟩
elsif ⟨C3⟩ then
```

```
    ⟨S3⟩
    -- and so on
else        -- the else part is optional
    ⟨Sn⟩
end if;
```

Each of the conditions, C1, C2, ... is tested in sequence until one evaluates to TRUE, whereupon the sequence of statements that it governs will be executed. If none of the conditions is TRUE, then the else part, if there is one, will be executed.

Using some of the symbols from the BNF notation in which the syntax of Ada is formally described, it is possible to make the above outline more concise:

```
if ⟨C1⟩ then
    ⟨S1⟩
{elsif ⟨Ci⟩ then
    ⟨Si⟩}
[else
    ⟨Sn⟩]
end if;
```

Here, the {} encloses components that may occur any number of times (including zero), while [] embraces elements that may occur once, or may be omitted.

The if statement should not be used where a case statement would be more appropriate, as it would be in

```
if PAINT = RED then
    ⟨S1⟩
elsif PAINT = BLUE then
    ⟨S2⟩
elsif PAINT = GREEN then
    ⟨S3⟩
    -- and so on.
end if;
```

In this example, each condition is a test on a mutually exclusive set of values of a discrete type, which is precisely what the case statement is intended for.

Not all occurrences of **else** followed by **if** should result in the use of

elsif, which is not merely a contracted form of **else if**. Here is a simple variation on an earlier example:

```
if X = Y then
  PUT("Numbers are equal");
else
  if X > Y then
    LARGER:=X;
    SMALLER:=Y;
  else              -- Y > X
    LARGER:=Y;
    SMALLER:=X;
  end if;
  PUT("Numbers are not equal");
end if;
```

As there is a statement which is common to both situations for which X and Y are not equal, it is not possible to use the **elsif** construction (unless, of course, the new call of PUT were to be repeated in both parts of the inner if statement).

In Chapter 3, the short-circuit control forms, **and then** and **or else** were introduced. These effectively enable an if statement to be eliminated (which is not possible in Pascal). So, instead of

```
if INDEX /= 0 then
  if LIST(INDEX) > MAX then
    MAX:=LIST(INDEX);
  end if;
end if;
```

we can write

```
if INDEX /= 0 and then LIST(INDEX) > MAX then
  MAX:=LIST(INDEX);
end if;
```

Unit 4.1 is a complete program, which utilizes if statements. It reads three numbers, each representing the lengths of the sides of a triangle. (It is assumed that these lengths can actually form a triangle.) The way that the logic is expressed makes the decision making clearer, but the resulting code could be made more efficient. Unless you really must bow to efficiency, *always* choose a clear exposition of your logic.

```
with SIMPLE_IO;  -- a non-standard package
use  SIMPLE_IO;

procedure MAIN is
  A, B, C:FLOAT;
begin
  PUT("Type the lengths of the 3 sides of a triangle: ");
  GET(A);
  GET(B);
  GET(C);
  if A=B and B=C then
    PUT("Equilateral");
  elsif A=B or A=C or B=C then
    PUT("Isosceles");
  else
    PUT("Scalene");
  end if;
  NEW_LINE;
end MAIN;
```

Unit 4.1   Use of the if statement.

4.2 The case statement [LRM 5.4]

The case statement enables one particular sequence of statements to be selected for execution from a number of such sequences. Each case statement has a *case expression*, which must be of a discrete type. When the statement is executed, the expression is evaluated, and the resulting value is used to identify the sequence of statements to be executed from a list of alternatives.

For an illustration of the syntax, here is a better way to express the colour selection introduced in 4.1:

```
case PAINT is
   when RED=>
      ⟨S1⟩
   When BLUE=>
      ⟨S2⟩
   When GREEN=>
      ⟨S3⟩
   When PINK=>
      ⟨S4⟩
   When YELLOW=>
      ⟨S5⟩
end case;
```

As in previous outlines, S1, S2, ... represents a sequence (of one or more) statements. On execution of the case statement, one, and only one, of these sequences will be selected for execution.

If a selection is made according to the value of a Boolean expression, then an if statement should be used rather than a case statement. So, this:

```
if I > J then
    ⟨S1⟩
else
    ⟨S2⟩
end if;
```

is preferable to:

```
case I > J is
  when TRUE=>
    ⟨S1⟩
  when FALSE=>
    ⟨S2⟩
end case;
```

However, for any other binary valued type, a case statement is preferable. Again, the major issue is a stylistic one, the aim, as always, being maximum readability. To the author, the first alternative above is much more acceptable. By the same token, this:

```
-- Declarations assumed:
-- type STATE is (OFF, ON);
-- SWITCH:STATE;

case SWITCH is
  when OFF=>
    POWER:=0.0;
  when ON=>
    POWER:=3.0;
end case;
```

is clearer than:

```
if SWITCH = OFF then
  POWER:=0.0;
else
  POWER:=3.0;
end if;
```

We all know that Booleans can only have two values. However, the last extract does not make it obvious that SWITCH only has two values;

the else part caters for all values that are not OFF, however many there may be.

That last point also relates to the correct use of the case statement. Whatever the type of the case expression, all of its possible values must somehow be included in the list of values from which to select. In the case of a sparsely used type, this would be rather inconvenient. For situations like this, it is possible to use the alternative **others**, which, if used, must be the last alternative. In the extract below, the case expression is of type INTEGER, which, whatever the implementation, will have a rather large range of values.

```
-- Declarations assumed:
-- type USER is (MANAGER, ANALYST, PROGRAMMER,
--                    INVALID);
-- ID:USER;
-- KEY:INTEGER;

case KEY is
  when 10365=>
    ID:=ANALYST;
  when 12477=>
    ID:=MANAGER;
  when 25869=>
    ID:=PROGRAMMER;
  when others=>
    ID:=INVALID;
end case;
```

If there is more than one choice governing a sequence of statements, they may be linked using the alternation character (or vertical bar), '|'.

```
-- Declarations assumed:
-- type MONTHS is (JAN, FEB, MAR, APR, MAY, JUN, JUL,
--                    AUG, SEP, OCT, NOV, DEC);
-- THIS_MONTH:MONTHS;
-- DAYS:INTEGER range 1..31;
-- LEAP_YEAR:BOOLEAN;

case THIS_MONTH is
  when JAN | MAR | MAY | JUL |
       AUG | OCT | DEC=>
    DAYS:=31;
  when APR | JUN | SEP | NOV =>
    DAYS:=30;
```

```
    when FEB=>
      if LEAP_YEAR then
        DAYS:=29;
      else
        DAYS:=28;
      end if;
  end case;
```

Of course, this could have been expressed more concisely using **others** instead of explicitly naming the months with 31 days, but it would have been stylistically poor, and, possibly dangerous! Using **others** (especially through laziness or sloppiness) reduces the error checking capability of the compiler, and may lead to erroneous code during program development. For example, an enumeration type may be changed; values may be added or removed. Any oversight in amending a case statement with a selector of that type will go undetected, if it has an **others** alternative.

The order in which the choices is listed does not matter in Ada, as long as **others**, if used, is placed last. Nevertheless, it does help comprehension if the enumeration order is followed, where possible.

A case alternative may be specified by a range, either explicitly, or via a subtype indication. Both are illustrated in this extract.

```
  -- Declarations assumed:
  -- type DAY is (MON, TUE, WED, THU, FRI, SAT, SUN);
  -- subtype WEEKEND is DAY range SAT..SUN;
  -- TODAY:DAY;
  -- type STATE_OF_MIND is (UNBEARABLE, TOLERABLE,
  --                        PLEASANT, FUN);
  -- MOOD:STATE_OF_MIND;

  case TODAY is
    WHEN MON=>
      MOOD:=UNBEARABLE;
    WHEN TUE..THU=>
      MOOD:=TOLERABLE;
    when FRI=>
      MOOD:=PLEASANT;
    when WEEKEND=>
      MOOD:=FUN;
  end case;
```

The last choice, which uses the subtype indication WEEKEND, represents the range SAT..SUN.

It has been noted that all values of the case expression must be included in the list of choices. We also know that each selection governs a sequence of statements, which must include at least one statement. What if we have a choice for which there are no actions? For occurrences like this, Ada provides the null statement, which is an actual statement. Unlike some other languages, Ada does not have an implied null or empty statement.

```
-- Declarations assumed:
-- type ACTION is (LEFT, RIGHT, UP, DOWN, STEADY);
-- COMMAND:ACTION;
-- procedures GO_LEFT, GO_RIGHT, GO_UP and GO_DOWN

case COMMAND is
  when LEFT=>
    GO_LEFT;
  when RIGHT=>
    GO_RIGHT;
  when UP=>
    GO_UP;
  when DOWN=>
    GO_DOWN;
  when STEADY=>
    null;
end case;
```

By qualifying the case expression, it is possible to restrict the number of values that have to be catered for within the case statement.

```
-- Declarations assumed:
-- WEEKEND and TODAY as before
-- procedures GO_SHOPPING and GO_BIRD_WATCHING

case WEEKEND' (TODAY) is
  when SAT=>
    GO_SHOPPING;
  when SUN=>
    GO_BIRD_WATCHING;
end case;
```

Of course, if TODAY has a value outside the range of WEEKEND when the case expression is evaluated, then CONSTRAINT_ERROR will be raised.

If the case expression belongs to a subtype, then only the values of the subtype have to be included in the choices, as in the case of the qualified expression above. That only applies if the subtype is static (if its range is known at compile-time). Otherwise, all values of the base type have to be represented in the case choices. Given the declarations:

```
-- Declarations assumed:
-- VAR_LIMIT:INTEGER;                 -- variable
-- CONST_LIMIT:constant INTEGER:=6;
subtype STATIC_SUB is INTEGER range 1..CONST_LIMIT;
subtype NON_STATIC_SUB is INTEGER range 1..VAR_LIMIT;
STATIC_VAR:STATIC_SUB;
NON_STATIC_VAR:NON_STATIC_SUB;
```

Then, if STATIC_VAR is used as a case expression, only the values 1..6 have to be represented in the case statement. For NON_STATIC_VAR, *all* values of the base type (INTEGER) have to be covered as possible choices, because the actual range is indeterminate at compile-time.

The choices in a case statement may themselves be expressions, as long as those expressions are static. Consequently, it is possible to have:

```
-- Declarations assumed:
-- type SEGMENT_VALUES is (LO, MID, HI);
-- subtype DIGIT_TYPE is INTEGER range 0..9;
-- DEC_DIGIT:DIGIT_TYPE;
-- SEGMENT:SEGMENT_VALUES;
-- BOUNDARY:constant DIGIT_TYPE:=4;

case DEC_DIGIT is
  when 0..BOUNDARY-2 =>
    SEGMENT:=LO;
  when BOUNDARY-1..BOUNDARY+1 =>
    SEGMENT:=MID;
  when BOUNDARY+2..9 =>
    SEGMENT:=HI;
end case;
```

4.3 Loop statements [LRM 5.5]

The loop statement of Ada is used for all situations where a sequence of statements is to be executed repeatedly. In all loops, the governed sequence of statements is preceded by **loop** and followed by **end loop.**

Without any qualification, or provision of some means of escape from its control, a loop statement implies indefinite repetition as exemplified in the program of Unit 4.2.

```
with TEXT_IO;
use  TEXT_IO;

procedure ECHO is
   CH:CHARACTER;
begin
   loop
      GET(CH);  -- read from keyboard
      PUT(CH);  -- write to screen
   end loop;
end ECHO;
```

Unit 4.2 An indefinite loop.

In conventional programming, such a construction is not usually used (deliberately!), as once the loop has been entered, there is no means of escape. In a concurrent environment, however, where there are several simultaneously extant tasks, this is not uncommon, as you will see in Chapter 11.

The exit statement [LRM 5.7]

By placing an exit statement within the range of a loop statement, i.e. as one of the statements in the sequence governed by the loop, control may be passed out of the loop, to the statement immediately following **end loop**. An **exit** may be followed by a Boolean condition, as in this modification to the loop of Unit 4.2.

```
loop
   GET(CH);
   exit when CH = ASCII.SHARP;
   PUT(CH);
end loop;
-- execution continues here after an exit
```

Now, the loop will be repeated until the character read by GET is '#'. When that happens, control immediately passes out of the loop, circumventing any statements between the **exit** and **end loop**.

If an **exit** is not qualified, then this signifies a mandatory transfer of control from the loop. This should only sensibly be used in conjunction with some decision structure, such as an if or case statement:

```
loop
  N:=N+1;
  SUM:=SUM+N;
  if N = MAX then
    PUT(SUM);
    exit;
  end if;
end loop;
```

Even here, a conditional exit would be better, with a little re-arrangement:

```
loop
  N:=N+1;
  SUM:=SUM+N;
  exit when N = MAX;
end loop;
PUT(SUM);
```

The conditions for terminating the loops we have seen so far are quite simple, and the use of an exit statement is not the best way of expressing them. We shall return to the exit statement later, when it can be put to better use.

Loop iteration schemes [LRM 5.5]

Ada provides two iteration schemes, which are written as a prefix to a loop statement. The while iteration is of the form:

```
while ⟨CONDITION⟩ loop
  ⟨SEQUENCE_OF_STATEMENTS⟩
end loop;
```

Before the sequence of statements in the loop is obeyed, the condition after the **while** is evaluated. If the result is TRUE, then the loop is entered, otherwise it is not executed at all and control passes to the statement after **end loop**. Assuming that the loop statements are executed, then at **end loop**, control passes back to the **while**, which causes the following condition to be re-evaluated. This process is repeated until the condition evaluates to FALSE. From this brief explanation, it should be clear that the condition should contain some element(s) which may be altered, directly or indirectly, by the execution of the statements within the loop. Otherwise, the loop will never terminate.

Here is how the last example of an exit statement can be re-written using a while loop iteration:

```
while N < MAX loop
   N:=N+1;
   SUM:=SUM+N;
end loop;
PUT(SUM);
```

For situations in which a loop is to be executed a specific number of times, the for iteration scheme should be used. Associated with each **for** is a loop parameter, a variable which assumes each value of a specified discrete range in turn. The program of Unit 4.3 contains a for loop.

```
with SIMPLE_IO;   -- a non-standard package
use  SIMPLE_IO;

procedure MAIN is
   X, MEAN:FLOAT;
   SUM:FLOAT:=0.0;
   N:POSITIVE;
begin
   PUT("How many numbers (integer) ? ");
   GET(N);
   for I in 1..N loop
     PUT("Type a number (real) : ");
     GET(X);
     SUM:=SUM+X;
   end loop;
   PUT("Mean is: ");
   PUT(SUM/FLOAT(N));
end MAIN;
```

Unit 4.3 Example of a for loop.

Briefly, the program ascertains the value of N, which is the number of times that the loop will execute. With each iteration, a number is read and is then added to the sum of all previously entered numbers. Finally, the program writes out the mean of the values read. One thing that may seem strange is that there is no explicit declaration of the loop parameter, I. In fact, a loop parameter is taken to be declared by its appearance in a for statement, its type being inferred from the discrete range that follows it (which may not necessarily be straightforward, as we shall see). One consequence of this is that the loop parameter only has any significance, as such, within the sequence of statements of the loop — it is said to be **in scope** from its point of declaration to the corresponding **end loop**. (More

will be said about scope in the next chapter.) So, the problem, which
arises in many languages, of the value of a loop control variable being
undefined on completion of a loop cannot occur in Ada, as the variable
itself is inaccessible outside the loop.

Within its scope, a loop parameter is "read only", which means that
its value cannot be changed by any program statement (including subprograms). This does not prevent the value of the loop parameter from
being used within the loop:

```
for I in 1..N loop
   SUM_SQUARE:=SUM_SQUARE + I*I;
end loop;
```

The range of discrete values that is specified for the loop parameter will
be covered in its entirety, from the first value in the range to the last, in
single valued increments. (It is possible to terminate the loop prematurely
using an exit statement.) As the loop variable cannot be altered by the
programmer, it is not possible for it to be incremented to any value other
than the next one in the given range.

Some examples of for iteration schemes, which use types or subtypes
defined earlier in this book, are listed below, together with comments on
the resulting iterations:

```
for SHADE in COLOUR loop
   -- RED..YELLOW
   -- this is preferable to:
   -- for SHADE in RED..YELLOW loop

for HUE in COLOUR range BLUE..PINK loop
   -- BLUE..PINK

for JOUR in DAY loop
   -- MON..SUN
   -- this is preferable to:
   -- for JOUR in MON..SUN loop

for REST_DAY in WEEKEND loop
   -- SAT..SUN
   -- which is preferable to:
   -- for REST_DAY in DAY range SAT..SUN loop
```

The reason for the stated preferences above is that it is always better to
use a subtype or type indication in expressing the range, for it implies the

application of the complete range associated with the (sub)type. Consequently, the loop is more general, in that should the type or subtype be changed, it will still apply to all values in the type.

Other examples of loops with for iteration schemes will be encountered in succeeding chapters.

On occasion, it is not possible to infer the type of the loop parameter from the given range. For example, if the types URGENCY and SPEED, defined in 3.9, were both applicable, then the scheme:

for RATE in LOW..HIGH loop

would be ambiguous (and would consequently fail to compile) as the type of LOW..HIGH cannot be uniquely determined. To overcome this, we can either use the type mark itself, or qualify the range (its first element is sufficient), as in:

for RATE in SPEED'(LOW)..HIGH loop

or, preferably:

for RATE in SPEED loop

An earlier example, in which the specified range was 1..N, presented no problem as the type of N was known. However, what if we were to write

for I in 1..10 loop

The range here is not necessarily of type INTEGER, but, because ranges like this are likely to be used very frequently, Ada will assume that the implied type is INTEGER. If you really mean some other integer type, it is up to you to say so, as in

for I in INT_TYPE'(1)..10 loop

in which INT_TYPE is an integer type introduced by the programmer in a way demonstrated in Chapter 8. It is always better to use an explicit type, so that any implementation dependences are more obvious.

The range limits may be specified by expressions (of compatible discrete types). If we had the iteration scheme:

for I in 2..N loop

where N is of subtype POSITIVE, then it would be possible for N to have the value 1. If this were the case, the range of I would be the "null range", as the first value is greater than the last. The effect on the iteration scheme would be that the loop would not be executed at all;

note that the values would not be assigned in the reverse order. If that is what you want, you indicate iteration in descending order by the addition of **reverse** after **in**:

>for I in reverse 1..10 loop

takes I through the values 10, 9, 8 and so on down to 1. Note that the range itself should *not* be inverted.

A loop range is only evaluated once, at the start of execution of the loop. If (for some obscure reason) we had:

>N:=6;
>for I in 1..N loop
> SUM:=SUM+I;
> N:=N-1;
>end loop;

the range for I would be fixed at 1..6 when the loop was initiated. Any subsequent change of N cannot affect the range.

There is no repeat..until

Ada does not provide a construct which corresponds to the repeat..until loop of Pascal. In most situations, a while loop may easily be substituted, or a conditional exit may be placed before **end loop**. To ensure that the sequence of statements within a loop, controlled by a **while**, is executed at least once (a major motivation for using **repeat**) the **while** condition must be initialized to TRUE. Also, care must be taken to ensure that the condition is not the inverse of that required. So, two ways of obtaining a repeat..until style of loop:

>loop
> ⟨SEQUENCE_OF_STATEMENTS⟩
> exit when TERM <= REL_ERROR;
>end loop;

or, using a while loop

>CONTINUE:=TRUE;
>while CONTINUE loop
> ⟨SEQUENCE_OF_STATEMENTS⟩
> CONTINUE:=TERM > REL_ERROR;
>end loop;

Unit 4.4 is a complete program that utilizes while loops in this way.

```
with SIMPLE_IO;  -- a non-standard package
use  SIMPLE_IO;

procedure SQ_ROOT is
  MAX_ERROR:constant FLOAT:=1.0E-6;
  HALF:constant FLOAT:=0.5;
  ARGUMENT, ROOT, LAST_ROOT:FLOAT;
  NUMBER_BAD, INACCURATE:BOOLEAN;
begin
OUTER:                                   -- once for each root
  loop
    NUMBER_BAD:=TRUE;
    while NUMBER_BAD loop
      PUT("Enter a real number (zero to terminate): ");
      GET(ARGUMENT);
      exit OUTER when ARGUMENT=0.0;       -- end of program
      NUMBER_BAD:=ARGUMENT < 0.0;         -- trap negative numbers
    end loop;                             -- while
    ROOT:=1.0;                            -- initial guess
    INACCURATE:=TRUE;
    while INACCURATE loop
      LAST_ROOT:=ROOT;                     -- remember last guess
      ROOT:=(ARGUMENT/ROOT + ROOT)*HALF;-- next guess
      INACCURATE:=abs(ROOT - LAST_ROOT) >= MAX_ERROR;
    end loop;
    PUT("Square root is : ");
    PUT(ROOT);
    NEW_LINE;
  end loop OUTER;
end SQ_ROOT;
```

Unit 4.4   Repeated calculation of square root.

Nested loops

Many algorithms call for the use of loops within loops. This is easily expressed in Ada, as any of the statements within the loop may itself be a loop. The usual rules of nesting apply, so that no loop may overlap another. In other words, an **end loop** is always associated with the last **loop**. A loop of any kind may be nested within any loop. Here are just two outlines of correctly nested loops, the first with two nested for loops:

```
for WORK_DAY in DAY loop
  -- some other statements here, if required
  for HOUR in 1..8 loop
    -- inner loop sequence of statements
    -- executed 56 times altogether
  end loop;     -- for HOUR
  -- more statements, if required
end loop;        -- for WORK_DAY
```

and the second with a while loop within a for loop:

```
for I in 1..N loop
   -- statements, if required
   while TERM > TOLERANCE loop
      -- inner loop sequence of statements
   end loop;    -- while
   -- more statements, if required
end loop;       for I
```

The range of a **for** iteration scheme is evaluated each time the for loop is encountered. Therefore, in the inner loop of:

```
for I in 1..N−1 loop
   for J in I+1..N loop
      -- inner statement sequence
   end loop;    -- for J
end loop;       -- for I
```

the inner loop is executed N−1 times. The first execution will be through the range 2..N, the second through 3..N, and so on.

One final feature of the loop statement is the ability to name any loop. Naming may be used to enhance the readability of nested loop structures, although indentation should suffice for that purpose. A situation, in which named loops are necessary, occurs when it is required to exit from a nested loop structure to an outer level. An unnamed **exit** only transfers control out of the current loop.

A loop is named by immediately preceding it with a valid indentifier and colon (to the left of the current indentation level), and the corresponding **end loop** *must* be followed by the same identifier.

```
SUMMATION:
   for I in 1..N loop
   SUM:=SUM+I;
   end loop SUMMATION;
```

Although the loop name may look like a label, it is not one! There is no way of transferring control to a loop name.

In order to exit from a specific loop, **exit** should be followed by the name of that loop:

```
OUTER:
   while MORE_LINES loop
      -- statements
```

```
    while MORE_CHARS loop
      -- inner statements
      exit when LINE_BAD;                      -- EXIT 1
      -- more statements
      exit OUTER when BUFFER_FULL;  -- EXIT 2
      -- further statements, if required
    end loop;
    -- EXIT 1 transfers control here
  end loop OUTER;
  -- EXIT 2 transfers control here
```

Unit 4.5 is a complete program, which employs some of the control statements introduced in this chapter. This program reads in expressions of the form:

NUMBER OPERATOR NUMBER OPERATOR ... NUMBER =

and prints the result rather in the manner of a pocket calculator. Each execution of the while loop reads a number followed by an operator. When the operator is an equals sign, which indicates a desire for the result, the execution of the loop terminates. Any valid arithmetic operator is applied during the subsequent execution of the loop, after the next number (its next operand) has been read.

```
with SIMPLE_IO;  -- a non-standard package
use  SIMPLE_IO;

procedure CALCULATOR is
  OPERAND:FLOAT;
  RESULT:FLOAT:=0.0;
  OPERATOR:CHARACTER:='+';
  EQUALS:constant CHARACTER:='=';
  NOT_EQUAL:BOOLEAN:=TRUE;
begin
  PUT("Type your calculation: ");
  while NOT_EQUAL loop
    GET(OPERAND);
    case OPERATOR is
      when '+' =>
        RESULT:=RESULT + OPERAND;
      when '-' =>
        RESULT:=RESULT - OPERAND;
      when '*' =>
        RESULT:=RESULT * OPERAND;
      when '/' =>
        RESULT:=RESULT / OPERAND;
      when others =>
        NEW_LINE;
        PUT("Invalid operator.");
        NEW_LINE;
        exit;
    end case;
```

```
    GET(OPERATOR);
    NOT_EQUAL:=OPERATOR /= EQUALS;
  end loop;
  NEW_LINE;
  PUT("Answer is : ");
  PUT(RESULT);
  NEW_LINE;
end CALCULATOR;
```

Unit 4.5 A simple calculator.

On entering: 2.0 + 3.0 * 4.0 =
the program will print the result 20.0 — it has no knowledge about operator precedence

Finally, *en passant*, it should be mentioned that there *is* a **goto** statement in Ada, much to the chagrin of purists. Because of the expressive power of other constructs provided by Ada (especially **exit**, **return** and exceptions), the justification for using a **goto** in Ada cannot be supported, as it can (occasionally) be for Pascal. A **goto** does make it easier to convert programs from less structured languages (like FORTRAN and BASIC) into Ada. In some circumstances, a literal translation may be necessary to preserve characteristics of the original as closely as possible. The result will not, of course, be a good Ada program.

Practising Ada 4

You are now in a position to write programs with rather more substance. Use all the control statements, in all their forms, before proceeding. Some suggestions for programs:

1 Write out the printing characters of type CHARACTER.

2 Write out all the integers between 1 and 99 that are multiples of 3 or 5 (but not both).

3 Read in a start value, final value and an increment for tabulating a variable, then produce a table of reciprocals, square roots and squares for all tabular values of the variable.

4 Read two integers and calculate the result of dividing the first by the second — using only addition and subtraction.

5 Read a real number and calculate the exponential of that number to 6 digits of accuracy, using the series:

$$\exp(x) = 1 + x + x^{**}2/2! + x^{**}3/3! + \ldots\ldots$$

6 Read a real number, x, which represents an angle in radians, and calculate the sine of that angle to 5 digits of accuracy using:

$$\text{sine}(x) = x - x^{**}3/3! + x^{**}5/5! - x^{**}7/7! + \ldots.$$

7 Read a Roman number and write out the decimal equivalent.

8 Read in a date of the form: dd mm yyyy and write out the date of the next day (in the same form)

9 Define a type to represent notes of a chromatic scale in music (e.g. C, C_SHARP, D, D_SHARP, E, F, F_SHARP, G etc.). Write a program that will read in an original key and a target key and then write out a transposition table.

(The musically inclined might like to extend this idea to include accidentals other than sharps − how would you incorporate them? One idea might be D_FLAT:constant NOTE:=C_SHARP; but how do you input/output values? Would a CHARACTER based approach, C#=Db, be better?)

Chapter 5

Blocks, subprograms and exceptions

The fundamental difference between blocks and subprograms is that the latter are program units, members of the class of distinct modules from which programs are constructed. Blocks, on the other hand, are used for localization within program units.

There are, however, so many similarities between blocks and subprograms that it is logical to treat them together. Indeed, computer scientists frequently apply the term "block" to both constructs. In this general usage a block is any module of code that has its own local declarations, which are only significant within the block itself. The last point relates to the scope and accessibility of declarations, a topic discussed at length in 5.2.

The handling of exceptions is an important feature of blocks and subprograms, so much so, that one of the main uses of blocks in Ada is to provide local exception handlers. Consequently, exceptions and their handlers are also introduced in this chapter.

5.1 Blocks [LRM 5.6]

A block is a sequence of statements that has its own local declarations and/or its own exception handler(s). It can be used anywhere within a sequence of statements, as one of the statements of the sequence.

It is always good practice to keep the range of influence of declarations as local as possible, so that they have no meaning (or can not be given a different one) in parts of a program to which they do not relate. The example of a block in Unit 2.4 showed that the variable TEMP was created specifically for the exchange of values in the block. Both before and after execution of the block, TEMP did not exist. (Of course, there might have been another TEMP declared somewhere else in the program, but that is for 5.2 to explain.)

In full, the structure of a block is:

```
[⟨BLOCK_SIMPLE_NAME⟩:]
  [declare
    ⟨DECLARATIVE_PART⟩]
  begin
    ⟨SEQUENCE_OF_STATEMENTS⟩
```

```
  [exception
    ⟨EXCEPTION_HANDLER(S)⟩]
  end [⟨BLOCK_SIMPLE_NAME⟩];
```

Remember that, in BNF notation, anything enclosed between [and] is optional. It was noted in Chapter 2 that a block does not require a declarative part or an exception handler. However, it is worth repeating that a block without at least one of these is a redundant construct.

From the above outline, the possibility of naming a block, rather like the naming of a loop, is revealed. If the block is named, then the block name *must* be included after the **end**. It always helps readability, if a block is given a name. There are other advantages of naming blocks, as we shall see.

The declarative part may contain any valid declaration items. However, if there is a need to declare program units (like subprograms and packages) within a block, then a block is not the appropriate structure — it should then be a program unit itself. Blocks should not be very long. They should include a sequence of statements with a coherent purpose, with which it is necessary to associate local declarations and/or exception handlers. In many situations where a block could be used, a subprogram would be more appropriate. This is the case with Unit 5.1!

```
with SIMPLE_IO;  -- a non-standard package
use  SIMPLE_IO;

procedure MAIN is
  N_MAX:POSITIVE;
  MEAN:FLOAT;
begin
  NEW_LINE;
  PUT("How many numbers: ");
  GET(N_MAX);
GET_THEM:
  declare
    NEXT:FLOAT;
    SUM:FLOAT:=0.0;
  begin
    for N_SO_FAR in 1..N_MAX loop
      PUT("Number (real) : ");
      PUT(N_SO_FAR);
      PUT(" = ");
      GET(NEXT);
      SUM:=SUM + NEXT;
    end loop;
    MEAN:=SUM / FLOAT(N_MAX);
  end GET_THEM;
  NEW_LINE;
  PUT("Mean= ");
  PUT(MEAN);
  NEW_LINE;
end MAIN;
```

Unit 5.1 A program containing a block.

The block in this example enables the variables NEXT and SUM to be localized (in the same way that Ada enforces localization of loop parameters like N_SO_FAR). The actions of the block are to read in a number of real values, compute their sum and mean, communicating the latter value to the enclosing program via the global variable MEAN. This will be rewritten as a procedure in 5.8, where an example is also given of a block for localizing exception handling.

5.2 Scope and visibility [LRM 8]

That the LRM devotes a whole chapter to these topics is an indication of their importance (and occasional intricacies). Some of the material relates to features yet to be discussed, in particular, that which concerns packages. For now, the discussion of these terms will be restricted to their relevance to blocks and subprograms.

In the ensuing explanations, it is useful to define the term *declarative region*, as used in the LRM, to mean a complete block or subprogram, with its own declarations, or it can be a loop statement, with a for loop parameter. A declaration in some declarative part is *local* to its particular declarative region, while a declaration in an enclosing declarative region is *global* to an inner one.

A declaration is in *scope* (i.e. it has a meaning) from the beginning of its declaration to the end of its declarative region. This scope includes any declarative regions nested within its own region.

An identifier becomes *visible* (i.e. can be referenced) immediately after its declaration. This invalidates declarations such as:

    N:INTEGER:=N; -- ILLEGAL

Even if N were a global (INTEGER) object, this new declaration of N would render the global N invisible at its beginning, for this is the start of the scope of the new N. The new N itself, cannot be referenced until after its declaration, hence the N used for initialization above has no meaning.

This brings us on to a general discussion of *homographs*, which are identifiers of the same name declared at more than one place. Any declaration of the same identifier within the same declarative part will generally be rejected as being erroneous. The overloading of enumeration literals and subprograms are exceptions to this, as we shall shortly see. If there is an outer homograph of an identifier (i.e. one in scope at the point of a new declaration) then the outer one ceases to be visible at the start of the declaration of the inner one. Alternatively, the inner homograph *hides* the outer one. The outline below explains some of these relationships:

```
procedure FUNNY is
   J:INTEGER:=3;                               |
begin                                       |  |
   -- J is 3                                |  |
INNER:                                      |  |
   declare                                  |  |
      I:INTEGER:=J; -- I:=3           |  |  |
      J:INTEGER:=6;               |  |  |     |
   begin                      |  |  |  |     |
      -- J is 6               |  |  |  |     |
   end INNER;                                |  |
   -- J is 3                                 |  |
end FUNNY;                        1  2  3  4  5  6
```

The numbered ranges above represent:

1 and 2 : visibility and scope (respectively) of INNER.J.
3 and 4 : visibility and scope (respectively) of I.
5 and 6 : visibility and scope (respectively) of FUNNY.J.

Any declaration hidden by the declaration of a homograph may be rendered visible by explicit selection, if its declarative region is named, and if the hidden homograph is, indeed, in scope (and therefore able to be hidden). To select an identifier, it must be prefixed by the name of its block, subprogram or loop, followed by a '.' . The example in Unit 5.2 is extreme, to say the least, in that it flouts one of the golden rules of good programming practice: never give an identifier a multiplicity of meanings.

```
with SIMPLE_IO;   -- a non-standard package
use  SIMPLE_IO;

procedure BAD_EXAMPLE is
   J:INTEGER:=0;
begin
   -- J=0
INNER_1:
   for J in 1..5 loop
      -- J is loop parameter, hiding outer J
      -- but visible by selection: BAD_EXAMPLE.J
   INNER_2:
      declare
         J:INTEGER:=INNER_1.J;
      begin
         J:=J * J;
         BAD_EXAMPLE.J:=BAD_EXAMPLE.J + J;
```

```
      end INNER_2;
      -- INNER_2.J no longer exists
    end loop INNER_1;
    -- INNER_1.J no longer exists
    PUT(J);            -- what will be output?
    NEW_LINE;
  end BAD_EXAMPLE;
```

Unit 5.2   Illustration of scope and visibility.

The program in Unit 5.2 illustrates the use of explicit selection. However, given that homographs should not generally occur (except when deliberately overloading) you would not normally need to use explicit selection. More will be said about scope and visibility later in this chapter, with reference to subprogram overloading and, again, in Chapter 7, in relation to packages.

One final word here; the nesting of blocks and subprograms should not be taken to excess, with the result that program structure is obscured for the sake of (over) localization.

5.3 Subprograms [LRM 6]

Subprograms, the collective term for procedures and functions, have a similar structure to blocks. The essential difference is that subprograms are program units, the execution of which is invoked by a call from some part of the program where the subprogram is in scope. Unlike blocks, subprograms may have parameters, which widens their applicability. Subprograms may be called recursively. It should be remembered, though, that for many applications, iteration provides a much more efficient alternative to recursion. The relative costs depend on how efficiently the hardware supports subprogram calls and parameter passing. Where speed is important, this may be significant: otherwise, the formulation of a solution should suit the problem in hand. If recursion is natural, in the application context, and if the corresponding code is concise (and readable), then it should be used.

Subprograms may be declared in any declarative part. Although it is possible, they should not be declared in a block, for reasons explained in 5.1. Subprograms themselves should be no longer than a page, otherwise they become hard to follow. Comments should always be included in the heading to state the purpose and characteristics of a subprogram. Now let us be more specific.

Functions

A function should be used wherever the purpose is to return a single value to the point of call, as is the case with functions like:

```
function CUBE(N:in INTEGER) return INTEGER is
-- calculates the cube of N
begin
   return N*N*N;
end CUBE;
```

This function takes an INTEGER parameter, N, and returns an INTEGER value, which is the cube of N. N is called a *formal parameter*, the name given to a parameter used in the declaration of a subprogram. Formal parameters must be declared using type or subtype identifiers, no other elements (including constraints) are allowed.

The function can be called from anywhere that an INTEGER value can be used (i.e. within an INTEGER expression). On making such a call, an *actual* parameter must be supplied, which must, itself, be an INTEGER expression. Some valid calls are:

```
PUT(CUBE(3));            -- provided there is a PUT for
                         -- INTEGER
K:=CUBE(I) + CUBE(J);    -- I and J must have values
PUT(CUBE(I*J));          -- both comments above apply
```

Following the **return** is an expression of the type that is returned by the function. There must be at least one **return** in a function, one of which must be executed when the function is called, otherwise the pre-defined exception, PROGRAM_ERROR, will be raised.

If there is more than one parameter, of the same type *and* the same mode (such as **in**), they can be listed together, as with X and Y in the function below.

```
function LARGER(X,Y: in FLOAT) return FLOAT is
-- returns the larger value of X and Y
begin
   if X > Y then
      return X;
   else
      return Y;
   end if;
end LARGER;
```

Functions in Ada are allowed to have parameters of mode **in**. This means that they can only be used as a means of entering values into the function, or initializing the formal parameters, in keeping with the mathematical notion of the argument of a function. Function parameters cannot be used to return values to actual parameters, nor can they be used as local variables within the function; both of these are possible in Pascal. Therefore, any attempt to assign a value to a function parameter will be rejected by the compiler.

Functions can, of course, have local variables, as in:

```
function SUM_SQUARE(N:in NATURAL) return NATURAL is
-- returns the sum of the square of the
-- values in the range 1..N
  SUM:NATURAL:=0;
begin
  for I in 1..N loop
    SUM:=SUM + I;
  end loop;
  return SUM;
end SUM_SQUARE;
```

The mode indicator, **in**, is optional. If a subprogram parameter has no explicit mode indication, then the compiler will assume that it is an **in** parameter. It can be argued that the **in** may be omitted for functions, where no other mode is allowed. This author feels that it is always better to state the mode explicitly.

Strangely, Ada does not insist that the name of a subprogram be repeated after the final **end** of the unit. It is a great aid to program understanding to repeat the subprogram name at the end, thereby rounding off the declaration neatly.

Procedures

Procedures share many of the characteristics of functions that we have seen. The main difference is that procedures do not return a value to the calling point; they are called by using the procedure name as a statement, rather than from within some expression. Procedures can only return values via parameters. Unit 5.3 includes a parameterless procedure declared in the main program (which is itself written as a parameterless procedure).

```
with SIMPLE_IO;  -- a non-standard package
use  SIMPLE_IO;

procedure MAIN is
  INT:INTEGER;

  procedure STARS is
  -- writes out a line of asterisks
    STAR_MAX:constant INTEGER:=30;
    STAR:constant CHARACTER:='*';
    subtype STAR_RANGE is INTEGER range 1..STAR_MAX;
  begin
    NEW_LINE;
    for COL in STAR_RANGE loop
      PUT(STAR);
    end loop;
    NEW_LINE;
  end STARS;

begin     -- MAIN
  STARS;
  PUT("Type an integer: ");
  GET(INT);
  STARS;
  PUT("Its square is: ");
  PUT(INT * INT);
  STARS;
end MAIN;
```

Unit 5.3   A program with a procedure.

5.4 Parameter modes [LRM 6.2]

Functions may only have parameters of mode **in**, but Ada provides three modes for procedure parameters, which are:

in

The value of the actual parameter is assigned to the formal parameter on entry to the subprogram. The parameter acts like a local *constant* (which cannot be changed).

out

This acts like a local variable within the procedure. It is *write only*, because its value cannot be read. On exit from the procedure, its value is assigned to the actual parameter variable. (The actual parameter can only be a variable.) If the formal parameter has not been given a value within the procedure, then the actual parameter variable becomes *undefined*. (This contrasts with the situation in other languages, in which the actual parameter remains unchanged if no assignment is made.)

in out

A parameter of this mode acts like a local variable that is initialized to
the value of the actual parameter variable on entry to the procedure.
(The actual parameter can only be a variable.) Within the procedure,
the value of the parameter may be read and modified. On exit from the
procedure, the value of the parameter is assigned to the actual
parameter variable. It can *not* be assumed that the actual parameter
and the formal parameter are the same.

For scalar types, the values of **in** and **in out** actual parameters are
copied into the formal parameters when the subprogram is called. On
termination of a procedure, **out** and **in out** formal parameters are copied
into their corresponding actual parameter variables. Therefore, the actual
and formal parameters do not keep in step, as is illustrated in Unit 5.4.

```
with SIMPLE_IO;   -- a non-standard package
use  SIMPLE_IO;

procedure MAIN is
  J:INTEGER:=3;

  procedure ADD_1(I:in out INTEGER) is
  begin
    I:=I + 1;
    PUT(J);      -- 3
  end ADD_1;

begin    -- MAIN
  PUT(J);        -- 3
  ADD_1(J);
  PUT(J);        -- 4
  NEW_LINE;
end MAIN;
```

Unit 5.4 Illustration of parameter transmission.

For more complex types, such as arrays and records, the parameter
transmission mechanism is undefined; it is left to the implementors to
decide. It may well be that, rather than copy all of a large structure
on subprogram entry and/or procedure exit, which can be very time-
consuming at run-time, the structure may be accessed by reference (as
with the **var** parameter of Pascal). In that case, all operations on formal
parameters will be applied directly to the actual parameters. This *may*
happen; it may not. Consequently, any program that assumes a particular
mechanism is unportable, and may be erroneous.

Don't be tempted to use **in out** parameters as local workspace variables.
Now that Ada has established exactly what a parameter is, an interface

with the calling environment, it cuts across this interpretation to use the parameters for other purposes. You should declare local variables within the procedure, if you need them. Their purpose is then obvious.

In a concurrent environment, in which several elements of a program appear to be executing simultaneously, it is much easier to understand and prove the behaviour of procedures that only affect their outside world on entry and exit. If a procedure is interrupted, for example, we do not have to worry about interference with its parameters by any other procedure. This argument helps to explain the rationale behind parameter transmission in Ada; it also mitigates against the use of global variables, which will shortly be attacked from another angle.

There is no limit on the number of parameters that a subprogram may have. However, a very large parameter list implies that a subprogram is too large, or that some structured type should be used to aggregate data. Certainly, a long list is cumbersome and difficult to read. Of course, that is not an excuse for removing parameters altogether and communicating via global variables. Far from it! In fact, subprograms should only access global variables when it is *really* necessary and when the nature of the access is obvious.

A subprogram that manipulates a global variable is said to exhibit a *side-effect*, i.e. it has influence on objects other than its parameters. One situation where side-effects are unavoidable is in i/o procedures, where some input or output stream is altered by calls of GET and PUT. Side-effects are particularly frowned upon in functions. It is usual to regard a function in a program as having the same characteristics as a mathematical function, operating only on some argument(s). Side-effects are particularly harmful in functions, if the result of calling the function is sensitive to the context of the call in an expression, as in:

```
function NASTY(I:in INTEGER)return INTEGER is
-- J is global
begin
  J:=J + I;
  return I * I;
end NASTY;
```

If we now have a (main program) calling sequence:

```
J:=1;
PUT(NASTY(J) + NASTY(J*J));
```

The result will be different from that obtained by:

```
J:=1;
PUT(NASTY(J*J) + NASTY(J));
```

which is not as it should be! (Verify that these two calls would result in the output of 17 and 5, respectively, and that the value of J would be different on completion of each sequence.)

5.5 Parameter associations and defaults [LRM 6.4]

Consider the following program extract:

```
I, J:INTEGER:=2;
K, L:INTEGER;

procedure COPY(P_IN:in INTEGER; P_OUT:out INTEGER) is
begin
   P_OUT:=P_IN;
end COPY;
begin
   -- at this point, we could call the procedure by:
   -- COPY(I,K); or COPY(J,L); or COPY(I,J); etc.
   -- but NOT by COPY(K,L); as K has no value.
end;
```

When a subprogram is called, it may be a point in the code that is lexically distant from the declaration. In the simple procedure above, for example, it would not be obvious from a call, taken in isolation, which parameter is being copied and which is the copy. In many situations, greater clarity is desirable at the point of call than can be obtained using *positional* parameter association like those above. For solving this problem, Ada also provides *named* parameter association, so that we can write:

```
COPY(P_IN => I, P_OUT  => K);
COPY(P_OUT => K, P_IN => J);
```

As long as the parameter names are well chosen, the meaning is enhanced by the name association. The above examples show that with named association, the order of listing the parameters does not have to follow the declaration order of the formal parameters. It is permitted (but not desirable) to mix positional and named associations in the same call, as long as the positional is used first, in the correct sequence, as in:

COPY(I, P_OUT => K);

Default parameters

Parameters of mode **in** may be given default expression (of the appropriate type) in the formal parameter list. If a default value is provided for a parameter, then that parameter may be omitted from the actual parameter list of the call, in which case, the parameter will be initialized to the default. To illustrate this, consider the procedure heading:

```
procedure ADD_STOCK
          (ITEM:in out ITEM_TYPE;
           DELIVERED, ORDERED:in STOCK_RANGE:=100;
           REORDER_LEVEL:in STOCK_RANGE:=50) ...
```

Assuming that the variable WIDGETS is of type ITEM_TYPE, then all of the following calls are valid:

```
ADD_STOCK(WIDGETS, 80, 120, 60);
          -- no defaults applied
ADD_STOCK(WIDGETS, 80, 120);
          -- default for REORDER_LEVEL
ADD_STOCK(WIDGETS);
          -- all defaults applied
ADD_STOCK(ITEM => WIDGETS,
          REORDER_LEVEL => 90);
          -- defaults for DELIVERED
          -- and ORDERED
```

Note that named association allows any of the defaults to be selected, as in the last call, while positional association only allows omission from the tail of the parameter list. A subprogram which only has parameters of mode **in**, all of which have default expressions, does not require any actual parameters when it is called!

Default parameter expressions should be used with care, as they hide some of the meaning of the subprogram call, where it is not obvious that there are any default parameters, never mind what values they might be. Default parameters should be used in situations where they represent the *normal* case, such that over-riding them is an exceptional occurrence. Extensive use is made of default parameters in TEXT_IO in just this manner, as we shall see in Chapter 10.

One final stylistic point about parameters concerns related subprograms, which have identical or similar parameter lists. Where this occurs, use the same parameter names and sequence throughout, as in:

```
-- SET_TYPE is a user-defined type
procedure UNION
      (LEFT, RIGHT:in SET_TYPE; RESULT:out SET_TYPE) --
procedure INTERSECTION
      (LEFT, RIGHT:in SET_TYPE; RESULT:out SET_TYPE) --
```

5.6 Subprograms and scope [LRM 8]

The scope rules already discussed apply to subprograms as well as blocks. However, some of the implications of the application of these rules to subprograms may not be obvious. First, as is common in block structured languages, the scope and visibility of identifiers that may be accessed by a subprogram are determined by where the subprogram is *declared*, not where it is called. This point is not always appreciated, and can lead to erroneous programs, particularly where subprograms operate on non-local variables.

Another point to note is which part of a subprogram declaration belongs to the declarative region in which it is declared, and which part is local to the subprogram itself. That is simple! The subprogram identifier is the property of the enclosing declarative region, and is global to the subprogram itself. The formal parameters, together with all other declarations within the subprogram, are all local to it.

Some of the consequences of these (and other) points are now illustrated. In some declaration part, we have:

```
type T is (ON, OFF);
procedure T(P:in out T) is -- INVALID
```

This would fail, because of the attempt to declare T as a procedure in the same declarative part in which it has already been declared as an enumeration type. What if the procedure were declared in some inner declarative region?

```
-- some declarative part
type T is (ON,OFF);
procedure INNER;
   procedure T(P:in out T) is -- INVALID
      --
   end T;
   --
end INNER;
```

It still fails, but now for a different reason. As soon as T is declared as the procedure name, the outer T ceases to be visible.

Another invalid declaration:

```
procedure P(I:in out INTEGER) is
      I:INTEGER; -- INVALID
```

This would be rejected because I is incorrectly declared twice within the same declarative part, as a parameter, then as a local variable.

To summarize the scope rules and their effects, this annotated program skeleton should be useful.

```
procedure MAIN is
  I, J, K:INTEGER;

  procedure P1(I:in INTEGER) is
    J:INTEGER:=2 * I;

    procedure P2(K:in INTEGER) is
      J:INTEGER:=3;
    begin -- P2
      -- locals: J(3)   K(parameter)
      -- globals: I(P1 parameter) P1 P2
      -- by selection: P1.J(2*P1.I)
      -- MAIN.I  MAIN.J  MAIN.K
    end P2;

  begin --P1
    -- locals: I(parameter)   J(2*I)   P2
    -- globals: K   P1
    -- by selection: MAIN.I   MAIN.J
  end P1;
```

```
procedure P3(J:in INTEGER) is
   I:INTEGER:=K+3;      -- MAIN.K+3
   K:INTEGER:=4;        -- K now re-defined
begin -- P3
   -- locals:I J(parameter)  K(4)
   -- globals: P1  P3
   -- by selection: MAIN.I  MAIN.J  MAIN.K
end P3;

begin -- MAIN
   -- locals: I  J  K  P1  P3
end MAIN;
```

If P3 were to call P1, then any reference to I, J and K in P1 will be interpreted by the scope and visibility relative to P1 (as shown above) and *not* with respect to P3.

Overloading [LRM 6.6]

By now, you should be familiar with the concept of overloading. Nevertheless, it may not be obvious when Ada will overload and when it will hide homographs, which are subprograms. An example was given in Chapter 2 of an additional overloading of procedure PUT. Although sharing the same name as several other procedures in TEXT_IO (and SIMPLE_IO), the distinction between this new one and all the others is easily made on the basis of its *parameter profile*, which is different from that of all previously existing PUT procedures. More should be said about this.

Two subprograms are said to have the same parameter (and result) type profiles, if they have the same number of parameters, with the same *base* types in the same positions (and for functions, the same result type). The names and transmission modes of parameters are irrelevant to the comparison of parameter type profiles. If two subprograms of the same name have identical profiles, then the inner one hides the outer one. (Two such subprograms cannot be declared in the same declarative part, except under particular circumstances.) So, we cannot have:

```
procedure DO_SOMETHING(X, Y:INTEGER) is --
procedure DO_SOMETHING(I:in INTEGER; J:out INTEGER)
is -- ILLEGAL
```

Identically named subprograms with different parameter and result profiles overload each other, and one does not hide any other.

A call to an overloaded subprogram must not be ambiguous. The
compiler must always be able to determine the subprogram to apply from
the actual parameters. Qualification or name notation may be required to
assist the resolution. For example, if we had:

```
with TEXT_IO;
use TEXT_IO;
procedure MAIN is
    type RESPONSE is ('Y', 'N', 'y', 'n');
    procedure PUT(R:in RESPONSE) is --
    -- and so on
begin
    -- main program
end MAIN;
```

then a call of:

```
PUT('Y');
```

would be ambiguous, as 'Y' is a value of the pre-defined type CHARAC-
TER as well as of type RESPONSE, and there is a PUT for CHARACTERs
in TEXT_IO. To resolve the ambiguity, we could write:

```
PUT(RESPONSE'('Y'));
```

which makes it clear which PUT to apply. A less satisfactory alternative
would be to use named notation, utilizing the fact that the two PUTs in
question have different parameter names:

```
PUT(R => 'Y');
```

That is nowhere near as informative as the first alternative.

The key to overloading, then, is not to be ambiguous, so that the
compiler (and you and others) know exactly what you mean.

Operators [LRM 6.7]

A function may be given a name (called a designator) which is the same
as that of one of the pre-defined operators. The new function must have
the same number of arguments as the pre-defined operator and it will
inherit the same precedence, which cannot be changed. The short-circuit

control forms **and then** and **or else** (which are not operators remember) cannot be explicitly overloaded, nor can "/=" be explicitly overloaded, as this is automatically performed by Ada when "=" is overloaded.

The following example illustrates a new overloading of "+":

> function "+" (LEFT:in INTEGER; RIGHT in FLOAT) return
> FLOAT is -- a new operator for FLOAT:=INTEGER + FLOAT
> begin
>   return FLOAT(LEFT) + RIGHT;
> end "+";

The function is called by using it like any other operator:

> X:=I+Y; -- assuming I:INTEGER; X, Y:FLOAT;

It is possible to write:

> X:="+"(I,Y);

but there is little to be said for this, unless you want to emphasize the difference between the pre-defined operators and subsequent overloadings, in which case there would be no point in overloading anyway.

Overloading provides a very convenient way of acquiring some very powerful operators. Operator overloading should only be applied, however, if the chosen operator symbol is relevant to the application, otherwise the program meaning is obscured.

The rules for overloading apply over all subprograms, including the operators. In theory, then, it is possible to hide an operator with an inner homograph. This should never be done.

5.7 Subprogram declarations and bodies [LRM 6.1, 6.3]

Subprograms comprise two logical parts, a declaration (or specification) and a body. Until now, all the examples have been both declarations and bodies combined. There are times when it is necessary to separate the two parts. In this section, we see both how to do it and why we might want to.

A subprogram declaration comprises the heading only: it terminates with a semicolon after the parameter list (or the subprogram name, if there are no parameters). Here are some declarations of subprograms declared in their entirety earlier in the chapter:

> function CUBE(N:in INTEGER) return INTEGER;
>   -- the declaration of a function

```
procedure STARS;
    -- the declaration of a parameterless procedure

-- the bodies would look exactly the same as the
-- complete declarations already given
```

Because the declaration contains all the information required by the compiler to check the validity of a call, it is possible to issue a call in an appropriate place, such as in the body of a subsequent subprogram, before the body itself appears in the text. The body of the subprogram must repeat *all* the information from the declaration to establish correspondence between the two parts. The headings of the declaration and body must comprise the same lexical elements in the same order. Contrast this with the overloading rules. Now, correspondence must be *exact* except for spacing. The following do not correspond:

```
procedure P(I, J:INTEGER) --
procedure P(I:INTEGER; J:INTEGER) --
procedure P(J, K:INTEGER) --
procedure P(I, J:in INTEGER) --
```

If the rules were not this strict, then overloading would not be feasible, for there could easily be mis-matches between declarations and bodies. A subprogram declaration and its corresponding body are unlikely to be physically adjacent, so having to repeat all the heading information in the body is a distinct aid to program comprehension. One restriction on declaration order (LRM 3.9) is, expressed simply, that any bodies must come after simpler declarations like types and objects.

One occassion when it is necessary to have a subprogram declaration is when there are mutually recursive subprograms, as there are in this outline for a recursive descent syntax analyser:

```
procedure EXPRESSION; -- declaration

procedure PRIMARY is
    -- declarations
begin
    -- recognize a literal, identifier
    -- or (EXPRESSION)
end PRIMARY;

procedure FACTOR is
    -- declarations
```

```
begin
   -- recognize PRIMARY {** PRIMARY}
end FACTOR;

procedure TERM is
   -- declarations
begin
   -- recognize FACTOR {mult. op. FACTOR}
end TERM;

procedure EXPRESSION is -- body
   -- declarations
begin
   -- recognize TERM {add op. TERM}
end EXPRESSION;
```

It is necessary to declare EXPRESSION to enable PRIMARY to include a call. No amount of re-ordering of these procedures would eliminate the need for a declaration.

If a subprogram is part of a package specification, then, as we will see, only the subprogram declaration can appear there.

In any declaration part with many subprograms, it can be much clearer if all the subprogram specifications are grouped together, with the bodies listed subsequently. It is then more readily apparent which subprograms are provided. How much better if we could remove the clutter of bodies completely!

Separation of subprogram bodies [LRM 10.2]

If a subprogram contains a number of local subprograms, then, for compilation of the parent subprogram, only the specifications of the local units are required. The bodies may (and should) be compiled separately.

To do this, at the point at which the body should reside, the subprogram heading is followed by **is separate**. This may be done whether or not there is a separate specification already declared. This creates a *body stub*. There is one restriction: that is that a subprogram body must be elaborated before it is called, otherwise the pre-defined exception PROGRAM_ERROR will be raised. The example below shows how the local procedures of RECORD_MANAGER can be separated by creating body stubs in the parent.

```
procedure RECORD_MANAGER is
   -- basic declarations
```

```
procedure ADD_RECORD(ID:in ID_TYPE;
                            ITEM:in REC_TYPE) is separate;
   -- a body stub

procedure DELETE_RECORD(ID:in ID_TYPE) is separate;
   -- a body stub

procedure GET_RECORD(ID:in ID_TYPE;
                            ITEM:out REC_TYPE) is separate;
   -- a body stub

begin
   -- body statements of RECORD_MANAGER
end RECORD_MANAGER;
```

Now there are three bodies to provide. These will be compiled separately, after RECORD_MANAGER has been compiled. It would be too much to expect the compiler to know exactly where they belong, so you must state the parent compilation unit, as in:

```
separate(RECORD_MANAGER)
procedure ADD_RECORD(ID:in ID_TYPE;
                            ITEM:in REC_TYPE) is
   -- local declarations
begin
   -- body statements
end ADD_RECORD;
```

Separately compiled bodies like this are known as *subunits*. Separate compilation does not affect the scope and visibility rules. The subprogram resides, for these purposes, where it is declared in the parent unit.

Compilation order is dictated by the scope rules. The parent must be compiled first, then the subprogram bodies. The compilation sequence for the above example can be illustrated diagrammatically as in Fig.5.1.

Fig. 5.1 Subunit compilation dependence.

This diagram shows that RECORD_MANAGER has to be compiled before the three subunits. Once the parent has been compiled, the subunits may be compiled — in any sequence.

As well as removing superfluous details from RECORD_MANAGER, we now have the means to assist with top-down design. The separately compiled subunits can be re-compiled without affecting the parent unit. Therefore, we can get the logic of the parent unit right, without having to worry about details. Then, the local subprograms can be gradually refined, without undoing the previous work.

Much more will be said about separate compilation in Chapter 7. Don't wait until then, though, to try it on your programs.

Documentation

An essential part of a subprogram declaration should be a description of the purpose, use and workings of that subprogram, so that there are no hidden facets of its behaviour. Specifically, the aspects that should be described include:
(i) the role of the subprogram
(ii) the use of the formal parameters, such as expectations of **in** and **in out** parameters, and remarks on **out** and **in out** parameters, particularly if there are circumstances under which output parameters may be undefined
(iii) the use of any global variables and consequent side effects
(iv) exceptions handled within the subprogram and, more importantly, exceptions to be handled by the caller
(v) any involvement of the subprogram in recursion, either self recursion, or a less obvious, mutually recursive chain

Striking a balance between conciseness and adequacy is not always easy. Verbose comments defeat the object of the exercise. If a long description is necessary, then look very hard at the subprogram itself. If it is so obscure, a re-write would be more appropriate.

5.8 Exceptions [LRM 11]

On many occasions in this book, mention has been made of pre-defined exceptions. Now is the time to look at what to do with them and how you can define and raise your own exceptions. Before proceeding, it is essential that you do not regard exceptions as flags (like Booleans) that can be tested as such. Exceptions are states, accessible only to exception handlers (and the Ada run-time system), which gives the program the opportunity of dealing with exceptional occurrences at run-time.

Pre-defined exceptions

There are five pre-defined exceptions that are part of the language. Two of them, you will probably be quite familiar with:

CONSTRAINT_ERROR is raised any time that a constraint is about to be violated. This may involve a range or an accuracy constraint.

NUMERIC_ERROR may be raised when a pre-defined numeric operation cannot deliver the correct result, such as a result being too large. You need to be careful with this, as it may have different effects on different implementations. For example, an implementation is allowed to use wider constraints for operands of its operations. This could result in CONSTRAINT_ERROR being raised on such a system, when the result is being assigned to a constrained type, rather than NUMERIC_ERROR on a different system.

PROGRAM_ERROR has various causes, such as calling a subprogram before its body has been elaborated, and exiting a function without executing a return.

STORAGE_ERROR is raised through various manifestations of storage exhaustion. It may relate to the run-time stack or a lack of memory for allocation to dynamic variables.

TASKING_ERROR has a number of causes, all to do, not surprisingly, with tasks.

There is also a group of exceptions made available through TEXT_IO (and SIMPLE_IO). All of these are described in Chapter 10. The most likely one that you will encounter at present is DATA_ERROR, which is invoked if an input data value for a GET does not conform to the syntax of the expected type, or is not in the range of that type (or subtype).

A useful rule of thumb with all of these exceptions is: don't assume the precise circumstances under which the pre-defined exceptions are raised.

User-defined exceptions [LRM 11.1]

To create exceptions with specific meanings, the programmer can declare exceptions in some appropriate declarative part. Exceptions are subject to the same scope and visibility rules as other items.

Exceptions are determined on compilation, not elaboration, therefore exceptions declared in recursive subprograms remain the same for all recursive invocations (which is what you would want).

Raising exceptions [LRM 11.3]

Under certain conditions, as we have seen, pre-defined exceptions are automatically raised by the Ada run-time system. User-defined exceptions are not raised automatically — only the programmer knows what they are for, so the programmer must raise them explicitly. It is also possible to raise the pre-defined exceptions explicitly. This should not be done, though, because when an exception is raised, it is not possible to tell if it was done by the program, or by the run-time system. Here is an example of declaring and raising an exception in a skeleton context:

```
-- some declarative part
   ARRAY_FULL:exception;
begin
   -- some statements
   if INDEX = MAX then
     raise ARRAY_FULL;
   end if;
   -- more statements
end;
```

which is better than:

```
begin
   -- some statements
   if INDEX = MAX then
     raise STORAGE_ERROR;
   end if;
   -- more statements
end;
```

Exception handlers [LRM 11.2]

From the syntactic outlines of blocks and subprograms, the position of exception handlers should be clear. As a reminder, the salient part of block and subprogram structure is:

```
begin
  ⟨SEQUENCE_OF_STATEMENTS⟩
exception
  ⟨EXCEPTION_HANDLER(S)⟩
end;
```

The exception handler has a form very much like that of the case statement:

```
begin
  -- statements
exception
  when ARRAY_FULL=>
    PUT("Array is full.");
  when CONSTRAINT_ERROR | NUMERIC_ERROR=>
    PUT("Number too large.");
  when others=>
    PUT("Something unexpected cropped up.");
end;
```

Unlike the case statement, an exception handler does not have its own **end**, as it always occurs immediately before an **end** of whatever construct houses it. By now, you will not be surprised to learn that, as with the case statement, you have to have a *very* good reason for using **others** in an exception handler. Each selection is followed by a sequence of statements, just as it is in the case statement. Any valid statement can be used in that sequence, including **return** to exit a subprogram:

```
function SAFE_DIVIDE(X, Y:in INTEGER) return INTEGER
is
-- always returns a value
-- if NUMERIC_ERROR or CONSTRAINT_ERROR is
-- raised, the function will return the
-- largest, or smallest integer, or 0
-- (as appropriate) to the calling point.
begin
  return X / Y;
exception
  when NUMERIC_ERROR | CONSTRAINT_ERROR =>
    if X > 0 then
      return INTEGER'LAST;
    elsif X < 0 then
      return INTEGER'FIRST;
```

```
        else
            return 0;
        end if;
    end SAFE_DIVIDE;
```

Dynamics of exception handling [LRM 11.4]

It remains to consider where an exception is handled in relation to the point at which it is raised. Wherever an exception is raised, normal program execution is abandoned and control passed to an exception handler. If an exception is not handled, the program will (eventually) terminate. Handling an exception causes normal program execution to continue but not from the point at which it was suspended. Exception handling dynamics depend on whether the exception was raised during execution of a sequence of statements, or if it was raised during elaboration of a declaration.

Exceptions raised during program execution

If an exception (pre-defined or programmer-defined) is raised during the execution of some statement in a sequence, control passes to the handler at the end of this sequence of statements.

If there is an exception part and if the raised exception is handled therein, control then passes to the enclosing unit, from which normal program execution resumes. If the exception is handled in a subprogram, the subprogram call is terminated and normal execution resumes at the statement following the call. For an exception handled in a block statement, the execution of the block is terminated and normal program execution resumes from the statement after the **end** of the block.

If an exception is not handled in the region in which it is raised, then it is raised again, either at the point of call for a subprogram, or immediately after the **end** for a block. This *propagation* of an exception continues until the exception has been handled; if it is not handled then program execution will terminate. If an exception is raised during the execution of the statements of a handler, or, if an exception is explicitly propagated (re-raised), it propagates *to the next level* as an unhandled exception.

The situation for a block is summarized in the skeleton below.

```
    begin -- enclosing region
    -- statements
```

```
BLOCK:
  begin
    -- An exception here transfers control
    -- to the handler for BLOCK.
  exception        -- handler for BLOCK
    -- If the exception is handled here,
    -- control passes to the statement
    -- immediately following the block,
    -- otherwise it goes to the handler
    -- of the enclosing region.
  end BLOCK;
  -- Control goes here after successful
  -- execution of BLOCK (any exceptions
  -- raised in the body of BLOCK would
  -- have been handled in BLOCK).
exception          -- handler for enclosing region
  -- Has a chance to deal with any
  -- unhandled exceptions from BLOCK.
end;       -- enclosing region
```

For a subprogram, control passes from the subprogram to the calling unit, rather than to the enclosing region. This is illustrated in a later example. The values of any parameters of an abandoned subprogram will be consistent with the rules given in 5.4.

Exceptions raised during elaboration of declarations

An exception that is raised during the elaboration of a declaration causes the elaboration to be abandoned. The subsequent action will, as for exceptions from statement execution, depend on whether it is raised in a subprogram or a block. For a subprogram, the exception is raised again at the calling point, while for blocks, it is raised again immediately after the **end** of the block. Note then, that these exceptions cannot be handled in the region in which they are raised. This is illustrated in:

```
procedure P is
  I:INTEGER;
begin
  -- some statements
BLOCK:
  declare
    N:NATURAL:=I;
```

```
begin
  -- some statements
exception
  -- handler of BLOCK
end BLOCK;
  -- some statements
exception
  -- handler of P
end P;
```

If the elaboration of the block declaration fails (on assignment to N, I could be negative) then control passes to the handler of P, *not* that of BLOCK.

For a more comprehensive example, study the skeleton below, which is used to show the propagation routes for exceptions raised in subprograms and blocks.

```
procedure MAIN is

  procedure P1 is
    -- elaboration error EL1
  begin
    -- execution error EX1
  B1:
    declare
      -- elaboration error EL2
    begin
      -- execution error EX2
    exception
      -- handler H1
    end B1;
    -- statements
  exception
    -- handler H2
  end P1;

  procedure P2 is
  begin
    P1;        -- second call of P1
  exception
    -- handler H3
  end P2;
```

```
begin          -- MAIN
  P1;          -- first call of P1
  P2;
exception
  -- handler H4
end MAIN;
```

The order of handlers visited, assuming that only one of the exceptions is raised during any single program execution and assuming that the exceptions are not handled at all, would be:

EXCEPTION	FIRST CALL OF P1			SECOND CALL OF P1			
EL1			H4			H3	H4
EX1		H2	H4		H2	H3	H4
EL2		H2	H4		H2	H3	H4
EX2	H1	H2	H4	H1	H2	H3	H4

So far, the examples have concentrated on what happens if an exception is *not* handled. The idea is, of course, to handle them and to regain control of program execution. As you can see, an exception, even if handled, causes an outward migration from its invocation. This is inconvenient if all you want to do is to repeat the execution of the offending statement (in the hope that all will be well second time around). It is here that blocks can be useful, particularly within a loop, as a general outline of such a structure within a subprogram shows:

```
procedure CONTROL is
  -- Local declarations. Exceptions raised during
  -- their elaboration must be handled by the caller.
begin
  loop                -- to maintain control
  B:                  -- block
    begin             -- to provide an exception handler
      --                 actual statements
      return;         -- return to calling point if all is well
    exception
      --                 local handler(s)
    end B;            -- end of block
  end loop;           -- have another go
end CONTROL;
```

The key to successful execution handling is to layer the program such that each layer is responsible for maintaining control over its own actions,

correct and erroneous. Unit 5.5 is a re-working of the block of Unit 5.1 as
a procedure, with exception handling added. It is presented in two parts,
with Unit 5.5a as the main program with a body stub of the procedure,
and Unit 5.5b as the (separately compiled) body of the procedure.

```
with SIMPLE_IO;   -- a non-standard package
use  SIMPLE_IO;

procedure MAIN is
  N_MAX:POSITIVE;
  MEAN:FLOAT;

  procedure DO_MEAN(NUMS:in POSITIVE; AVE: out FLOAT)
                    is separate;
  -- body stub of a procedure to read NUMS numbers
  -- and return the mean via AVE. It does not handle
  -- NUMERIC_ERROR;

begin     -- MAIN
  loop
  BLOCK:
    begin
      PUT("How many numbers: ");
      GET(N_MAX);
      NEW_LINE;
      exit;                     -- all is well
    exception
      when DATA_ERROR=>
        PUT_LINE("Number must be an integer.");
      when CONSTRAINT_ERROR=>
        PUT_LINE("Number must be positive.");
    end BLOCK;
  end loop;
  DO_MEAN(N_MAX, MEAN);
  PUT("Mean= ");
  PUT(MEAN);
  NEW_LINE;
exception
  when NUMERIC_ERROR | CONSTRAINT_ERROR =>
    PUT_LINE("No result. Number too large.");
end MAIN;
```

Unit 5.5a Main program for re-working of Unit 5.1. The block has been replaced by a
procedure (compiled separately) and exceptions added.

The main program ascertains how many numbers there are to process,
handling any erroneous input. When valid input has been obtained,
DO_MEAN is called. Note that in the outermost handler, two pre-
defined exceptions are handled. Either of these could be raised, depending
on the implementation. PUT_LINE is a procedure defined in TEXT_IO
(and re-exported by SIMPLE_IO), which is equivalent to a call of PUT
to output a string, followed by a call of NEW_LINE.

```
separate(MAIN)                -- Identify the parent unit.
                              -- No semi colon required.
procedure DO_MEAN(NUMS:in POSITIVE; AVE:out FLOAT) is
-- Reads NUMS real numbers and calculates their
-- sum and mean.
-- Handles DATA_ERROR only.
-- Caller must handle NUMERIC_ERROR, which
-- could be invoked by a numeric operation.

  NEXT:FLOAT;
  SUM:FLOAT:=0.0;
begin
  for N_SO_FAR in 1..NUMS loop
  GET_FLOAT:
    loop
    NUM_BLOCK:
      begin
        PUT("Number (real) : ");
        PUT(N_SO_FAR);
        PUT(" = ");
        GET(NEXT);
        exit;                 -- leaves GET_FLOAT loop
      exception
        when DATA_ERROR=>
          PUT_LINE("Not a valid real number. (Must have a .)");
      end NUM_BLOCK;
    end loop GET_FLOAT;
    SUM:=SUM + NEXT;
  end loop;
  MEAN:=SUM / FLOAT(NUMS);
end DO_MEAN;
```

Unit 5.5b   Separately compiled procedure DO_MEAN.

The procedure DO_MEAN is responsible for reading the individual numbers and accumulating their sum. If anything goes wrong with the entry of a real number, DATA_ERROR will be raised, and it is DO_MEAN's responsibility to deal with it. However, if anything goes wrong with the addition or division, that is more serious and is left for the caller to sort out. In MAIN, DATA_ERROR will be raised if an input item is not an integer and CONSTRAINT_ERROR will be raised if it is negative. You might think that the resulting structure is cumbersome. It is! Nevertheless, it can be very effective.

Use of exceptions

Despite the unwieldiness of exception handling structures, exceptions do make the logic of error detection easier, and obviate the need for constructions like:

    CALL_SUB(PARAMS, OK);
    if OK then ...

With the exception mechanism of Ada, omissions in error handling are less likely to occur — if they do, their effects will be more obvious.

Exceptions should not be used when they are not necessary. Think of them as being provide for *exceptional* occurrences, not regular ones. A typical example of exceptional behaviour is when a stack overflows. Don't use exceptions as a substitute for testing, like evaluating I/J to see if J is zero! Also, you *could* say:

```
TOMORROW:=DAY'SUCC(TODAY);
exception
  when CONSTRAINT_ERROR=>
    TOMORROW:=DAY'FIRST;
end;
```

but it would be much better to write:

```
if TODAY = DAY'LAST then
  TOMORROW:=DAY'FIRST;
else
  TOMORROW:=DAY'SUCC(TODAY);
end if;
```

The attributes FIRST, LAST and SUCC are discussed in Chapter 8, but you don't need to understand them to follow the argument.

Exceptions are useful for error recovery from deeply nested structures, as the run-time stack automatically unwinds as an exception is propagated. A good example is the recursive descent analyser outlined earlier in 5.7. If a parse fails, we might want to abandon it cleanly and be in a position to start another one. With exceptions, this is easy and no **goto** is required.

Exceptions and scope

The pre-defined exceptions are always in scope, while user-defined exceptions are subject to the same scope rules as other declarations. This leads to the interesting question of what happens to an exception that is propagated out of scope, either through not being handled (as in the next example), or through re-raising.

```
begin            -- outer region
BLOCK:
  declare
    LOCAL_ERROR:exception;
```

```
begin
  -- statements
  raise LOCAL_ERROR;
  -- no local exception handler
end BLOCK;
```
```
exception        -- outer region
  when others=>
    -- handles all exceptions, including
    -- anonymous ones.
end;      -- outer region
```

When LOCAL_ERROR is propagated out of BLOCK, it is still an exception that has to be handled, but it cannot be referred to by its name, which has no significance outside BLOCK. Here, then, we would have to use **others** to handle it. You should not, however, declare an exception locally if you are not going to handle it locally.

So, there is still not a really good reason for using **others**. It does have its uses, though, particularly in tasking, where an unhandled exception would cause a task to terminate — not always a desirable occurrence. A handler with an **others** choice would prevent that from happening, by trapping all exceptions (even anonymous ones).

Finally, an example program to draw together some of the points made in this chapter. Unit 5.6 shows a recursive function for computing factorials, with a driver program. (Although this is not an efficient way of computing factorials it is a simple example of recursion.)

```
with SIMPLE_IO;  -- a non-standard package
use  SIMPLE_IO;

procedure MAIN is
  FAC_ERROR:exception;   -- must be in scope in FACTORIAL

  function FACTORIAL(N:in POSITIVE) return POSITIVE is
  -- Recursively computes the factorial of N.
  -- If NUMERIC_ERROR is raised (number too large)
  -- or STORAGE_ERROR raised (stack overflow), they
  -- will be handled by the function, but FAC_ERROR
  -- will then be raised.
  -- The caller must handle FAC_ERROR.

    procedure REPORT_AND_RAISE is
    -- Provides output for exception handlers.
    -- Raises FAC_ERROR.
    begin
      NEW_LINE;
      PUT("Value of N at point of failure: ");
      PUT(N);
      NEW_LINE;
```

```
              PUT_LINE("Try a smaller integer.");
              raise FAC_ERROR;
            end REPORT_AND_RAISE;

        begin
          if N = 1 then
            return 1;
          else
            return N * FACTORIAL(N-1);
          end if;
        exception
          when NUMERIC_ERROR | CONSTRAINT_ERROR =>
            PUT("Number too large for implementation.");
            REPORT_AND_RAISE;
          when STORAGE_ERROR=>
            PUT("Run-time stack exhausted: N too large.");
            REPORT_AND_RAISE;
        end FACTORIAL;

      begin        -- MAIN
        loop
        CONTROL:
          declare
            INT:INTEGER;
          begin
            PUT("Type integer for factorial. (0 Terminates): ");
            GET(INT);
            exit when INT = 0;
            PUT("Factorial is: ");
            PUT(FACTORIAL(INT));
            NEW_LINE;
          exception
            when DATA_ERROR=>
              PUT("Must be an integer.");
              NEW_LINE;
            when CONSTRAINT_ERROR=>
              PUT("Must be smaller or a positive integer.");
              NEW_LINE;
            when FAC_ERROR=>
              null;                -- No actions for this handler.
          end CONTROL;
        end loop;
        PUT_LINE("Program terminated normally.");
      end MAIN;
```

Unit 5.6 Exception handling with a recursive function.

The function includes handlers for NUMERIC_ERROR (or
CONSTRAINT_ERROR) and STORAGE_ERROR, both of which are
fatal errors. (Note the use of the local procedure REPORT_AND_RAISE
to deal with common actions.) As recovery is not possible from them, we
want the stack to unwind without any further work being done. To do
this, each handler raises FAC_ERROR, which is not handled by the
function itself, so that it is propagated to the main program. If the
individual exceptions had been re-raised, then *each* handler in the re-

cursive chain would process it as the stack collapses. A simpler way of achieving the same effect would have been to have no handler in the function at all, leaving the main program to handle any exception when the recursive calls have been completed. If that were the case, though, it would not be possible to determine the value of N at which a problem arises — knowledge of this value could be very important.

There is no single correct program for any given application. Unit 5.6 is no exception to this (pardon the pun), being only one way to achieve a particular level of robustness using exceptions.

Practising Ada 5

You should now be in a position to use subprograms, blocks and exceptions effectively. Your aims henceforth should be modularity, readability and error tolerance through exception handling. Exercise separate compilation of subprograms as much as possible. Have fun with these:

1 Write functions for exp and sine (defined in Practising Ada 4). Compile them separately and write main programs to call them. Handle all possible exceptions at appropriate places.

2 Write a procedure which, given three FLOAT parameters, will order the values such that, on returning to the calling point, the first parameter will hold the smallest value, and the third parameter the largest.

3 Write a procedure which, given a positive integer, will write that integer in reverse. (Write two versions, one recursive, the other iterative.)

4 Write a function which: reads an integer, validates it as an octal number (i.e. no digit > 7) and returns the validated integer. (Might a procedure be better?) Write another function which, given a valid "octal" integer, returns the integer representing the decimal equivalent.

5 Write a function as an operator, "+", which takes a CHARACTER, and an INTEGER as arguments, and returns the character which is the given integer away (if there is one!).

6 Write a limit function, which will take three arguments: a real number (R); a lower bound for the output; an upper bound for the output. The function will return R if R is between the specified bounds, otherwise it will return the upper or lower bound, as appropriate. The bounds should have default values of −1.0 and 1.0. Call the function with 1, 2 and 3 actual parameters. (Check for misuse.)

Chapter 6

Composite and access types

Ada provides two composite, or structured, types: arrays and records. There is no pre-defined set type. Dynamic data structures are also provided under the nomenclature of access types. Compared to other languages, Ada provides many facilities for manipulating arrays and records; consequently, there is a lot to learn. However, as always, you don't need to use all the features straight away — bring them into play one at a time. This is not a text about data structures, but it is worth mentioning that, from the point of view of good practice and style, a data structure should always be appropriate to your particular application.

6.1 Constrained array types [LRM 3.6]

Arrays are homogeneous structures in which *all* elements are of the same component type, which may be any type, including other structured types. There may be any number of indexes, or subscripts, but all must be of discrete types (not necessarily the same). Each component is accessible individually via the index(es).

One-dimensional arrays

An example of array type and object declarations:

```
type LIST is array (1..10) of INTEGER;
L_1, L_2:LIST;
```

Assignment may involve individual elements of a vector, or it may be performed on whole arrays:

```
L_1(3):=64;
I:=L_2(6);        -- I must be INTEGER
L_2:=L_1;         -- All elements of L_1 copied to L_2.
```

In whole array assignments like the last one, all elements of the array on the right hand side (L_1 here) must be defined, otherwise CONSTRAINT_ERROR will be raised.

Ada allows the use of anonymous array types such as

    FV_1:array (1..4) of FLOAT;
    FV_2, FV_3:array (1..4) of FLOAT;

However, arrays only have the same type if they are declared using the same type identifier. Therefore, FV_1, FV_2 and FV_3 are all of different types. Remember that Ada will treat the second declaration as the declaration of FV_2 followed by the declaration of FV_3 as a separate entity. Although the types of the arrays themselves are different, their component types are all the same, so it is possible to have:

    FV_2(2):=FV_3(3);

whereas it is not permitted to say

    FV_2:=FV_3;   -- INVALID

The programmer should always think of variables being of a particular, named type.

The only use for anonymous array types is for constant arrays, which are to be used for table look-up:

    type COURSE_COMPASS is (N, NE, E, SE, S, SW, W, NW);
    POINT_PORT:constant array (COURSE_COMPASS) of
        COURSE_COMPASS:=(NW, N, NE, E, SE, S, SW, W);
    POINT_STARBOARD:constant array (COURSE_COMPASS) of
        COURSE_COMPASS:=(NE, E, SE, S, SW, W, NW, N);

The above assignments to the array constant are known as *aggregates*, complete sets of values for an array object, which are fully explained in 6.3

Multi-dimensional arrays

The only limits on the number of dimensions an array may have are conceptual and stylistic. Often, what *can* by represented by a multi-dimensional array is better described by a hierarchical collection of vectors. So:

    type VOLUME is array (1..200, 1..60, 1..80) of CHARACTER;

although legal, would be better as:

```
type LINE is array (1..80) of CHARACTER;
type PAGE is array (1..60) of LINE;
type BOOK is array (1..200) of PAGE;
```

Given the declarations:

```
L_1, L_2:LINE;
P_1, P_2:PAGE;
B_1, B_2:BOOK;
```

then the following assignments are valid:

```
L_1(1):='X';            -- CHARACTER
L_2:=L_1;               -- LINE
P_1(1):=L_1;            -- LINE
P_2:=B_1(6);            -- PAGE
P_1(1)(1):='Y';         -- CHARACTER - correct but not good
B_1(1)(2)(3):='Z';      -- CHARACTER - correct but even
                        -- worse
```

Having made the data structure clearer, each component type should have its own subprograms to process it, so that manipulating a BOOK only involves PAGEs, and no smaller items. Similarly, the processing of PAGEs should only involve LINEs, and so on.

Arrays with more than one dimension may have indexes of different types:

```
-- Assumes types DAY and COLOUR of 3.8
type PAINT_COUNT is array (DAY range MON..FRI, COLOUR)
of NATURAL;
TALLY:PAINT_COUNT;
```

A valid indexing operation is shown in the assignment:

```
TALLY(TUE, RED):=25;
```

6.2 Unconstrained array types

The array types introduced in the previous section were all *constrained*. In other words, they had defined, fixed bounds. Ada permits the definition of array types, for any number of dimensions, which have no specific bounds, only the *types* of the indexes are specified:

```
-- assumes type MONTHS of 4.2
type VECTOR is array (INTEGER range ⟨⟩) of FLOAT;
type PART_YEAR is array (MONTHS range ⟨⟩) of INTEGER;
```

(The ⟨⟩ construction is pronounced "box".) The first of these declarations defines a type for a one-dimensional array of FLOATs, with an INTEGER index. The second definition is for an array of INTEGERs with any subscript of type MONTHS, or a subtype thereof. These declarations do not imply the whole range of the specified index type, but indicate the upper and lower bounds of the (contiguous) range that may be used. From an unconstrained type definition we can declare subtypes and array objects, *all* of which must be constrained. So, subsequent valid declarations are:

```
subtype BIG_VEC is VECTOR (0..999);
subtype TINY_VEC is VECTOR (1..10);
V1:VECTOR (1..20);                        -- 20 FLOATs
B:BIG_VEC;                                -- 1000 FLOATs
QUARTER_1:PART_YEAR (JAN..MAR);           -- 3 INTEGERs
T:TINY_VEC;                               -- 10 FLOATs
```

Note that the range constraint (of the correct type) must be supplied in subtype and object declarations from unconstrained arrays types. The declaration of B does not require a constraint, as it inherits the constraint of the subtype.

In multi-dimensional arrays, *all* dimensions must be either constrained or unconstrained:

```
type MATRIX is array (POSITIVE range ⟨⟩,
                      POSITIVE range ⟨⟩) of FLOAT;
type WRONG_UN is array (INTEGER range ⟨⟩, DAY)
                of INTEGER;     -- INVALID
```

Although the subtypes BIG_VEC and TINY_VEC have different index ranges, they are nevertheless subtypes of the same VECTOR, so are compatible for certain operations described in 6.4.

Array attributes [LRM 3.6.2]

In passing, we have encountered a few of the *attributes* of discrete types, like INTEGER'FIRST and DAY'SUCC(TODAY). (These and other attributes are discussed in Chapter 8). Arrays also have a number of attributes that enable the programmer to access their characteristics conveniently.

If AOT is an array object, or a *constrained* array type, then the corresponding attributes are:

AOT'FIRST(N)	-- lower bound of Nth index
AOT'LAST(N)	-- upper bound of Nth index
AOT'LENGTH(N)	-- size (number of values) of Nth index
AOT'RANGE(N)	-- the range of the Nth index

N may be a static expression (i.e. one that does not involve variables – see Chapter 8) that yields a positive integer value, no larger than the number of dimensions of the array. Be careful not to think of RANGE as being the same as LENGTH. LENGTH gives the *number* of values that the Nth index has, while RANGE represents the complete range of values of the Nth index, from FIRST to LAST. As we shall soon see, this can be very useful.

For a one-dimensional array, the index specification may be omitted, so that AOT'FIRST is equivalent to AOT'FIRST(1).

Given the declaration:

    VEC:VECTOR (0..19);

the attribute values would be:

VEC'FIRST	= 0
VEC'LAST	= 19
VEC'LENGTH	= 20
VEC'RANGE	= 0..19

Assuming the above declaration (and declarations of SUM and MEAN as FLOAT variables) we can write:

```
SUM:=0.0;
for I in VEC'RANGE loop
   SUM:=SUM + VEC(I);
end loop;
MEAN:=SUM / FLOAT(VEC'LENGTH);
```

The characteristics of the array do not have to be explicitly coded as literals or constants but can be derived directly from the array itself using its attributes. Therefore, should the bounds of VEC be subsequently changed, the code will still be valid for computing the mean value over all its elements.

This idea is generalized into a function, shown as Unit 6.1, which can be called with *any* array of type VECTOR, without any need to supply additional parameters for the bounds.

```
-- Assume the body stub appears in MAIN,
-- where VECTOR is declared.

separate(MAIN)
function MEAN_OF_VEC(VEC:in VECTOR) return FLOAT is
  SUM:FLOAT:=0.0;
begin
  for I in VEC'RANGE loop
    SUM:=SUM + VEC(I);
  end loop;
  return SUM/FLOAT(VEC'LENGTH);
end MEAN_OF_VEC;
```

Unit 6.1 A function for any VECTOR.

When operating on more than one unconstrained array, you have to be careful to ensure that the arrays are compatible for the operation you are performing. Consider the function in Unit 6.2, which returns the vector that results from summing its argument vectors.

```
-- Again, assume VECTOR is declared in MAIN.

separate(MAIN)
function VEC_SUM(A, B:in VECTOR) return VECTOR is

-- returns the result of the sum of vectors A and B.
-- ASSUMPTION: A and B have identical RANGEs,
-- otherwise CONSTRAINT_ERROR will be raised.
-- NUMERIC_ERROR (or CONSTRAINT_ERROR) could be
-- raised by a +.
-- ALL exceptions must be handled by the caller.

  SUM:VECTOR(A'RANGE);
begin
  for I in A'RANGE loop
    SUM(I):=A(I) + B(I);
  end loop;
  return SUM;
end VEC_SUM;
```

Unit 6.2 Returns the sum of two VECTORs.

This will work correctly, as long as the ranges of A and B are the same. If they are different, then some additional action must be taken. The ranges themselves cannot be tested for equality, therefore the FIRST and LAST attributes must be tested before the for loop:

```
if A'FIRST /= B'FIRST or
   A'LAST /= B'LAST then
   raise INCOMPATIBLE;
end if;
```

The caller would probably want to handle the exception, although it could be handled locally, returning, say, a null vector or a copy of A.

If both arrays have the same number of elements (LENGTH is the same for both) then it is possible to produce a result, which would be the sum of the corresponding elements. This is what is done in Unit 6.3.

```
-- INCOMPATIBLE:exception; declared in MAIN

separate(MAIN)
function VEC_SUM_2(A, B:in VECTOR) return VECTOR is

-- returns the result of the sum of the vectors A and B.
-- ASSUMPTION: A and B must have the same number of
-- elements, otherwise the exception INCOMPATIBLE will
-- be raised.
-- NUMERIC_ERROR (or CONSTRAINT_ERROR) could be
-- raised by a +.
-- ALL exceptions must be handled by the caller.

  SUM:VECTOR(0..A'LENGTH-1);
begin
  if A'LENGTH /= B'LENGTH then
    raise INCOMPATIBLE;
  end if;
  for I in SUM'RANGE loop
    SUM(I):=A(I + A'FIRST) + B(I + B'FIRST);
  end loop;
  return SUM;
end VEC_SUM_2;
```

Unit 6.3 A more general function.

As a final example in this section, Unit 6.4 is a complete program, which includes a function for sorting arrays of type I_VECTOR.

```
with SIMPLE_IO;  -- a non-standard package
use  SIMPLE_IO;

procedure MAIN is
  type I_VECTOR is array (INTEGER range <>) of INTEGER;
  V_1, V_2:I_VECTOR(1..10);

  procedure GET_VECTOR(V_DATA:out I_VECTOR) is

  -- Reads integers into V_DATA, one for each element.
  -- Handles DATA_ERROR, but no other exception.

  begin
    PUT("Type in ");
    PUT(V_DATA'LENGTH);
    PUT(" Integers.");
    NEW_LINE;
    for I in V_DATA'RANGE loop
    CONTROL:
      loop
        begin
          PUT(I);
```

```
                PUT(": ");
                GET(V_DATA(I));
                exit;
              exception
                when DATA_ERROR=>
                  PUT("Must be an integer. Re-type it.");
                  NEW_LINE;
            end;
          end loop CONTROL;
        end loop;
    end GET_VECTOR;

    procedure PUT_VECTOR(V_DATA:in I_VECTOR) is

    -- Outputs V_DATA, one element per line.
    -- CONSTRAINT_ERROR could be raised if array
    -- element(s) undefined. Caller must handle.

    begin
      NEW_LINE;
      for I in V_DATA'RANGE loop
        PUT(V_DATA(I));
        NEW_LINE;
      end loop;
    end PUT_VECTOR;

    function SORT_VEC(V_IN:in I_VECTOR) return I_VECTOR is

    -- Sorts elements of V_IN into RESULT in ascending
    -- order. RESULT will have the same RANGE as V_IN.
    -- Will work for an I_VECTOR of any RANGE.
    -- CONSTRAINT_ERROR could be raised by undefined
    -- element(s) of V_IN. Caller must handle.

      RESULT:I_VECTOR(V_IN'RANGE):=V_IN;
    begin
      for SORT_POS in RESULT'FIRST .. RESULT'LAST-1 loop
        for COMPARISON in SORT_POS + 1 .. RESULT'LAST loop
          if RESULT(SORT_POS) > RESULT(COMPARISON) then
          SWAP:
            declare
              TEMP:INTEGER:=RESULT(SORT_POS);
            begin
              RESULT(SORT_POS):=RESULT(COMPARISON);
              RESULT(COMPARISON):=TEMP;
            end SWAP;
          end if;
        end loop;
      end loop;
      return RESULT;
    end SORT_VEC;

begin     -- MAIN
  GET_VECTOR(V_1);
  PUT("Initial list:");
  PUT_VECTOR(V_1);
  V_2:=SORT_VEC(V_1);
  PUT("Sorted list:");
  PUT_VECTOR(V_2);
end MAIN;
```

Unit 6.4   A program with a sort procedure for any I_VECTOR.

6.3 Array aggregates [LRM 4.3]

From the example of a constant array in 6.1, you already know what an array aggregate is. It is used for assigning a *complete* set of values to an array object — every element of the array must be represented. First, we look at one-dimensional array aggregates.

Given the declaration

>   type IV6_TYPE is array (1..6) of INTEGER;

then we can use aggregates for initialization and assignment:

>   IV_1:IV6_TYPE:=(0, 0, 0, 0, 0, 0);
>   IV_2:IV6_TYPE;
>   begin
>   IV_2:=(1, 2, 3, 4, 5, 6);

The examples so far have illustrated the use of positional association, in which the leftmost value is assigned to the array element with the lowest index. As with subprogram parameter associations, named notation may be used:

>   IV_3:IV6_TYPE:=(1=>1, 2=>2, 3=>3, 4=>4, 5=>5, 6=>6);

The order of enumerating the elements in named notation is up to the programmer. Stylistically, though, some sort of logical sequence should be used so as not to confuse the reader.

Where a number of contiguous elements is to be set to the same value, a range may be used in named notation:

>   IV_4:IV6_TYPE:=(1..6 =>0);

or, more generally:

>   IV_5:IV6_TYPE:=(IV6_TYPE'RANGE =>0);

For assigning the same value to non-contiguous elements, the alternation character, '|', can be used:

>   IV_6:IV6_TYPE:=(1 | 6 =>0, 2..5 =>1);

Which sets the first and last elements to zero and the others to one. Actually, Ada provides **others** for use in named notation aggregates, but, as you would by now expect, you must have a good reason for using it. Inspired by laziness, we could have said:

>   IV_4:IV6_TYPE:=(others=>0);

Here is a more excusable example, where the alternative would be to enumerate the many intervening ranges. As it stands, the example is readable — the most important criterion.

```
PRIMES:constant array (1..32) of BOOLEAN
    :=(1  | 2  | 3  | 5  | 7  | 11 |
       13 | 17 | 19 | 23 | 29 | 31 =>TRUE,
       others =>FALSE);
```

If **others** is used, it must be placed last, indicating all the remaining (unspecified) elements. It is not permissible to mix positional and named notation in one-dimensional array aggregates, except for **others**, which can be used with either scheme.

Array **constants** may derive their bounds from the aggregate, if the type indication is unconstrained. The index of the first element will be determined by the notation used in the aggregate as illustrated in the examples. **Others** can only be used where the bounds are determinable by some other means.

```
type NEW_VEC is array (INTEGER range 〈〉) of INTEGER;
type DAY is (MON, TUE, WED, THU, FRI, SAT, SUN);
type D_A is array (DAY range 〈〉) of INTEGER;
NV_1:constant NEW_VEC:=(1, 2, 3, 4, 5);
    -- NV_1(INTEGER'FIRST):=1;
    -- ......
    -- NV_1(INTEGER'FIRST + 4):=5;
NV_2:constant NEW_VEC:=(1=>0, 2=>1, 3=>2);
    -- NV_2(1):=0;
    -- ......
    -- NV_2(3):=2;
DINT:constant D_A:=(1, 2, 3);
    -- DINT(MON):=1;
    -- ......
    -- DINT(WED):=3;
```

As can be seen with named notation, the range is determinable from the component choices, while for positional, the first value is assigned to the element corresponding to the first value of the index type. Array *variables* must be constrained by the use of a constrained subtype or the provision of a constraint before the assignment of an initial value. The bounds cannot be determined from this initial value.

It is always better to introduce more certainty into a program by using array subtypes (which must, of course, be constrained). Another way of specifying the constraint for the constants above would have been to *qualify* the aggregate with a subtype indication (identifier):

```
subtype SMALL_VEC is NEW_VEC(1..5);
S:constant NEW_VEC:=SMALL_VEC'(0, 2, 4, 6, 8);
  -- S(1):=0;
  -- ......
  -- S(5):=8;
```

However, this represents a rather roundabout way of expressing your intentions. Nevertheless, it does introduce the idea of qualifying aggregates, which you will see used later in other contexts.

Both the element values and the component choice (in named notation) may be expressions, subject to correct typing.

```
-- some outer declarative region
BOUNDARY, LIMIT, I:POSITIVE;
  -- assume values are assigned to all of these

  -- some inner declarative region
  type BOOL_VEC is array (INTEGER range ⟨⟩) of BOOLEAN;
  FLEXIBLE:BOOL_VEC(1..LIMIT):=
    (1..BOUNDARY=>TRUE,
    BOUNDARY+1..LIMIT =>FALSE);
  type VEC_5 is array (1..5) of INTEGER;
  I_POWER:VEC_5:=(1, I, I**2, I**3, I**4, I**5);
```

FLEXIBLE will have bounds determined by the value of LIMIT, when its declaration is elaborated. The value of BOUNDARY also establishes those elements that are initially TRUE and those that are FALSE. I_POWER will always be the same size, but its initial value depends on the value of the global variable, I. Ada does not provide implied do loops within aggregates, as FORTRAN does for array i/o.

If an array has only one element, then any aggregate assigned to it must use named notation, so that it cannot be interpreted as a parenthesized expression:

```
SOLO:VECTOR(1..1):=(1=>3);
```

If the aggregate had been (3), then this could have been interpreted as the INTEGER 3, and not as an array of one element, which has that value. As ever, the types on either side of an assignment must be the same.

Multi-dimensional array aggregates

For arrays with more than one dimension, the complete aggregate is made up of a number of sub-aggregates of one fewer dimensions. The aggregate for each dimension may be specified using named or positional association (not both), however, different dimensions may employ different notations. An example, taken from the LRM illustrates these points:

```
type MAT is array (1..2, 1..3) of FLOAT;
M_1:MAT:=((1.1, 1.2, 1.3), (2.1, 2.2, 2.3));    -- all positional
M_2:MAT:=(1=>(1.1, 1.2, 1.3),                   -- row is
                                                -- named but
         2=>(2.1, 2.2, 2.3));                   -- column is
                                                -- positional
M_3:MAT:=(1=>(1=>1.1, 2=>1.2, 3=>1.3),
          2=>(1=>2.1, 2=>2.2, 3=>2.3));         -- all named
```

Using named association throughout results in a rather unreadable aggregate.

6.4 Array operations and type matching

Before looking at the operations that can be performed on arrays, it is necessary to examine the type compatibility of arrays and related matters.

Type compatibility

Arrays of the same type that have the same number of elements but *not* necessarily the same index ranges are assignment compatible. Consider the declarations:

```
V_2:VECTOR(1..10);
V_3:VECTOR(-10..-1);
V_4:VECTOR(100..109);
```

As there is a one-to-one correspondence between elements, one of the above arrays may be assigned to another, as in:

```
V_2:=V_3;       -- V_2(1):=V_3(-10)  etc.
V_3:=V_4;       -- V3(-10):=V_4(100) etc.
```

The same compatibility rule applies to (in)equality testing, therefore it is possible to have:

```
if V_2=V_3 then ......
```

This view of compatibility is not restricted to one-dimensional arrays. For multiple dimensions, each index must have the same number of values (i.e. LENGTH must be the same for corresponding indexes):

```
M_1:MATRIX(1..5, 1..9);
M_2:MATRIX(-2..2, -4..4);
```

The following are valid:

```
M_1:=M_2;                    -- M_2 must be defined
if M_1=M_2 then ......       -- M_1 and M_2 must be defined
```

If an attempt is made to use an array for assignment or comparison, when not all of its elements are defined, then CONSTRAINT_ERROR will be raised.

Array slices [LRM 4.1.2]

One-dimensional arrays may be subjected to slicing, which indicates a contiguous subset of its elements to be used in the same context as the original. For example, using V_2, V_3 and V_4 as declared above:

```
V_2(1..5):=(5, 4, 3, 2, 1);      -- V_2(1):=5 etc.
V_3(-5..-1):=V_2(6..10);         -- V_3(-5):=V_2(6) etc.
V_4(100..100):V_2(1..1);         -- V_4(100):=V_2(1)
```

In the last assignment, both sides are array slices of one element, and are of type VECTOR, *not* type INTEGER. V_4(100..100) is not, therefore, the same as V_4(100), which is a single INTEGER element of V_4.

Array slices can obviate a need for a loop, as in the second assignment above, which is equivalent to:

```
for I in -5..-1 loop
   V_3(I):V_2(I + 11);
end loop;
```

All assignment statements require the complete evaluation of the right hand side before the actual assignment is made. Assignments involving array slices are no exception, which helps us to understand what happens with overlapping slices. The effect is demonstrated by the following extract of code to shift some elements in a vector down one position.

```
-- assume that 1 <= J <= 10
V_2(J+1..10):=V_2(J..9);
```

which is equivalent to:

```
      for I in reverse J..9 loop
         V_2(I+1):=V_2(I);
      end loop;
```

Note the need for **reverse** in expressing the loop equivalent of the slice assignment.

Type conversion [LRM 4.6]

It is possible to convert explicitly from one array type to another, provided that:
(i) the component types are the same
(ii) the numbers of dimensions are the same
(iii) the type of the indexes is the same
Type conversion may also be applied to slices of one-dimensional arrays, as long as the above conditions are satisfied. It is not, of course, necessary to convert explicitly between subtypes and their parent types.
   Given the declarations:

```
      type V_TYPE is array (INTEGER range ⟨⟩) of INTEGER;
      subtype S_TYPE is V_TYPE(1..10);
      type D_TYPE is array (0..9) of INTEGER;
      V_VEC:V_TYPE(1..20);
      S_VEC:S_TYPE;
      D_VEC:D_TYPE;
```

then the following assignments are valid:

```
      D_VEC:=D_TYPE(S_VEC);
      S_VEC:=S_TYPE(D_VEC);
      V_VEC(1..10):=S_VEC          -- no conversion required
      V_VEC(1..10):V_TYPE(D_VEC);
      D_VEC:=D_TYPE(V_VEC(11..20));
```

If the conversion is to an unconstrained type, as in the penultimate example above, the conversion inherits the bounds of the subject of the conversion, which in this case is D_VEC.
   Some examples of declarations of arrays with more than one dimension:

```
      -- assume the previous declarations are visible
      type M_TYPE is array (INTEGER range ⟨⟩,
                            INTEGER range ⟨⟩) of FLOAT;
      type T_TYPE is array (1..4, 1..6) of FLOAT;
      type A_D_TYPE is array (1...10) of D_TYPE;
```

```
M_MAT:M_TYPE(0..3, 0..5);
T_MAT:T_TYPE;
A_D_VEC:A_D_TYPE;
```

Valid assignments involving these include:

```
M_MAT:=M_TYPE(T_MAT);
A_D_VEC(1):=D_VEC;        -- no conversion required
S_VEC:=S_TYPE(A_D_VEC(3));
A_D_VEC(4)(1..5):=A_D_TYPE(S_VEC(6..10));
```

The last example may require a little explanation. First, the right hand side denotes a five element slice of S_VEC, which is then converted to become a slice of type A_D_TYPE. The result is subsequently assigned to a five element slice of the fourth component of A_D_VEC.

Array operations [LRM 3.6.2]

The array attributes introduced in 6.2 can be applied to all array objects (and constrained array types). Assignment and the equality and inequality operators can also be applied to all array objects (but obviously not types), whatever the dimensionality.

All one-dimensional arrays may be (con)catenated using the pre-defined operator "&" [LRM 4.5.3]. This operator is overloaded for the following parameter combinations, in which A_TYPE denotes an array type and C_TYPE a component type.

LEFT operand	RIGHT operand	RESULT
A_TYPE	A_TYPE	A_TYPE
A_TYPE	C_TYPE	A_TYPE
C_TYPE	A_TYPE	A_TYPE
C_TYPE	C_TYPE	A_TYPE

Here are some valid applications of "&" on previously defined vectors:

```
V_2:=(1, 2, 3, 4, 5, 6, 7, 8, 9, 10);
V_2:=V_2(6..10) & V_2(1..5);
     -- V_2(1):=V_2(6);
     -- ......
     -- V_2(5):=V_2(10);
     -- V_2(6):=V_2(1);
     -- ......
     -- V_2(10):=V_2(5);
     -- V_2 is now (6, 7, 8, 9, 10, 1, 2, 3, 4, 5)
```

```
V_2:=(1, 2, 3, 4, 5, 6, 7, 8, 9, 10);
V_2:=0 & V_2(1..9);
        -- V_2 becomes (0, 1, 2, 3, 4, 5, 6, 7, 8, 9);
V_4(100..101):=VECTOR'(6 & 8);
```

The lower bound of the result of catenation is the same as that of the left operand (unless it is null). If the upper bound of the result exceeds the range of the index, then CONSTRAINT_ERROR will be raised. The catenation operator is classed as a binary adding operator. Other examples will be given when we look at strings.

For one-dimensional arrays with components of a discrete type, all the relational operators can be applied. The BOOLEAN result is determined by an element by element comparison, using the underlying order of the component type to establish the result of element comparisons. Some relationships determined on this basis are illustrated for different component types using aggregates for arrays of four components:

```
-- assumed declaration of type DAY is (MON, etc.)
(MON, TUE, THU, FRI) (MON, TUE, WED, SAT)
   -- TRUE because THU is greater than WED
(1, 99, 36, 25) < (2, 0, 0, 0)
   -- TRUE because 1 is less than 2
```

The ordering for strings is similarly determined by the enumeration of the characters in type CHARACTER. Therefore "BOX TREE" will be less than "BOXERDOG" because a space is less than 'E'.

Finally, the Boolean operators "and", "or", "xor" and "not" can be applied to one-dimensional arrays of BOOLEAN components. (The short-circuit control forms cannot be so used.) The operations are applied component by component.

```
type BIT_4 is array (0..3) of BOOLEAN;
EVEN:BIT_4:=(TRUE, FALSE, TRUE, FALSE);
ODD_HIGH, EVEN_LOW, ODD:BIT_4;
MASK_2:BIT_4:=(FALSE, FALSE, TRUE, TRUE);
```

Valid operations:

```
ODD:=not EVEN;
                -- (FALSE, TRUE, FALSE, TRUE)
ODD_HIGH:=ODD and MASK_2;
                -- (FALSE, FALSE, FALSE, TRUE)
```

```
EVEN_LOW:=EVEN and not MASK_2;
               -- (TRUE, FALSE, FALSE, FALSE)
```

The ability to use logical operators with BOOLEAN arrays makes this structure eminently suitable for the representation of sets of some discrete type. The index would be the discrete type in question, giving one array element per possible member of the set. To denote the presence (or absence) of a particular member, its component is set to TRUE (or FALSE). The logical operators make it very easy to express the basic set operations, union being the application of "or", "and" gives the intersection while "and" followed by "not" evaluates the set difference. These operations would be implemented very efficiently. Unit 7.2 in the next chapter expands on this theme.

Strings [LRM 2.6, 3.6.3]

The pre-defined type STRING is defined as:

```
type STRING is array (POSITIVE range ⟨⟩) of CHARACTER;
```

String literals are constructed using string quotes and may be used for denoting array values, in lieu of an aggregate. Some examples of declarations and operations:

```
      BLANK:constant CHARACTER:=";
      subtype WORD is STRING (1..10);
      STR_1:STRING(1..5):="ELLIE";
      STR_2:STRING(1..4):=('B', 'E', 'T', 'H');
      STR_3:STRING(1..4):="ANNA";
      ME:WORD:=(1=>'P', 2=>'A', 3=>'U', 4=>'L',
               5..10=>BLANK);
      THEM:WORD:=(WORD'RANGE => BLANK);
      TROUBLE:WORD:=(WORD'RANGE => BLANK);
      US:WORD;
begin
      THEM:=STR_1 & BLANK & STR_2; -- "ELLIE BETH"
      US:="CHRIS" & BLANK & ME(1..4);-- "CHRIS PAUL"
      TROUBLE(1..8):=STR_3 & STR_3;  -- "ANNAANNA   "
      ME(1..3):=ME(2..4);            -- "AULL       "
      -- ......
end;
```

String literals can also be used with user-defined character (enumeration) types:

ANS_STRING:array (1..4) of ANSWERS:="NnYy";   -- see 3.8

6.5 Records [LRM 3.7]

Records are heterogeneous structures comprising a number of components called fields (not necessarily of the same type), which are selected by identifier — the name of the field. Within any given record, field names must be distinct. Different records, though, may use the same component names. However, while the Ada compiler will not get confused, *you* might, if you adhere to such practices.

A record component or field, is defined within the record type declaration, where it is associated with a particular type. Record components can be of any type, including structured types.

A default expression can be specified for fields of a record, so that, on creation of a record object, values will be automatically assigned to those components with a default, unless, of course, the defaults are over-ridden. It is often a good idea to apply defaults to all fields of a record, although this is not necessary, as it can prevent errors arising from the attempted use of undefined components.

A record declaration is introduced by **record** and is terminated by **end record** — the name of the record cannot, unfortunately appear in the termination. Here is a typical (well-worn) record definition, following an enumeration type declaration:

```
-- some declarative part
type MONTH_TYPE is (JAN, FEB, MAR, APR, MAY, JUN,
                    JUL, AUG, SEP, OCT, NOV, DEC);
type DATE is
record
   DAY:INTEGER range 1..31;
   MONTH:MONTH_TYPE:=JAN;
   YEAR:INTEGER range 1900..1999:=1986;
end record;
D_1, D_2, D_3:DATE;
```

On elaboration of the above record object declarations, each of the three will have the default values applied.

Record operations [LRM 3.7.4, 4.3]

Compared to arrays, records have far fewer applicable operations. Records do not have any attributes of interest here. Assignment may be made to whole records, or to selected fields, as shown in the next example. Equality and inequality may be used with record operands, but no other operators are applicable (they would have no obvious meaning, anyway). Type conversion from one record type to another is only possible between derived types — see Chapter 8. Record values, like array values, can be specified by aggregates. Record aggregates may (if you have a justifiable reason) mix positional and named notation, provided that the positional notation comes first. **others** may be used in record aggregates in the same way that it can be used in array aggregates. However, as it can only be used for elements of the same type, it is of rather limited use with records.

Some valid operations that follow the last set of declarations:

```
        D_1.DAY:=16;          -- Component assignment
        D_1.MONTH:=JUN;       -- to the selected fields
        D_1.YEAR:=1978;       -- of record D_1.
        D_2:=D_1;             -- whole record assignment:
                              -- all of D_1 is copied
                              -- into D_2.
        D_3:=(13, MAR, 1983); -- positional aggregate
        D_2:=(YEAR=>1979,
             MONTH=>DEC,
             DAY=>28);        -- named aggregate
```

Remember that an aggregate must define a complete record, therefore it is not possible to use one to assign a value only to the DAY component, even though the other components have default values.

Anonymous record types are not allowed in Ada (whereas they are in Pascal). It is not possible, therefore, to define a (anonymous) record as a component within the definition of a record. Record fields that are, themselves, records must have a type identifier for the component already defined. (This is how you should do it, even in Pascal.) To be consistent, the language does not allow anonymous arrays to be used for record component types — type identifiers must always be used.

Unit 6.5 is a program with type declarations and subprograms for a geometric application.

```
with SIMPLE_IO, FLOAT_MATH_LIB;   -- non-standard packages
use  SIMPLE_IO, FLOAT_MATH_LIB;

procedure MAIN is

   type POINT is
   record
     X,
     Y:FLOAT;
   end record;

   type LINE is
   record
     END_1,
     END_2:POINT;
   end record;

   P_1, P_2:POINT;
   L_1, L_2:LINE;

   procedure GET_POINT(ITEM:out POINT) is

   -- Reads in 2 co-ordinates for a point.
   -- DATA_ERROR could be raised - NOT handled.

   begin
     PUT("Type X  Y co-ordinates: ");
     GET(ITEM.X);
     GET(ITEM.Y);
   end GET_POINT;

   procedure GET_LINE(ITEM:out LINE) is

   -- Reads in the two points that form a line.
   -- Calls GET_POINT twice.
   -- DATA_ERROR could be raised in GET_POINT.
   -- NOT handled here either.

   begin
     PUT("End 1: ");
     GET_POINT(ITEM.END_1);
     PUT("End 2: ");
     GET_POINT(ITEM.END_2);
   end GET_LINE;

   function DISTANCE(PT_1, PT_2:in POINT) return FLOAT is

   -- Returns the distance between P_1 and P_2.
   -- NUMERIC_ERROR (or CONSTRAINT_ERROR) could be raised
   -- by the arithmetic operations. They are NOT handled.

   begin
     return SQRT( ( PT_1.X - PT_2.X)**2
              + ( PT_1.Y - PT_2.Y)**2);

   end DISTANCE;
```

```
function LENGTH(A_LINE:in LINE) return FLOAT is

-- Returns the length of A_LINE. Calls
-- DISTANCE. This does not handle exceptions either.

begin
  return DISTANCE(A_LINE.END_1, A_LINE.END_2);
end LENGTH;

begin        -- MAIN
  GET_POINT(P_1);
  GET_POINT(P_2);
  GET_LINE(L_1);
  L_2:=(L_1.END_1, P_2);
  PUT("Distance from Point 1 to Point 2= ");
  PUT(DISTANCE(P_1, P_2));
  NEW_LINE;
  PUT("Length of line= ");
  PUT(LENGTH(L_1));
  NEW_LINE;
  PUT("Distance between ends of lines= ");
  PUT(DISTANCE(L_1.END_2, L_2.END_2));
  NEW_LINE;
end MAIN;
```

Unit 6.5   Records for geometric objects.

Obviously, many other facilities could have been added, such as more shapes:

    type CIRCLE is
    record
      ORIGIN:POINT;
      RADIUS:FLOAT;
    end record;

Note that in the definition of POINT, X and Y are components of the same type. They could have been defined, equivalently, as:

    type POINT is
    record
      X, Y:FLOAT;
    end record;

Even where more than one field has the same type, it helps readability if each is placed on a separate line, as in the program of Unit 6.5.

Where record components are records, it would be possible to have complex field selections, such as

    L_1.END_1.X

which selects the X field of the END_1 component of the record L_1.

However, as noted for the equivalent situation with arrays, it is better to avoid complex component selections, by providing subprograms for operating at one level of selection only.

While on the subject of complexity, let us look at arrays as record components, and arrays of records, so that you understand the selection of the exact component that you want.

```
STACK_MAX:constant NATURAL:=32;
subtype STACK_RANGE is INTEGER range 1..STACK_MAX;
subtype STK_PTR_RANGE is INTEGER
    range 0..STACK_MAX;
type STACK_STRUCTURE is array (STACK_RANGE) of
    INTEGER;
type STACK is record
    ITEMS:STACK_STRUCTURE;
    TOP:STK_PTR_RANGE:=0;
end record;
STAX:array (1..10) of STACK;
-- some possible component selections
-- STAX(1)                -- type STACK
-- STAX(2).ITEMS          -- type STACK_STRUCTURE
-- STAX(6).TOP            -- type STK_PTR_RANGE
-- STAX(3).ITEMS(5)       -- type INTEGER
```

This shows what *can* be done, rather than what should be done. Complex selections like this would be hidden, as remarked earlier, by a hierarchy of subprograms, with each selection level having its own routine(s).

6.6 Discriminated records

Records may have *discriminants*, which enable them to be parameterized. Only discrete types are allowed for discriminants. A discriminant is effectively used to pass information into a record, so that it can be used in certain component type specifications, in default expressions, or for record variant selection. It is usual for at least one component of a discriminated record to depend on a discriminant, but this is not required by the language.

The specification of discriminant(s) appears in parentheses after the record name in its declaration, with a syntax reminiscent of that of subprogram parameters. The type of the discriminant (discrete, remember) must be specified using a type identifier, so that it is not possible to add a constraint. Continuing the analogy with parameters, discriminants may have default expressions. Before looking at the consequences of this, here are some examples.

First, assume that we want to represent queues of different sizes. If the elements of the queue are represented by an array, and we have pointers to the first and last items in the queue, as well as a count of the number of items currently in the queue, we could write:

```
-- type Q_ITEM is the type of queue members
type Q_LIST is array (POSITIVE range ⟨⟩) of Q_ITEM;
type QUEUE(CAPACITY:POSITIVE) is
record
  ITEM:Q_LIST(1..CAPACITY);
  FRONT,
  BACK,
  WAITING:NATURAL:=0;
end record;
```

It is important to note that, although discriminants can be used to specify index ranges, they cannot be used to specify the ranges of subtypes. So, WAITING could not have been declared as:

```
WAITING:NATURAL range 0..CAPACITY:=0;   -- INVALID
```

The only other permitted use of discriminants in component type specifications is as a discriminant to a *component* of the discriminated record itself. To create queue objects, we can declare:

```
CPU_Q:QUEUE(100);                       -- positional
DISK_Q:QUEUE(CAPACITY=>20);             -- named
```

Note a further similarity with subprogram parameters, in that values for discriminants may be supplied using positional or named notation. (It is possible to mix notations, with the same restrictions and advice given for parameters.) The first of the above declarations creates a queue for 100 items, while DISK_Q can accommodate up to 20. Neither queue can have its capacity changed, once it has been created.

It is not possible to assign to a discriminant, nor, to be consistent, does Ada allow a discriminant to be passed as an **out** or **in out** parameter. Under certain circumstances, discriminant values can be changed, but only by whole record assignment, as we shall soon see.

Record aggregates may be assigned to discriminated records, as long as any discriminants are placed first, in declaration order. Values for discriminants must *always* be provided in aggregates, even in situations where they cannot be changed. For example, if Q_ITEM is an integer type, we might have:

> TINY_Q:QUEUE(5):=(5, (1, 2, 3, 0, 0), 1, 3, 3);

A discriminant must always have a value, known as a constraint, when a discriminated record object is elaborated. If there is no default expression, then the value must be supplied at the declaration. It is also possible to create subtypes for particular discriminant values:

> subtype SMALL_QUEUE is QUEUE(10);
> BANK_Q:SMALL_QUEUE;   -- size 10

No constraint has to be provided in the declaration of BANK_Q, as it is inferred from the constraint of the subtype. No other value may be subsequently given to the discriminant.

For record constants, as in the case of array bounds, discriminant values can be obtained from the aggregate that defines the value of the constant. As already said, this aggregate must include a value for (all) discriminants.

> EMPTY_Q:constant QUEUE :=(10, (1...10=>0), 0, 0, 0);

creates a constant empty queue with a capacity for ten items.

Discriminants can be accessed (for reading only) just like any other record component, by selection:

> TOTAL_CAPACITY:=CPU_Q.CAPACITY
>   + DISK_Q.CAPACITY;

A nice example of a discriminated record (taken from the LRM) is one for defining a square matrix, in which the ranges of the two indexes *have* to be identical. This declaration uses the unconstrained array type MATRIX defined earlier in this chapter.

> type SQUARE(SIZE:POSITIVE:=10) is
> record
>   GRID:MATRIX(1..SIZE, 1..SIZE);
> end record;

Note that a default expression has been given for the discriminant. The following declarations are now valid:

> BOARD:SQUARE(8);   -- 8 * 8
> BORED:SQUARE;   -- 10 * 10

BOARD has been declared with a value of eight for the discriminant, thus over-riding the default. BOARD will *always* be an eight by eight matrix. BORED, on the other hand, has relied on the default value of the discriminant. This leads to an important difference between BOARD and BORED. While BOARD is constrained to its initial size, BORED is not so constrained. We can, if we so wish, *change* its size (by whole record assignment, of course):

```
BORED:=(2, ((1.1, 1.2), (2.1, 2.2)));     -- 2*2
BORED:=BOARD;                             -- 8*8
```

A Boolean attribute, CONSTRAINED, is provided to determine whether or not a record is constrained. A record with default expressions for its discriminants will not yield CONSTRAINED objects unless a constraint is provided on declaration, as with BOARD above. If we had

```
SMALL_BOARD:SQUARE:=(3, ((1.0, 2.0, 3.0),
                         (4.0, 5.0, 6.0),
                         (7.0, 8.0, 9.0)));
```

the SMALL_BOARD is not constrained by the *assignment* of an initial value — its SIZE may be subsequently changed.

Some of this takes on added significance when we consider the passing of discriminated records as parameters. If a formal parameter is unconstrained, then it will inherit its characteristics from the actual parameter. Consider the procedure below, which removes a row and a column from a SQUARE. The actual parameter must obviously be unconstrained for this to succeed.

```
procedure GUILLOTINE(VICTIM:in out SQUARE) is
   NEW_SIZE:constant POSITIVE:=VICTIM.SIZE-1;
   subtype NEW_RANGE is POSITIVE range 1..NEW_SIZE;
   SHRUNK:MATRIX(NEW_RANGE, NEW_RANGE);
begin
   for ROW in NEW_RANGE loop
     for COL in NEW_RANGE loop
       SHRUNK(ROW, COL):=VICTIM.GRID(ROW, COL);
     end loop;
   end loop;
   VICTIM:=(NEW_SIZE, SHRUNK);
 end GUILLOTINE;
```

This procedure may be called with BORED, but a call with BOARD would cause CONSTRAINT_ERROR to be raised.

Variant records [LRM 3.7.3]

An important use of discriminants is to enable records to have variant parts, i.e. different sets of fields for different circumstances. Variant records should only be used for closely related objects, which exhibit variations, and not for the convenience of making a number of unrelated items share the same type (because, for example, you find strong typing inconvenient!). A typical example is:

```
type   VEHICLE_TYPE   is   (CAR,   PICK_UP,   BUS,
M_CYCLE);
subtype NAME is STRING(1..12);
SPACES:constant NAME:=(NAME'RANGE=>'');
subtype YEAR_TYPE is POSITIVE range 1900..1999;
type VEHICLE (CLASS:VEHICLE_TYPE:=CAR) is
record
  MODEL:NAME:=SPACES;
  BUILT:YEAR_TYPE:=1986;
  case CLASS is
    when CAR=>
      SEATS:POSITIVE range 1..9:=4;
    when PICK_UP=>
      CAPACITY:FLOAT range 0.0..10.0;
    when BUS=>
      PASSENGERS:POSITIVE range 1..80:=52;
    when M_CYCLE=>
      null;
  end case;
end record;
```

The static, or common, part must precede the variant part of the record definition. Note that the variant part is structured exactly like a case statement, which requires an **end case** immediately before the **end record** (unlike Pascal). Component choices may use the same notations as case statement choices, so that '|' can be used for separating alternatives and ranges can be specified using '..'. And, of course, **others** can be used (as the last choice) but shouldn't! All possible values of the case selector must be catered for. In common with the case statement, as we have seen, the specification of choices and ranges must be static expressions (which cannot include variables).

Wherever possible, the case discriminant should be an enumeration type, as it lends considerable readability to the code.

The requirement that component identifiers be distinct applies over all variants of a record. If a variant has no additional components, as is the case for M_CYCLE above, then **null** must be used (another syntactic similarity with the case statement). Only one variant part may occur in a record. However, a component within a variant may, itself, include a variant part (subject to the same rules as the outer variant part: there may only be one; it must come last and all component identifiers must be distinct). Again, what is possible in Ada, is not always an indication of what is desirable. If you have a structure that is so complex, then it should be declared hierarchically, with the inner variant as a separate variant record type.

The points made earlier about discriminants in general still apply to discriminants in variant records — they are no different. So, a variant cannot be changed on its own, it can only be changed by whole record assignment. Consequently, it is not possible to set a variant selector to one value and select fields of a different variant (as it is in Pascal). Given the earlier vehicular declarations, Ada will not allow references to CAPACITY or PASSENGERS fields of a CAR variant.

The use of CONSTRAINED and the rules about constrained and unconstrained discriminants also remain applicable. So, if we had the declarations:

```
FORD:VEHICLE;
ROLLS_ROYCE:VEHICLE(CAR);
```

ROLLS_ROYCE is constrained to be a car forever, whereas, FORD can be subjected to a conversion into a PICK_UP:

```
FORD:=(PICK_UP, "Ford Escort", 1987, 1.5);
```

6.7 Access types [LRM 3.8, 4.8]

Access types are used to reference *dynamic objects*, i.e. ones which are created during execution of the program, when required. All the objects seen so far have been *static*, being created at the time of elaboration of their declarations. Dynamic objects are created by an *allocator*. Static objects are referred to directly by name, whereas dynamic objects are accessed indirectly by a *pointer*. It is these pointers that are called "access types" in Ada.

An access type may be declared as a pointer to any type. As you would expect in a strongly typed language, an access type is specific to one type of object. The value **null** may be assigned to any access type object to indicate that it is not pointing to anything. **null** is also the default initial value of access types, which ensures that pointers only acquire their values through the (controlled) use of allocators.

Access types are useful for a certain purpose in packages, and for working with some tasking applications (see Chapters 7 and 11 respectively). However, it is for creating *dynamic data structures* that they are most widely used. Two common examples of such structures are the dynamic linked list and the (ordered) binary tree. The discussion of access types here, will therefore concentrate on this general use, looking specifically at linked lists.

Linked lists are used quite frequently for a number of reasons. First, no size limit has to be specified, so the list can expand and contract to suit the immediate requirement. Also, they are very flexible structures, which can be easily updated, at little cost.

A dynamic linked list comprises a number of nodes, each of which contains the required information, together with a pointer to the next node in the list. Fig. 6.1 shows a linked list of integers, maintained in ascending order.

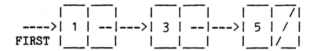

Fig. 6.1 A linked list of integers.

FIRST is a pointer to the first node in the list (the head). All other nodes are accessed (eventually) via this one. The pointer field of the last node is set to **null**, to indicate that no more nodes remain.

First of all, let us see how the nodes are defined in Ada. Each NODE will be a record with two components, INFO (an INTEGER) and NEXT (a POINTER). NEXT will have to point to a node just like the record that contains it, so that it appears that a NODE has to be defined in terms of itself. To overcome this circularity, Ada permits the node type to be introduced as an *incomplete type declaration*, which is sufficient to enable an access type to be declared for it. The full declaration of the node can then follow. So, for our linked list, we have:

```
type NODE;                    -- incomplete type declaration
type POINTER is access NODE;
type NODE is
record
   INFO:INTEGER;
   NEXT:POINTER;              -- set to null by default
```

```
end record;
FIRST:POINTER;                    -- set to null by default
```

When these declarations have been elaborated, we have one pointer, FIRST, that is pointing nowhere, its having been initialized to **null** automatically. In practice, it is always better to initialize pointers explicitly. The reason Ada initializes pointers is to prevent any possibility of accessing (and corrupting) memory locations not actually allocated.

We now set about creating the list of Fig. 6.1 (the hard way), one node at a time. The code, which illustrates various aspects of dynamic variable allocation, goes something like:

```
FIRST:=new NODE;             -- Allocator creates a new
                             -- NODE and makes FIRST
                             -- point to it.
FIRST.all:=(3, null);        -- FIRST.all is the record
                             -- (type NODE) that FIRST
                             -- points to.
                             -- FIRST is a POINTER.
FIRST.NEXT:=new NODE' (5, null);
                             -- Allocation and initialization
                             -- can be combined by qualifying
                             -- the expression. This adds
                             -- the 5 after the 3. The pointer
                             -- to the new node is assigned
                             -- to the NEXT field of the node
                             -- pointed to by FIRST.
FIRST:=new NODE' (1, FIRST.NEXT);
                             -- Creates the third node, which
                             -- points to the node currently
                             -- pointed to by FIRST. The new
                             -- node then becomes pointed to
                             -- by FIRST.
```

The list has now been created. For each dynamic variable, the allocator **new** has to be called, with the type of the dynamic object specified, *not* the access type. **new** creates the dynamic object and returns a pointer to it to the invocation point.

De-referencing is automatic in Ada — no special syntactic device is required to distinguish between the pointer and the object to which it points, as long as the meaning is clear from the context. Therefore,

FIRST.NEXT denotes the NEXT field of the NODE object *pointed to* by FIRST. If we do want to refer to the *whole* object to which FIRST points, then we have to use **all**. So, FIRST.all is a complete record (in this case, the first in the list) of type NODE. (FIRST.NEXT is really an abbreviation for FIRST.all.NEXT.) If we had the declarations:

> P_1, P_2:POINTER;

then you must appreciate the distinction between:

> P_1:=P_2;

and

> P_1.all:=P_2.all;

The first assignment copies the pointer value, P_2, into P_1, so that P_1 now points to the *same object* that P_2 points to. (P_1 no longer points to the object that it was previously referencing — if that object has no other reference to it, it is now inaccessible!) The second assignment copies the record pointed to by P_2 into the record pointed to by P_1. If P_1 and P_2 were referencing different objects *before* the assignment, then they will continue to do so afterwards, although both objects will have the same value.

If you are not used to pointers, take care, but do not be disheartened if things do not always work as you intend. Access types are very useful (and fun to work with).

One effect that may not be obvious, is demonstrated by:

> CONST_POINT:constant POINTER:=new NODE'(0,null);

As you would expect with a constant, the value of CONST_POINT cannot be changed, so that it will always point to the same dynamic variable. However, the value of the object itself *can* be changed, so of the following assignments, the first is invalid, while the second is quite acceptable:

> CONST_POINT:=FIRST;   -- INVALID
> CONST_POINT.all:=FIRST.all;   -- allowed

A similar effect is demonstrated by the following procedure heading.

```
procedure POINT_PROC(PTR:in POINTER) is
  LOCAL_PTR:POINTER:=PTR;
begin
  LOCAL_PTR.NEXT:=null;
end POINT_PROC;
```

LOCAL_PTR is a local variable, which is initialized to the value of the actual parameter passed to PTR. PTR itself is a parameter of mode **in**, so the actual parameter cannot therefore be altered within the subprogram. However, any object to which the actual parameter points, *can* be changed. Consider then, the effect of calling the procedure thus:

POINT_PROC(FIRST);

where FIRST points to the list of Fig. 6.1. FIRST cannot be changed by the call, but the NEXT field of the NODE to which it points is set to **null**, thereby deleting the two following nodes!

Access types themselves may be tested for (in)equality, which determines whether or not the *pointers* are the same. No other operators may be applied to pointers but, if valid, operators can, of course, be applied to the objects to which they point.

Memory management [LRM 4.8]

The memory used for dynamic variables is separate (and separately managed) from that used for static (not access) variables. When an allocator is evaluated, the memory required is allocated from the dynamic memory area. What happens, though, when a dynamic variable is no longer required? Generally, there are two approaches to this. The first is for the language to provide a *garbage collector* as part of its run-time system. Its purpose is to identify and reclaim unwanted (or unusable) dynamic memory. Ada implementations *may* provide a garbage collector. The second approach is to give the responsibility of reclamation or *de-allocation* to the programmer. For this purpose, Ada provides a pre-defined generic library procedure, UNCHECKED_DEALLOCATION, which must be used to instantiate procedures specific to all dynamic types in an application. Any compilation unit which requires this generic must name it in a with clause.

For our linked list example, we would write:

```
with UNCHECKED_DEALLOCATION;
procedure MAIN is
   -- other declarations
   procedure DISPOSE_NODE is new
      UNCHECKED_DEALLOCATION (NODE, POINTER);
```

The name of the generic is a constant reminder to the programmer to check that a de-allocated node is not referenced by any pointer other than the one specified to a call of the instantiated procedure, as in:

DISPOSE_NODE(FIRST);

which reclaims the memory allocated to FIRST.all and sets FIRST to **null**. Note that this call would only reclaim the first node in the list. If FIRST.NEXT were still pointing to the remainder of the list shown in Fig. 6.1, then those two nodes would not be reclaimed. What is more, if there is no other pointer to those nodes, there would be no way of accessing them at all, whether to recover them, using DISPOSE_NODE, or to utilize the truncated structure.

There is more to memory management for dynamic variables, such as how to work with a garbage collector. Consult the LRM [4.8] for further information.

Unit 6.6 is a program which contains the type definitions given earlier, together with procedures for inserting integers into an ordered list and printing the contents of such a list. Always, when working with dynamic data structures, specific action is required for the empty structure. The program creates a specific de-allocation procedure, which is used by DELETE to reclaim nodes removed from the list.

```
with SIMPLE_IO;                -- a non-standard package
with UNCHECKED_DEALLOCATION;   -- for visibility
use  SIMPLE_IO;

procedure MAIN is
  type NODE;
  type POINTER is access NODE;

  type NODE is
  record
    INFO:INTEGER;
    NEXT:POINTER:=null;                  -- redundant, but explicit
  end record;

  LIST:POINTER:=null;            ,-- and again
  NOT_FOUND:exception;
  MORE_WORK:BOOLEAN:=TRUE;

  procedure INSERT(FRONT:in out POINTER; ITEM:in INTEGER) is

  -- Inserts ITEM into the list pointed to by FRONT.
  -- The list is maintained in ascending order.

    HERE:POINTER;
  begin
    if FRONT = null or else ITEM < FRONT.INFO then
      FRONT:=new NODE'(ITEM, FRONT);
```

```
        else
          HERE:=FRONT;
          while HERE.NEXT /= null and HERE.INFO < ITEM loop
            HERE:=HERE.NEXT;
          end loop;
          if ITEM = HERE.INFO then
            PUT(ITEM);
            PUT_LINE(" is already in the list.");
          elsif ITEM < HERE.INFO then          -- insert before HERE
            HERE.NEXT:=new NODE'(HERE.all);
            HERE.INFO:=ITEM;
          else                                 -- insert after HERE
            HERE.NEXT:=new NODE'(ITEM, HERE.NEXT);
          end if;
        end if;
      end INSERT;

      procedure DELETE(FRONT:in out POINTER; ITEM:in INTEGER) is

      -- Removes ITEM from the list.
      -- NOT_FOUND is raised, if ITEM not present.
      -- The caller must handle it.

        DEL_NODE, PRE_NODE:POINTER;

        procedure DISPOSE_NODE is new
                   UNCHECKED_DEALLOCATION(NODE, POINTER);

      begin
        if FRONT = null then
          PUT_LINE("List empty.");
          raise NOT_FOUND;
        end if;
        -- list is not empty if we get here
        DEL_NODE:=FRONT;
        if ITEM = FRONT.INFO then
          FRONT:=FRONT.NEXT;
        elsif ITEM < FRONT.INFO then
          raise NOT_FOUND;
        else
          while ITEM /= DEL_NODE.INFO and DEL_NODE.NEXT /= null loop
            PRE_NODE:=DEL_NODE;
            DEL_NODE:=DEL_NODE.NEXT;
          end loop;
          if ITEM /= DEL_NODE.INFO then
            raise NOT_FOUND;
          end if;
          PRE_NODE.NEXT:=DEL_NODE.NEXT;          -- bypass the node
        end if;
        DISPOSE_NODE(DEL_NODE);
      end DELETE;

      procedure PRINT_LIST(FRONT:in POINTER) is

      -- Prints the elements of the list

        THIS:POINTER:=FRONT;
      begin
        if FRONT = null then
          PUT_LINE("The list is empty.");
```

```
    else
      PUT_LINE("The list is:");
      while THIS /= null loop
        PUT(THIS.INFO);
        NEW_LINE;
        THIS:=THIS.NEXT;
      end loop;
  end if;
end PRINT_LIST;

procedure GET_ACTION is

-- The main driving routine.

  INT:INTEGER;
  ACTION:CHARACTER;

  procedure GET_INT(ITEM:out INTEGER) is

  -- Ensures the input of a valid integer.

  begin
    loop
      begin
        NEW_LINE;
        PUT("Type the integer: ");
        GET(ITEM);
        NEW_LINE;
        exit;
      exception
        when DATA_ERROR=>
          PUT_LINE("Must be an integer.");
        when CONSTRAINT_ERROR=>
          PUT_LINE("Integer too large.");
      end;
    end loop;
  end GET_INT;

begin          -- GET_ACTION
  NEW_LINE;
  PUT("Next action (I D P X): ");
  GET(ACTION);
  NEW_LINE;
  case ACTION is
    when 'I'=>
      GET_INT(INT);
      INSERT(LIST, INT);
    when 'D'=>
      begin              -- block for exception handler
        GET_INT(INT);
        DELETE(LIST, INT);
      exception
        when NOT_FOUND=>
          PUT(INT);
          PUT_LINE(" not found in the list.");
      end;
    when 'P'=>
      PRINT_LIST(LIST);
    when 'X'=>
      MORE_WORK:=FALSE;
```

```
    when others=>
       PUT_LINE("Invalid action code.");
    end case;
  end GET_ACTION;

begin            -- MAIN
  while MORE_WORK loop
    GET_ACTION;
  end loop;
end MAIN;
```

Unit 6.6   Operations on an ordered linked list.

6.8 Renaming [LRM 8.5]

At this point, it is appropriate to introduce renaming, the ability to declare an *alias* for some object in a declarative part. (We shall see other aspects of renaming in the next chapter.) Renaming does not create a separate object. It should be used where it makes the meaning clearer (and not more obscure), or it may be used for greater run-time efficiency. First, an example using nested record structures.

```
-- type DATE as before
type WORKER is
record
  D_O_B:DATE;
  -- other components of no concern here
end record;
subtype EMP_RANGE is POSITIVE range 1..99;
EMPLOYEE:array (EMP_RANGE) of WORKER;

procedure PROCESS_EMPLOYEE
                     (EMP_NO:in EMP_RANGE) is
  THIS_DOB:DATE renames EMPLOYEE(EMP_NO).D_O_B;
  -- From this point on, throughout the scope of
  -- this renaming declaration, it is possible
  -- to use, for example, THIS_DOB.DAY instead
  -- of EMPLOYEE(EMP_NO).D_O_B.DAY.
end PROCESS_EMPLOYEE:
```

Of course, some (but not all) the motivation for a renaming like this would be eliminated by a hierarchical processing strategy advocated earlier.

As a final example, if TABLE is a two-dimensional array of INTEGER, then we could say:

```
for I in TABLE'RANGE(1) loop
  for J in TABLE'RANGE(2) loop
    declare
      TIJ:INTEGER renames TABLE(I,J);
    begin
      if TIJ < 10 then
        TIJ:=TIJ + 1;
      end if;
      -- and so on
    end;
  end loop;
end loop;
```

In the block, the addrress of the array element is only calculated once for each block execution, rather than three times as might be necessary if a compiler cannot detect the repetition. Consequently, this rendering could be more efficient at run-time. Incidentally, note that if the values of I and J were to be changed within the range of the renaming declaration (in this particular example, they are loop parameters, so cannot be so changed) then TIJ would still represent the original TABLE(I, J) determined on elaboration of the renaming declaration.

Practising Ada 6

Practise data structure definition and manipulation in Ada. Choose structures which are appropriate to the application. Your programs should, of course, all be modular by now and have effective exception handling. Try these for size:

1 Read in two binary integers and print their sum (in binary).
2 Write operators to add and mutiply any two compatible two-dimensional matrices of type FLOAT. It is your responsibility to check compatibility.
3 Write functions that return the following substrings of a given STRING (if possible):
(i) the leftmost N characters
(ii) the rightmost N characters
(iii) the N characters beginning with character M
4 Read, validate and print dates (hold them as records). Read two dates and print the number of days that separate them.
5 Define a type for representing complex numbers. Write subprograms to read, write, add, subtract and multiply them.

6 A triangle is defined by: (i) the lengths of its three sides, a, b and c; OR (ii) the lengths of two sides, a, b, and the intervening angle, C. Write code to read data for a triangle in either form. Add a function to calculate the area of a triangle given as an argument (in either format).

The formulae are, respectively: (i) $S*(S-a)*(S-b)*(S-c)$ where $S=(a+b+c)/2.0$;   (ii) $0.5*a*b*sine(C)$.

7 Read in a string and print it in reverse using a stack. (Use a linked list, then use an array for the stack.)

8 Write subprograms to construct and print ordered binary trees of integers. Each node will have an integer and two pointers — one to the root of the left subtree and the other to the root of the right subtree (empty subtrees will be **null**). The characteristic of an ordered binary tree is that all information to the left of a given node is less than the information at the node itself while information to the right is greater.

Chapter 7

Packages [LRM 7]

Of the four program units, the package is the most important one for constructing Ada programs. The package is not a new concept in programming languages, having been provided by SIMULA in the 1960s. Experience with SIMULA has proved the package to be a powerful means of extending a general purpose language into specific application areas, with very high level, application orientated features for the user.

In Ada, the role of the package is emphasized by the fact that much of what we regard as the basic language is effectively provided by packages, in particular the package STANDARD (see Appendix B). The Ada programs that we write use the pre-defined types and operations for our own particular purpose. If we want to extend the language by defining further types, together with operations specific to them, then this would be done by writing our own package, which can be made available to all programs that we or others write, in the same way that STANDARD is always available.

So, the package should be used to assemble a collection of types, objects and operations, which form a coherent group. In addition to making things visible for other units to use, the package enables other items to be completely hidden from these other units. By so doing, the Ada package directly supports the concept of information hiding introduced in Chapter 1.

Before looking at how packages are normally used, as *library units*, the structure of a package is discussed in more detail.

7.1 Package structure — specification [LRM 7.2]

In Chapter 2, it was shown that packages have two parts to them, a specification and a body. Subsequently, Chapter 5, revealed that subprograms may also, if the programmer wishes, have a separate specification and body. With packages, however, the programmer has no option: the specification must *always* be provided and it must precede any corresponding body. (There need not, though, under circumstances explained below, be a package body.)

The specification of a package specifies the elements that the package

147

makes available to other program units, or, expressing it another way, it defines what the package *exports* to the outside world. A package specification can only contain what the LRM calls "basic_declarative_items", which can be taken as meaning any valid Ada declaration, other than the body of a program unit. If there are any subprogram, package or task specifications within a package specification, then the corresponding bodies must be included in the corresponding package body. If a package specification contains only type and object declarations (i.e. no other specifications) then a body is not required, as in:

```
-- some declarative part
package HARDWARE_TYPES is

    type BYTE_PART is (LO_NIBL, HI_NIBL);
    type WORD_PART is (LO_BYTE, HI_BYTE);
    type NIBBLE is ('0', '1', '2', '3', '4', '5', '6', '7', '8', '9', 'A',
        'B', 'C', 'D', 'E', 'F');
    type BYTE is array(BYTE_PART) of NIBBLE;
    type WORD is array(WORD_PART) of BYTE;
    ZERO:constant NIBBLE:='0';
    ONES:constant NIBBLE:='F';
    BYTE_ZERO:constant BYTE:=(ZERO, ZERO);
    BYTE_ONES:constant BYTE:=(ONES, ONES);
    WORD_ZERO:constant WORD
      :=(BYTE_ZERO, BYTE_ZERO);
    WORD_ONES:constant WORD
      :=(BYTE_ONES, BYTE_ONES);
end HARDWARE_TYPES;

-- all the above types and objects are visible
-- from this point by selection, e.g.
MY_WORD:HARDWARE_TYPES.WORD
:=HARDWARE_TYPES.WORD_ZERO;
begin

MY_WORD(HARDWARE_TYPES.LO_BYTE)
  :=HARDWARE_TYPES.BYTE_ONES;

-- ......
end;
```

Note that, in common with the treatment of subprograms, the repetition of the package name after the **end** is optional, but should always be provided to aid readability.

The scope of declarations in a package specification extends over the range of the declarative region in which the specification itself is declared. However, as the above example shows, the declarations are *directly* visible. Rather than employ selection, a use clause could have been inserted after the package specification:

```
package HARDWARE_TYPES

    -- as before
end HARDWARE_TYPES;

use HARDWARE_TYPES;
MY_WORD:WORD:=WORD_ZERO;

begin

    MY_WORD (LO_BYTE):=BYTE_ONES;
    -- . . . . . .
end;
```

This is clearly more concise and readable. However, **use** should not be applied as a matter of course, as we shall see.

Because a package is used to group related entities together, it can stand alone as a collection with a coherent theme. If the package is embedded within a main program, it can only be used within that main program. On the other hand, if it is compiled as a library unit, then it may be used by different programs. This is discussed further in the next section.

7.2 Packages as library units (Introduction)

Packages are normally compiled as library units, which is the status of TEXT_IO and SIMPLE_IO, into the library maintained by the Ada system that you are using. The procedure that represents a main program is also a library unit.

There is quite a lot to say about library units and the way that an Ada program should be modularized and compiled. Most of the discussion is postponed until 7.7. At this point, sufficient information is provided to enable you to implement and use your packages as library units.

Library units all exist at the same level — effectively, it is as if they are all declared at the end of the pre-defined package STANDARD, which is always visible to all other units. If your main program wants to utilize the facilities provided by a library unit, it is necessary to have a *with clause* to state the dependency, as we have seen in the programs that have been dependent on TEXT_IO and SIMPLE_IO. The effect of the **with** is to extend the scope of the named library unit(s) over the dependent unit. The *packages themselves* then become visible throughout the dependent units, however, the items they export have to be made visible by selection or by a *use clause*.

Owing to its fundamentally important nature, STANDARD is accorded a special status, which ensures its visibility, always. Consequently, it does not have to be (nor should it be) named in a with clause. All the items exported by STANDARD are, themselves, directly visible, so that no selection or **use** is required with STANDARD. One of the items exported by STANDARD is the package ASCII. Because it is in STANDARD, ASCII does not have to be referenced in a with clause. However, like any library units of our own creation, the items exported by ASCII are only visible by selection or by including a use clause.

In all the remaining examples in this chapter, it will be assumed that the packages are library units. To be complete, let us go back to the example in the last section and assume that the package specification has already been compiled into the library — the package specification itself will not need to be altered in any way. Any dependent unit then has to specify the unit name (HARDWARE_TYPES) in a with clause, before the dependent unit itself. Thus, we could write:

```
with HARDWARE_TYPES, TEXT_IO;
use HARDWARE_TYPES, TEXT_IO;

procedure MAIN is

    MY_WORD:WORD:=WORD_ZERO;

begin

    MY_WORD(LO_BYTE):=BYTE_ONES;
    -- ......
end MAIN;
```

Note that MAIN depends on the two library packages specified in the with clause. The **use** also specifies both packages. Here, it has been placed immediately after the **with**. If you are going to have a use clause, this is the best place for it, as it is in a more prominent position than it would be if it were half way down some declarative part. It is not a good idea to apply the use clause indiscriminately, as it can obscure the meaning of a program. If MAIN were dependent on five library units, all of which were named in a use clause, then it would be far from obvious, from MAIN itself, which facilities were provided by what package.

7.3 Package structure — bodies [LRM 7.3]

A package body must always come after its specification and, remember, all bodies must come after "basic_declarative_items" in any declarative part. A package body has the structure:

```
package body ⟨NAME⟩ is
    ⟨DECLARATIVE_PART⟩
[begin
    ⟨SEQUENCE_OF_STATEMENTS⟩
[exception
    ⟨EXCEPTION_HANDLER(S)⟩ ]]
end [⟨NAME⟩];
```

The declarative part contains any valid declarations, which will be local to the body only. The specification and body of a package are considered to be the same declarative region, therefore it is not permissible to declare identifiers in the package body that have already been declared in the specification.

When it comes to scope and visibility, declarations in the body are treated very differently from those in the specification. Declarations within the body are only in scope from the point of their declaration to the end of the body and are subject to the normal visibility rules (within the body), therefore they are in scope and accessible (subject to normal hiding rules) from any subprograms contained in the package body. Declarations in the specification are also directly visible in the package body but they are also potentially visible to the outside world, for the specification contains the declarations of those items exported by the package. All declarations in the package body are completely hidden from all external program units and cannot be rendered visible by any means. This is one aspect of information hiding in packages.

From the structural outline, the square brackets (denoting optional features) indicate that, unlike in blocks and subprograms, the **begin** and following statement part need not be present in a package body. An empty statement part in a block or subprogram (or task) would be meaningless. In packages this is not so. The statement part of a package, if there is one, is executed once, when the package body is elaborated, and is provided for any initializations of package objects that cannot be performed in their declarations.

A package is a passive unit, which is used by other (active) program units. It is a library unit, it exists throughout the execution of the program, providing types and objects to other program units and subprograms that may be called by these other units. (A package may also export other packages, as is the case with STANDARD and, as we shall see in Chapter 10, TEXT_IO.) The hidden variables of a package (i.e. those declared in the body) can only be changed as a result of calls to visible subprograms of the package. Between such calls, their values are preserved.

Unit 7.1 is a package which contains a stack onto which CHARACTERs may be PUSHed and from which they may be POPped, one at a time. The package exports the subprograms PUSH, POP and STACK_EMPTY, together with two exceptions. The stack itself is hidden from view, as it is declared in the package body. Note the commentary in the package specification. More will be said about this later.

```
package CHAR_STACK_1 is

   -- Description:
   -- The package provides a fixed size stack which
   -- can accommodate up to 32 CHARACTERs.
   -- Exceptions:
   -- UNDERFLOW may be raised by POP, if the stack is
   -- empty.
   -- OVERFLOW may be raised by PUSH, if the stack is
   -- already full.
   -- No other exceptions should be raised.
   -- Implementation dependences:
   -- None.

   procedure POP(CHAR:out CHARACTER);
      -- Pops the top CHARACTER from the stack into CHAR

   procedure PUSH(CHAR:in CHARACTER);
      -- Pushes CHAR onto the stack

   function STACK_EMPTY return BOOLEAN;
      -- Returns TRUE if stack empty

   UNDERFLOW, OVERFLOW:exception;
end CHAR_STACK_1;

package body CHAR_STACK_1 is
   STACK_MAX:constant:=32;
   type STACK_ITEMS is array (1..STACK_MAX) of CHARACTER;
   type STACK_TYPE is
   record
     TOP:NATURAL range 0..STACK_MAX:=0;
     ITEM:STACK_ITEMS;
```

```
end record;
STACK:STACK_TYPE;

procedure POP(CHAR:out CHARACTER) is
begin
  if STACK.TOP = 0 then
    raise UNDERFLOW;
  end if;
  CHAR:=STACK.ITEM(STACK.TOP);
  STACK.TOP:=STACK.TOP - 1;
end POP;

procedure PUSH(CHAR:in CHARACTER) is
begin
  if STACK.TOP = STACK_MAX then
    raise OVERFLOW;
  end if;
  STACK.TOP:=STACK.TOP + 1;
  STACK.ITEM(STACK.TOP):=CHAR;
end PUSH;

function STACK_EMPTY return BOOLEAN is
begin
  return STACK.TOP = 0;
end STACK_EMPTY;

end CHAR_STACK_1;
```

Unit 7.1 A package to provide a stack.

This is an example of a package with no statement part. The initialization of STACK_TOP *could* have been performed by a single statement in a statement part, but it is better to perform the initialization at the declaration.

To use the package (a library unit, remember), we might have:

```
with TEXT_IO, CHAR_STACK_1;
use TEXT_IO;

procedure MAIN is

  CHAR:CHARACTER;
  -- etc.

begin

  -- some statements
  GET(CHAR);
  CHAR_STACK_1.PUSH(CHAR);    -- pushes a copy of
                              -- CHAR onto stack
  -- more statements
  while not CHAR_STACK_1.STACK_EMPTY loop
                              -- write whole stack
```

```
        CHAR_STACK_1.POP(CHAR);   -- pops the top of stack
                                  -- into CHAR
        PUT(CHAR);
    end loop;
    -- yet more statements
end MAIN;
```

Another package, which utilizes a slightly expanded CHAR_STACK_1 is developed in 7.7.

7.4 Private types [LRM 7.4]

So far, you have learned that items declared in the package body are completely hidden, while those in the specification are potentially visible to all would-be users. There are many occasions when we want to export a type but impose restrictions on the way that the type can be used. To illustrate this, consider an example.

A typical use of a package is to introduce a new type and a set of operations for operands of that type. Using such a package, we can provide our own set type. Say, for example, that we require to be able to represent sets of CHARACTERs. There are various ways of implementing sets — the most suitable structure here might be an array of BOOLEANs, with one element in the array for each value of CHARACTER. If a character is present in the set, then its corresponding element will be TRUE, otherwise it will be FALSE.

Unit 7.2 is a package containing the definition of the set type and some operations for objects of the defined type. In practice, more operations would be useful, together with further overloadings of the operators to allow operands of type SET_OF_CHAR or CHARACTER, as demonstrated for "+". Note how convenient it is that Ada allows logical operators to be applied to one-dimensional BOOLEAN arrays.

```
with TEXT_IO;
package CHAR_SET_1 is

    -- Description:
    -- This package defines a type for representing sets
    -- of CHARACTERs, a constant for an empty set, and
    -- a number of subprograms as described below.
    -- Exceptions:
    -- None expected.
    -- Implementation dependences:
    -- None.

    type SET_OF_CHAR is array(CHARACTER) of BOOLEAN;
    EMPTY:constant SET_OF_CHAR:=(others=>FALSE);
```

```
   function SET_OF(CHAR:in CHARACTER) return SET_OF_CHAR;
      -- constructs a singleton set from a CHARACTER

   function "+"(LEFT, RIGHT:in SET_OF_CHAR) return SET_OF_CHAR;
      -- returns the union of LEFT and RIGHT

   function "+"(LEFT:in SET_OF_CHAR; RIGHT:in CHARACTER)
               return SET_OF_CHAR;
      -- returns LEFT with RIGHT added to it

   function "-"(LEFT, RIGHT:in SET_OF_CHAR) return SET_OF_CHAR;
      -- returns the difference: LEFT-RIGHT

   function "*"(LEFT, RIGHT:in SET_OF_CHAR) return SET_OF_CHAR;
      -- returns the intersection of LEFT and RIGHT

   function SUBSET(LEFT, RIGHT:in SET_OF_CHAR) return BOOLEAN;
      -- returns TRUE if LEFT is subset (improper) of RIGHT

   procedure PUT(ITEM:in SET_OF_CHAR);
      -- writes members of the given set, ITEM

end CHAR_SET_1;

package body CHAR_SET_1 is

   function SET_OF(CHAR:in CHARACTER) return SET_OF_CHAR is
     RESULT:SET_OF_CHAR:=EMPTY;
   begin
     RESULT(CHAR):=TRUE;
     return RESULT;
   end SET_OF;

   function "+"(LEFT, RIGHT:in SET_OF_CHAR) return SET_OF_CHAR is
   begin
     return LEFT or RIGHT;
   end "+";

   function "+"(LEFT:in SET_OF_CHAR; RIGHT:in CHARACTER)
               return SET_OF_CHAR is
   begin
     return LEFT or SET_OF(RIGHT);
   end "+";

   function "-"(LEFT, RIGHT:in SET_OF_CHAR) return SET_OF_CHAR is
   begin
     return LEFT and not RIGHT;
   end "-";

   function "*"(LEFT, RIGHT:in SET_OF_CHAR) return SET_OF_CHAR is
   begin
     return LEFT and RIGHT;
   end "*";

   function SUBSET(LEFT, RIGHT:in SET_OF_CHAR) return BOOLEAN is
   begin
     return (LEFT or RIGHT) = RIGHT;
   end SUBSET;

   procedure PUT(ITEM:in SET_OF_CHAR) is
   begin
```

```
        if ITEM = EMPTY then
          TEXT_IO.PUT("Set is empty.");
        else
          for CH in CHARACTER loop
            if ITEM(CH) then
              TEXT_IO.PUT(CH);
            end if;
          end loop;
        end if;
        TEXT_IO.NEW_LINE;
      end PUT;

    end CHAR_SET_1;
```

Unit 7.2   A package for a set type and operations.

The package could be used as outlined:

```
    with TEXT_IO, CHAR_SET_1;
    use TEXT_IO, CHAR_SET_1;

    procedure MAIN is

      S_1, S_2, S_3:SET_OF_CHAR;
      S_4:SET_OF_CHAR:=EMPTY;

    begin
      S_1:=SET_OF('A');
      -- other statements to construct sets
      S_2:=S_1 + S_4;
      PUT(S_2 * S_3);
      if S_1 = S_2 then
        PUT("S_1 and S_2 are the same.");
      end if;
      -- and so on
    end MAIN;
```

The details of the package are not central to the main argument here. One peripheral point worthy of note, though, is that SUBSET was not written as an overloading of the operator "<=". Remember that the relational operators are defined for one-dimensional arrays of discrete types. Consequently, if we were to define a more specific meaning of "<=", it would hide the pre-defined meaning but all *other* relational operators would retain their original meanings. This could be confusing and dangerous.

The discussion about "<=" is not entirely irrelevant to the main concern of this section. While the package satisfies the requirements for providing a set type and operations, it can be open to abuse, or misuse.

The package makes the type SET_OF_CHAR available in such a way that units using it can do with the type whatever they will. In other words, they can treat it just like any other array of BOOLEANs, performing assignments to individual elements, for example. One advantage of the package concept is the prospect of being able to offer some degree of security by restricting the operations that can be performed on an exported type.

Because SET_OF_CHAR is being exported, it cannot be removed from the package specification into the body — that would hide it completely! We need to be able to hide the *details* of the type, rather than the type itself. This is where *private types* come in. Any type in a package specification can be designated **private**, with no details being provided at that point. Obviously, the details must go somewhere, such that they are inaccessible. The place for them is in a private part of the package specification, which is a section invisible to package users that follows the visible part of the specification.

Unit 7.3 is an outline of a modified version of CHAR_SET_1 to make SET_OF_CHAR a private type.

```
with TEXT_IO;
package CHAR_SET_2 is

   -- comments as before

   type SET_OF_CHAR is private;     -- no details provided here
   EMPTY:constant SET_OF_CHAR;      -- no value; a deferred constant

   -- subprogram specifications as before

private
   type SET_OF_CHAR is array(CHAR) of BOOLEAN;
   EMPTY:constant SET_OF_CHAR:=(others=>FALSE);
end CHAR_SET_2;

package body CHAR_SET_2 is
   -- exactly the same as the body of CHAR_SET_1
end CHAR_SET_2;
```

Unit 7.3 (Outline) Making the set type private.

Note that EMPTY is also only fully declared in the private part — it is a *deferred constant*. To declare it fully in the visible part of the specification would require knowledge of its parent type, which is not available at that point.

Because of the incompleteness, a private type can only be used in the visible part of the specification for the definition of: deferred constants, further types and subtypes and for subprogram parameter and result types. It cannot be used to define variables.

Within the package, once the full declaration has been made, there are no restrictions on what the package itself can do with objects of a private type. Users of the package, however, can only perform the following operations on objects of an exported private type:

(i) Assignment

(ii) Equality/inequality testing (but no other relational operations)

(iii) calling subprograms exported by the package, or defined by the user. These subprograms may have parameters of the private type and functions may return values of the type. No subprograms (such as operators) are inherited.

The user has no access to the details of the type, so assignment to an individual element of a private type that happens to be an array is not permitted.

Subprograms exported by the package can, of course, utilize details of a private type. User subprograms are not accorded that privilege, which often makes it difficult to augment the facilities provided by the package. Look at the subprograms in the package CHAR_SET_2 and determine which of these could not be provided by the user.

The following extract is an example of valid utilization of the package:

```
with TEXT_IO, CHAR_SET_2;
use TEXT_IO, CHAR_SET_2;

procedure MAIN is

   S_1, S_2, S_3:SET_OF_CHAR:=EMPTY;
   CHAR:CHARACTER;

   function SUPERSET(LEFT, RIGHT:in SET_OF_CHAR)
                     return BOOLEAN is
   begin
     return LEFT*RIGHT = RIGHT;
   end SUPERSET;

begin     -- MAIN
   while not END_OF_LINE loop
     GET(CHAR);
     S_1:=S_1 + SET_OF(CHAR);
   end loop;
   PUT(S_1);
   -- more statements
   S_3:=S_1 * S_2;
```

```
    if SUPERSET(S1, S3) then ......
    end if;
    -- and so on
  end MAIN;
```

An added advantage of the private type is the freedom that it gives the writer of the package to change the details without affecting the user at all. So, if we wanted to implement sets as linked lists, rather than as arrays, then this could easily be arranged. (Although this would not affect the overall use and behaviour of the package, some consequent differences could arise, particularly with regard to the raising of exceptions, memory utilization and exception speed.)

Assuming the change to the data structure was made, then the package specification would obviously have to be re-compiled, along with the body. This would then necessitate the re-compilation of all dependent units, as is explained in 7.7. One way of obviating this consequence is to make the private type an access type. To do this, it is declared as an access type in the private part of the specification, following an incomplete declaration of the type to which it points. The full declaration of the dynamic variable type can be placed in the package body, hence the full declaration can be altered without affecting the specification at all, thereby achieving the desired effect. A package that works along these lines is given in Unit 7.7, by which time, you will know a little more about private types, which will help to create a better package. It is worth saying that, convenient though avoiding re-compilation can be, making the private type an access type can make the package itself less readable and more difficult to write.

Before moving on, look at Unit 7.4. Here we have a (small) package that exports a type, a constant, a single operation (addition) and a function. In the private part, we can see that the type is, in fact, an integer one.

```
package P is
  type T is private;
  FIRST_VALUE:constant T;
  function NEXT_ONE(THIS:in T) return T;
  function "+"(LEFT,RIGHT:in T) return T;
private
  type T is new INTEGER;
  FIRST_VALUE:constant T:=0;
end P;

package body P is

  -- in here, we can do anything that is allowed
  -- for integers on objects of type T.
```

```
function NEXT_ONE(THIS:in T) return T is
begin
   return T'SUCC(THIS);
end NEXT_ONE;

function "+"(LEFT,RIGHT:in T) return T is
begin
   return T(INTEGER(LEFT) + INTEGER(RIGHT));
end "+";

end P;
```

Unit 7.4 A controlled integer and its implications.

T is a *derived type*, which is explained in detail in the next chapter. For now, it is sufficient to record that it is a new type, distinct from INTEGER, which inherits all the INTEGER operations. However, T is a private type, so these inherited operations can only be used within the package itself, and are not available to users. The re-definition of "+" in the package causes the inherited (pre-defined) operator of the same name to be hidden, hence the long-winded expression after **return**. This expression could also have been written as:

LEFT — (−RIGHT);

As for the user of the package, the only operation available is "+". The user could write a function for "*", which would use repeated application of the exported "+" operator. However, with no ability to negate, subtraction and division are another story! So, this is an example of how effective the restrictions on private types can be.

7.5 Limited private types [LRM 7.4.4]

Strange as it might seem at first, private types can still allow too much freedom to the package user. The writer of the package might feel that the operations of assignment and inequality/equality testing are either inappropriate or dangerous for a certain type. For this purpose, it is possible to designate a type as **limited private**. This only leaves the application of exported and user-defined subprograms as the permissible operations. Any subprograms that the user writes can only utilize the subprograms supplied by the package, therefore the package writer has extremely tight control over the use of the type.

Rather than introduce a new example, let us think again of the stack package of Unit 7.1. All that the package exports is the two procedures PUSH and POP. If we were to require more than one stack, then, using

CHAR_STACK_1, we would need to use more than one package, one for each required stack. The alternative approach is to allow the package to export a stack type. Now is the time for careful reflection.

CHAR_STACK_1 was praised because it does *not* make its stack visible — the details are hidden in the body. This advantage has to be preserved, while putting the stack in the visible part of the specification. To achieve this aim, the stack should be declared as a limited private type. By so doing, the only operations that can be applied to stack objects of the exported type are PUSH and POP (and any subprograms the user is able to create from them).

CHAR_STACK_1 is transformed into CHAR_STACK_2 in Unit 7.5, along the lines just discussed. Another change that is required is to make the stack a parameter of PUSH and POP, so that the procedures can be applied to different stacks.

```
package CHAR_STACK_2 is

  -- Comments omitted: authors'prerogative

  type STACK_TYPE is limited private;
  procedure POP(STACK:in out STACK_TYPE; CHAR:out CHARACTER);
  procedure PUSH(STACK:in out STACK_TYPE; CHAR:in CHARACTER);
  UNDERFLOW, OVERFLOW:exception;
private
  STACK_MAX:constant:=32;
  type STACK_ITEMS is array(1..STACK_MAX) of CHARACTER;
  type STACK_TYPE is
  record
    TOP:NATURAL range 0..STACK_MAX:=0;
    ITEM:STACK_ITEMS;
  end record;
end CHAR_STACK_2;

package body CHAR_STACK_2 is

  procedure POP(STACK:in out STACK_TYPE; CHAR:out CHARACTER) is
  begin
    if STACK.TOP = 0 then
      raise UNDERFLOW;
    end if;
    CHAR:=STACK.ITEM(STACK.TOP);
    STACK.TOP:=STACK.TOP - 1;
  end POP;

  procedure PUSH(STACK:in out STACK_TYPE; CHAR:in CHARACTER) is
  begin
    if STACK.TOP = STACK_MAX then
      raise OVERFLOW;
    end if;
    STACK.TOP:=STACK.TOP + 1;
    STACK.ITEM(STACK.TOP):=CHAR;
  end PUSH;

end CHAR_STACK_2;
```

Unit 7.5 A package for creating more than one stack.

It is unfortunate that each stack that is created is of exactly the same size. It would be more convenient if the same package could be used to create stacks of any size (and different sizes). If the full declaration of a private type reveals it to be a record, then, as we saw in the last chapter, this record can have discriminants. The discriminant(s) of a private type must be declared at the point of the private declaration in the visible part of the package specification, *as well as* in the full declaration in the private part. Using a discriminant for STACK_TYPE, to indicate stack size, we arrive at CHAR_STACK_3 in Unit 7.6.

```
package CHAR_STACK_3 is

  -- Documentation here

  type STACK_TYPE(MAX:POSITIVE:=32) is limited private;
  procedure POP(STACK:in out STACK_TYPE; CHAR:out CHARACTER);
  procedure PUSH(STACK:in out STACK_TYPE; CHAR:in CHARACTER);
  UNDERFLOW, OVERFLOW:exception;
private
  type STACK_ITEMS is array(POSITIVE range <>) of CHARACTER;
  type STACK_TYPE(MAX:POSITIVE:=32) is
  record
    TOP:NATURAL:=0;
    ITEM:STACK_ITEMS(1..MAX);
  end record;
end CHAR_STACK_3;

package body CHAR_STACK_3 is

  -- only one change from body of CHAR_STACK_2, in PUSH

  procedure POP(STACK:in out STACK_TYPE; CHAR:out CHARACTER) is
  begin
    if STACK.TOP = 0 then
      raise UNDERFLOW;
    end if;
    CHAR:=STACK.ITEM(STACK.TOP);
    STACK.TOP:=STACK.TOP - 1;
  end POP;

  procedure PUSH(STACK:in out STACK_TYPE; CHAR:in CHARACTER) is
  begin
    if STACK.TOP = STACK.MAX then       -- the only change in the body
      raise OVERFLOW;
    end if;
    STACK.TOP:=STACK.TOP + 1;
    STACK.ITEM(STACK.TOP):=CHAR;
  end PUSH;

end CHAR_STACK_3;
```

Unit 7.6 A package for creating different size stacks.

By supplying a default value for the discriminant, the erroneous declaration of an unconstrained stack by the user is avoided. Such details are very important when designing packages. Note the small change in PUSH, such that the test for overflow tests the discriminant of the stack concerned. The user of this package could now make declarations like:

```
ST_1:CHAR_STACK_3.STACK_TYPE(100);  -- size 100
ST_2:CHAR_STACK_3.STACK_TYPE(8);    -- size 8
ST_3:CHAR_STACK_3.STACK_TYPE;       -- size 32
```

The exported procedures PUSH and POP can be applied to *all* stacks of type CHAR_STACK_3.STACK_TYPE, regardless of size. Remember that discriminants cannot be used to define the ranges of subtypes, so that TOP has to be declared as of type NATURAL, rather than:

NATURAL range 0..MAX

As a final example of the use of limited private types, Unit 7.7 is a rather sparse package that exports a type for complex numbers together with some applicable subprograms. There is a choice of data structures for representing complex numbers, the most obvious of which are a record with two fields (preferred by this programmer), or a vector with two elements. Typically, if we are uncertain about which to use, we would try one data structure and then change it, if it proves to be unsuitable. Earlier, I alluded to the fact that such a change can be effected, without necessitating the re-compilation of the package *specification*. All we have to do is make the type in question a private type in the visible part of the specification, and then declare it as an access type to some incomplete type in the private part of the specification. The incomplete declaration of COMP_TYPE is all that is required for COMPLEX to be declared as an access type, and for the package specification to be compiled and its usage analysed. The full type declaration for COMP_TYPE must appear in the package body.

This does have some repercussions on the package design, in particular, the type designation of COMPLEX. It would not be sufficient to make it a private type, as this would not prevent equality testing. As we saw in the last chapter, equality testing of access types applies to the pointers themselves, rather than the objects to which they refer. Therefore, COMPLEX has to be designated **limited private** and the package export its own function for equality testing. This does, of course, mean that the user cannot assign COMPLEX objects either, hence the implementation of ADD_COMP as a procedure, rather than as an overloaded operator. Also, care has to be taken to ensure that no operation is performed on non-existent objects. Users cannot use an allocator directly, of course,

because they do not know anything about the real nature of COMPLEX
— why should they? Complications like this do bring into question the
use of an access type for the private type. If there is an over-riding need
to avoid re-compilation of dependent units, then so be it; the package
interface and/or its readability may suffer unduly as a result.

```
with SIMPLE_IO;
use  SIMPLE_IO;
package COMPLEX_STUFF is

   -- This package provides a restricted set
   -- of facilities for creating and processing
   -- complex numbers.
   -- UNDEFINED can be raised, if an operand
   -- of ADD_COMP or "=", or the object for
   -- PUT_COMP does not exist (i.e. has not
   -- been created by MAKE_COMP).
   -- The user must handle UNDEFINED.
   -- NUMERIC_ERROR could be raised by
   -- ADD_COMP. The caller must handle it.


   type COMPLEX is limited private;
   UNDEFINED:exception;

   procedure MAKE_COMP(COMP:out COMPLEX; RE, IM:in FLOAT);
      -- Creates a complex number object and initialises it.

   procedure ADD_COMP(RESULT:out COMPLEX; LEFT, RIGHT:in COMPLEX);
      -- Adds two complex numbers and creates the result.

   procedure PUT_COMP(COMP:in COMPLEX);
      -- Writes the complex number, COMP.

   function "="(LEFT, RIGHT:in COMPLEX) return BOOLEAN;
      -- Tests two complex numbers for equality.

private
   type COMP_TYPE;                    -- incomplete declaration
   type COMPLEX is access COMP_TYPE;

end COMPLEX_STUFF;

package body COMPLEX_STUFF is

   type COMP_TYPE is                -- completion
   record
     REAL,
     IMAG:FLOAT:=0.0;
   end record;

   procedure MAKE_COMP(COMP:out COMPLEX; RE, IM:in FLOAT) is
   begin
     COMP:=new COMP_TYPE'(RE, IM);
   end MAKE_COMP;

   procedure ADD_COMP(RESULT:out COMPLEX; LEFT, RIGHT:in COMPLEX) is
   begin
     if LEFT = null or RIGHT = null then
       raise UNDEFINED;
```

```
      end if;
      MAKE_COMP(RESULT, LEFT.REAL+RIGHT.REAL, LEFT.IMAG+RIGHT.IMAG);
   end ADD_COMP;

   procedure PUT_COMP(COMP:in COMPLEX) is
   begin
      if COMP = null then
         raise UNDEFINED;
      end if;
      PUT(COMP.REAL);
      PUT(COMP.IMAG);
      NEW_LINE;
   end PUT_COMP;

   function "="(LEFT, RIGHT:in COMPLEX) return BOOLEAN is
   begin
      if LEFT = null or RIGHT = null then
         raise UNDEFINED;
      end if;
      return LEFT.all = RIGHT.all;
   end "=";

end COMPLEX_STUFF;
```

Unit 7.7   A package for complex numbers.

To use the package requires no additional knowledge. Indeed, the user has no way of telling that COMPLEX is, in fact, an access type.

```
with COMPLEX_STUFF;
use COMPLEX_STUFF;

procedure MAIN is

   C1, C2, C3:COMPLEX;

begin

   MAKE_COMP(C1, 1.0, 2.0);
   MAKE_COMP(C2, 1.0, −2.0);
   ADD_COMP(C3, C1, C2);
   PUT_COMP(C3);
   -- and so forth
end MAIN;
```

The loss of the ability to assign and, consequently, provide overloadings of the arithmetic operations has to be judged against the advantages, which are the ability to change the implementation of COMPLEX, with minimum ramifications, and much greater control over what can be performed. For some applications, one, or both of these may be sufficiently important to outweigh the disadvantages to the user.

7.6 The use of packages

It is not possible to list all the purposes for which a package should be used. There are, though, some general points that are worth bearing in mind. It has been said that packages should be used for grouping related items together. They should also be made as general as possible, hence the evolution of CHAR_STACK_3. (Generics provide an even more powerful means of generalization.) Packages should always be used as a means of hiding any implementation dependent features, as in TEXT_IO.

If you follow a top down approach to program design, then the package should not be a difficult construct to apply. Start thinking in terms of packages: as a package writer, as well as a package user.

As for the actual writing of packages, there are some general guidelines. All details that are of no concern to users should be hidden from view, but not to the extent that the package becomes inconvenient to use. In other words, packages must be very carefully designed, in such a way that the needs of the users are anticipated and met, with safe and reliable use assured. Good design and information hiding protect the package from misuse.

Packages should have simple interfaces, with as few visible items as possible (but without violating any of the above principles).

Documentation is an essential part of a package specification, as there are some very important things that the specification alone does not describe. The specification of a package is not only used to determine what is visible to other program units but it is often the most readily available description for the human user. For a package, the comments in the specification should include the following information:
(i) a description of its purpose
(ii) a statement of any side-effects on global variables
(iii) a note of the exceptions exported, with comments as to where and why they are raised
(iv) a list of any other exceptions that may be raised (pre-defined and/or global), where and why this may occur and whether or not they are handled. In particular, does the user have to handle exceptions?
(v) a list of all implementation dependent aspects

7.7 Separate compilation [LRM 10]

This is not a new subject, but a continuation of the explanations of the separate compilation of subprograms in Chapter 5 and of library units in 7.2. For packages, separate compilation is normal, whether they form library units or not. Before proceeding further, it is important to establish the correct nomenclature.

To recap, library units include package specifications and subprogram declarations, with or without their respective bodies. Library units are global to the main program.

A *compilation unit* is either a library unit, or a *secondary unit* accompanied by any necessary with clause. A secondary unit may either be the body of a library unit (subprogram or package) or a *subunit*. Subunits, as we saw in Chapter 5, include the actual (or proper) bodies of subprograms which have been designated **separate**. The term "subunit" should now be extended to include package (and, later, task) bodies similarly designated. Subunit bodies must be prefixed by **separate**, with the name of the parent unit in parentheses.

Fig. 7.1 shows the hierarchical classification of the various components of a compilation in Ada, extended to include tasks and generics, so that it is complete.

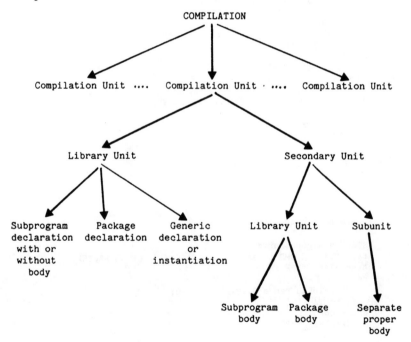

Fig. 7.1   The components of an Ada compilation.

If all this terminology is still confusing, Unit 7.8, in all its constituent parts, demonstrates what it all means in practice.

This example has a very short main program, which forms Unit 7.8h. The program calls subprograms to: read an arithmetic expression in infix (normal algebraic) notation, such as "a+b*c"; convert the infix expression to postfix (or reverse Polish), "abc*+" for our example; write the result of the conversion. The package EXPRESSION_HANDLER exports a type for expressions, as well as subprograms for reading and writing expressions, and IN_TO_POST to effect conversions. IN_TO_POST uses the algorithm commonly referred to as "Dijkstra's shunting algorithm", which utilizes a stack for temporary storage of operators during conversion. Stack facilities are provided by courtesy of the package CHAR_STACK, a slightly enhanced version of CHAR_STACK_1. The compilation units show how the program units could be separated. Note the occasional use of renaming in IN_TO_POST.

```
package CHAR_STACK is

   -- Basically the same as Unit 7.1.
   -- TOP_OF_STACK has been added to
   -- make the package a little more
   -- useful.
   -- A call of TOP_OF_STACK could cause
   -- UNDERFLOW to be raised.

   procedure POP(CHAR:out CHARACTER);
   procedure PUSH(CHAR:in CHARACTER);
   function STACK_EMPTY return BOOLEAN;
   function TOP_OF_STACK return CHARACTER;
   UNDERFLOW, OVERFLOW:exception;

end CHAR_STACK;
```

Unit 7.8a   Library unit

```
package body CHAR_STACK is

   STACK_MAX:constant:=32;
   type STACK_ITEMS is array (1..STACK_MAX) of CHARACTER;
   type STACK_TYPE is
   record
     TOP:NATURAL range 0..STACK_MAX:=0;
     ITEM:STACK_ITEMS;
   end record;
   STACK:STACK_TYPE;

   procedure POP(CHAR:out CHARACTER) is
   begin
     if STACK.TOP = 0 then
       raise UNDERFLOW;
     end if;
     CHAR:=STACK.ITEM(STACK.TOP);
     STACK.TOP:=STACK.TOP - 1;
   end POP;
```

```
      procedure PUSH(CHAR:in CHARACTER) is
      begin
        if STACK.TOP = STACK_MAX then
          raise OVERFLOW;
        end if;
        STACK.TOP:=STACK.TOP + 1;
        STACK.ITEM(STACK.TOP):=CHAR;
      end PUSH;

      function STACK_EMPTY return BOOLEAN is
      begin
          return STACK.TOP = 0;
        end STACK_EMPTY;

        function TOP_OF_STACK return CHARACTER is
        begin
          if STACK_EMPTY then
            raise UNDERFLOW;
          end if;
          return STACK.ITEM(STACK.TOP);
        end TOP_OF_STACK;

      end CHAR_STACK;
```

Unit 7.8b   Secondary unit (library unit body)

```
      package EXPRESSION_HANDLER is

        -- Description:
        -- A package that exports a type for creating
        -- expressions of characters, reading them,
        -- writing them and converting infix expressions
        -- to postfix.
        -- Operators: * / + - (dyadic only)
        -- Operands : a..z | A..Z
        -- Other documentation omitted for brevity.

        type EXPRESSION is limited private;

        procedure GET_EXP(EXP:out EXPRESSION);
          -- reads in an expression as CHARACTERs

        procedure PUT_EXP(EXP:in EXPRESSION);
          -- outputs an expression

        procedure IN_TO_POST(INFIX:in EXPRESSION;
                             POSTFIX:in out EXPRESSION);
          -- converts INFIX to the equivalent POSTFIX expression

      private
        MAX_CH:constant:=80;
        subtype CH_RANGE is NATURAL range 0..MAX_CH;
        type EXPRESSION is
        record
          LENGTH:CH_RANGE;
          CH:STRING(1..MAX_CH);
        end record;
      end EXPRESSION_HANDLER;
```

Unit 7.8c   Library unit

```
with TEXT_IO;
use  TEXT_IO;
package body EXPRESSION_HANDLER is
  procedure GET_EXP(EXP:out EXPRESSION) is
  begin
    loop
      begin
        PUT("Type in an arithmetic expression.");
        NEW_LINE;
        GET_LINE(EXP.CH, EXP.LENGTH);
        exit;
      exception
        when CONSTRAINT_ERROR =>
          PUT("??? Expression too long. Limit is: ");
          PUT(MAX_CH);
          PUT(" Try again.");
          NEW_LINE;
      end;
    end loop;
  end GET_EXP;

  procedure PUT_EXP(EXP:in EXPRESSION) is
  begin
    for CH_POS in 1..EXP.LENGTH loop
      PUT(EXP.CH(CH_POS));
    end loop;
    NEW_LINE;
  end PUT_EXP;

  procedure IN_TO_POST(INFIX:in EXPRESSION;
                       POSTFIX:in out EXPRESSION)
                       is separate;  -- BODY STUB

end EXPRESSION_HANDLER;
```

Unit 7.8d Secondary unit (library unit body)

```
with CHAR_STACK;
use  CHAR_STACK;
separate(EXPRESSION_HANDLER)
procedure IN_TO_POST(INFIX:in EXPRESSION;
                     POSTFIX:in out EXPRESSION) is

  NEXT_IN:CH_RANGE:=0;
  NEXT_POST:CH_RANGE renames POSTFIX.LENGTH;
  TOP_OUTER:CHARACTER;
  INVALID_CHAR:exception;
  type SYMB_TYPE is (OPERAND, OPERATOR, L_PAREN, R_PAREN, INVALID);
  subtype PREC_RANGE is NATURAL range 0..3;

  procedure TO_POST(CHAR:in CHARACTER) is
    -- Adds CHAR to POSTFIX
  begin
    NEXT_POST:=NEXT_POST + 1;
    POSTFIX.CH(NEXT_POST):=CHAR;
  end TO_POST;

  function TYPE_OF(CHAR:in CHARACTER) return SYMB_TYPE is separate;
    -- BODY STUB
    -- The function returns the type of the given CHARACTER
```

```
         function PRECEDENCE(OP:in CHARACTER) return PREC_RANGE is separate;
           -- BODY STUB
           -- Returns the precedence of the operator OP

     begin              -- IN_TO_POST
       NEXT_POST:=0;
       while NEXT_IN < INFIX.LENGTH loop
         NEXT_IN:=NEXT_IN + 1;
         declare
           THIS_CH:CHARACTER renames INFIX.CH(NEXT_IN);
           TOP:CHARACTER;
         begin
           case TYPE_OF(THIS_CH) is
             when OPERAND=>
               TO_POST(THIS_CH);
             when OPERATOR=>
               while not STACK_EMPTY and then
                     PRECEDENCE(THIS_CH) <= PRECEDENCE(TOP_OF_STACK) loop
                 POP(TOP);
                 TO_POST(TOP);
               end loop;
               PUSH(THIS_CH);
             when L_PAREN=>
               PUSH(THIS_CH);
             when R_PAREN=>
               while TOP_OF_STACK /= '(' loop
                 POP(TOP);
                 TO_POST(TOP);
               end loop;
               POP(TOP);
             when INVALID=>
               raise INVALID_CHAR;
           end case;
         exception
           when INVALID_CHAR =>
             PUT("??? Expression contains the invalid character: ");
             PUT(THIS_CH);
             NEW_LINE;
             PUT("Character ignored.");
             NEW_LINE;
         end;
       end loop;
       while not STACK_EMPTY loop
         POP(TOP_OUTER);
         TO_POST(TOP_OUTER);
       end loop;
     end IN_TO_POST;
```

Unit 7.8e Secondary unit (subunit: proper body)

```
     separate(EXPRESSION_HANDLER.IN_TO_POST)
     function TYPE_OF(CHAR:in CHARACTER) return SYMB_TYPE is
     begin
       case CHAR is
         when 'a'..'z' | 'A'..'Z' =>
           return OPERAND;
         when '^' | '*' | '/' | '+' | '-' =>
           return OPERATOR;
```

```
      when '(' =>
        return L_PAREN;
      when ')' =>
        return R_PAREN;
      when others =>
        return INVALID;
    end case;
  end TYPE_OF;
```

Unit 7.8f   Secondary unit (subunit: proper body)

```
  separate(EXPRESSION_HANDLER.IN_TO_POST)
  function PRECEDENCE(OP:in CHARACTER) return PREC_RANGE is
  begin
    case OP is
      when '^' =>
        return 3;
      when '*' | '/' =>
        return 2;
      when '+' | '-' =>
        return 1;
      when '(' =>
        return 0;
      when others =>
        null;            -- should never occur!
    end case;
  end PRECEDENCE;
```

Unit 7.8g   Secondary unit (subunit: proper body)

```
  with EXPRESSION_HANDLER;
  use  EXPRESSION_HANDLER;
  procedure MAIN is
    IN_EXP, POST_EXP:EXPRESSION;
  begin
    GET_EXP(IN_EXP);
    IN_TO_POST(IN_EXP, POST_EXP);
    PUT_EXP(POST_EXP);
  end MAIN;
```

Unit 7.8h   Library unit (subprogram forming main program)

It is important that the dependence of a compilation unit on some other unit be explicitly stated, otherwise the compilation will fail. However, it is equally important that no inapplicable dependences be declared. This is why, in Unit 7.8, it is not necessary for EXPRESSION_HANDLER itself to be dependent on CHAR_STACK. Only IN_TO_POST requires that package. Had this subprogram not been separate, though, then the body of EXPRESSION_HANDLER would have to have CHAR_STACK in its context clause, along with TEXT_IO.

For TYPE_OF and PRECEDENCE, the *full* name of the parent unit has to be specified, as IN_TO_POST itself is not a library unit whereas its owner is.

There is no single valid compilation sequence for the compilation units of Unit 7.8. The general rules are, remember, that specifications must always be compiled before bodies, and that a unit named in a **with** context clause must be compiled before the dependent unit(s). The mandatory precedences are illustrated in Fig. 7.2, in which a line from one unit to another indicates that the higher unit must be compiled first.

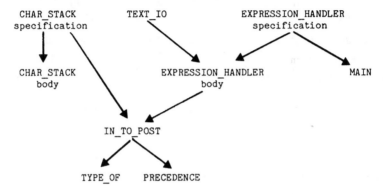

Fig. 7.2 Compilation dependences of Unit 7.8.

If a compilation unit is re-compiled, then any unit that depends on it must also be re-compiled. Hence, in Unit 7.8, TYPE_OF and MAIN can be re-compiled without repercussion, whereas re-compilation of the *body* of EXPRESSION_HANDLER will require the re-compilation of IN_TO_POST and its subunits. If the *specification* of the same package is re-compiled, then its body and MAIN will have to be re-submitted for compilation (along with the units dependent on the body, as noted above).

Complicated dependences should be avoided, as they can lead to compilation failures. They also reveal something about the programmer's thought processes!

While correctly used **with** clauses provide the compiler with sufficient information to determine the correct compilation sequence, they do not ensure a correct *elaboration* sequence. Consider the following example adapted from Nissen and Wallis [6].

```
package A is
  I:INTEGER:=111;
end A;
```

```
with A;
use A;
package B is
  J:INTEGER:=I;
end B;

package body A is
begin
  I:=-999;
end A;
```

The compilation dependences dictate that the specification of A must be compiled before the specification of B. The body of A must be compiled after the specification of A but it does not matter if it is compiled before or after the specification of B. Applying the same logic to the elaboration sequence, then there is more than one possible outcome, for, if the body of A is elaborated *before* the specification of B, B.J will be initialized to −999, otherwise, the same variable is initialized to 111. If a compiler detects an incorrect order dependence, it may cause PROGRAM_ERROR to be raised during elaboration (but the LRM does *not* require a compiler to go to this trouble). Consequently, there are three possible outcomes from the elaboration of this small example!

A pre-defined pragma, ELABORATE, is provided to specify, immediately after the with clause of a compilation unit, the library unit bodies to be elaborated beforehand. So, in the last example, we would have:

```
with A;
pragma ELABORATE(A);
use A;
package B is
-- and so on
```

to force the body of A to be elaborated before the specification of B.

This may all seem a little involved. Nevertheless, it clearly underlines the important distinction between compilation and elaboration. We may want some subprogram or package body to be the last unit to be compiled, so that it may be re-compiled without affecting other units. However, if the *elaboration* of any other unit requires that body (for example, the other unit may call a separate subprogram body, or it may require that a package body be elaborated as in the example), then this must be stated.

In practice, it is better to avoid elaboration dependences altogether. They could be taken to be an indication of muddled thought processes!

7.8 Renaming [LRM 8.5]

We briefly met the idea of renaming in the last chapter. Here, the idea is
extended to apply to packages and subprograms. Exceptions can also be
renamed, as will be seen in Chapter 10.

No feature of a programming language should be used if it obscures
meaning. Renaming is not an exception to this rule. One example of its
use can be illustrated with reference to Unit 7.8e, which could have
begun:

```
with CHAR_STACK;
separate(EXPRESSION_HANDLER)
procedure IN_TO_POST(INFIX:in EXPRESSION;
                          POSTFIX:in out EXPRESSION) is
  PUSH(C:in CHARACTER) renames CHAR_STACK.PUSH;
  -- and similarly for POP
  -- ......
end IN_TO_POST;
```

Unit 7.8e Secondary unit (subunit: proper body)

This shows how the subprograms of CHAR_STACK can be called via
new names declared within IN_TO_POST. The new declaration does not
hide the earlier alias. Note that when subprograms are renamed, their
parameter and result profiles must match in type and transmission mode
but the parameter names may be different. (Default expressions may also
be different, but no example is given here.)

When the use clause was introduced, it was with a warning against
indiscriminate use. Renaming provides a means of having identifiers of
reasonable length which retain an obvious meaning, localized to a particular declarative region. This is particularly important where a unit is
prefixed by a number of packages. Ambiguities that could arise owing to
library packages exporting the same identifier, can also be resolved by
renaming, whereas **use** would cause the compiler to reject the ambiguity.

Enumeration literals, and attributes defined as functions (such as
FIRST and SUCC) can be renamed as functions:

function PUCE return COLOUR renames PINK;
function DAY_AFTER(D:in DAY) renames DAY'SUCC;

Renaming cannot be applied to types, although a similar effect can be
achieved by the introduction of an unconstrained subtype:

subtype BITS_8 renames HARDWARE_TYPES.BYTE:

There is one, final, important aspect of renaming, which concerns scope and visibility. Renaming does not hide any alias that is visible at the renaming point, as has been said, however, the new name may be subject to different scope and visibility. For example, in

```
with HARDWARE_TYPES;
use HARDWARE_TYPES;

procedure MAIN is

    FULL:BYTE renames BYTE_ZERO;
    -- irrelevant declarations

begin

    -- irrelevant statements
    declare
        BYTE_ZERO:BYTE;   -- this hides BYTE_ZERO of the
                          -- package, unless selected.
                          -- Although representing the
                          -- same object, FULL is still
                          -- directly visible.
end MAIN;
```

A more important aspect of this is the use of renaming to extend the visibility of package declarations through other packages, as will be demonstrated in Chapter 10.

7.9 Exceptions raised in packages

There is nothing really different (or exceptional) about exceptions raised in packages, from the behaviour cited in 5.8. If an exception is raised during the elaboration of a library package, then execution of the main program is abandoned. If a package appears in some declarative part, then an exception raised during its elaboration will cause that declarative part to fail, with the consequences explained in Chapter 5.

An exception that is raised during the execution of the statement part of a package will cause normal execution to be abandoned and control to pass to the handler in the package body, if there is one. If the exception is handled, then this completes the elaboration of the body, otherwise, it will be regarded as a failure of the elaboration, which is then treated as explained in the paragraph above.

Should an exception be raised during the execution of a package subprogram, this will be handled and/or propagated in the manner described in Chapter 5.

Practising Ada 7

From now on, you must think and act in packages. Concentrate on providing packages that you and others will want to use. A package must be convenient, reliable and robust. Create packages out of earlier assignments, such as: complex numbers (use Unit 7.7 as a guide — extend its features — the type need not be an access type, but should be limited private); matrix operations; string processing. Use top down design methodologies and separately compile, where appropriate. More ideas:

1 Write a package for sets of INTEGERs. Use Units 7.3 and 7.2 as a guide. An array is not a suitable structure here! The operators will be more complex to code. Unit 6.6 should be helpful.

2 Take one of the stack packages and change the stack implementation from an array to a linked list.

3 Change the implementation of COMPLEX in Unit 7.7 to an array with two elements (indexed by a type with values REAL and IMAGINARY). Do you really not have to re-compile dependent units?

4 Write a package that exports a type for representing binary integers together with operations on those integers.

5 Create a package of mathematical constants and functions that might be useful in your application area.

Chapter 8

More on types

Now that you have seen most of the major language features, it is time to return to aspects of Ada's strong typing which were not discussed in Chapter 3. Among these is the important concept of the derived type, which is followed by a general treatment of type conversion. Attention is focused again on the numeric types, in particular the definition and implementation of real number types. Also, some more useful attributes of the scalar types are introduced.

8.1 Derived types [LRM 3.4]

A derived type definition, characterized by the reserved word **new**, introduces a new type which is derived from, and inherits its characteristics from a parent type. Derived types should be used for types which are structurally equivalent and also related, where it is important to segregate objects of different types. We might have:

```
-- some declarative part
type METRES is new FLOAT;
type SECONDS is new FLOAT range 0.0..FLOAT'LARGE;
type M_PER_SEC is new FLOAT;
type M_PER_SEC_SEC is new FLOAT;
subtype SMALL_METRES is METRES range 0.0..10.0;
LENGTH, DISTANCE:METRES;
LITTLE_WAY:SMALL_METRES;
TIME:SECONDS;
V_INIT, V_TERMINAL:M_PER_SEC;
ACCELERATION:M_PER_SEC_SEC;
```

The derived type may, but need not, introduce a constraint, as is the case with SECONDS above. The assignments below illustrate the significance of the derived types.

```
LENGTH:=12.5;           -- literals inherited
LITTLE_WAY:=5.0;        -- literals inherited
DISTANCE:=LENGTH;       -- compatible assignment
```

```
ACCELERATION:=9.81;        -- literals inherited
V_INIT:=10.0;              -- literals inherited
V_TERMINAL:=V_INIT;        -- compatible assignment
LENGTH:=LITTLE_WAY;        -- compatible subtype
DISTANCE:=TIME;            -- INVALID. WILL NOT
                           -- COMPILE
V_TERMINAL:=DISTANCE/TIME; -- INVALID.
                           -- WILL NOT COMPILE
```

The last two assignments will not be accepted owing to type conflicts. Derived types inherit all the values and operations that belong to the parent type, which in this case is FLOAT. Of course, it is possible to provide additional overloadings of the pre-defined operators to, say, divide a METRES value by a SECONDS and return an M_PER_SEC value. Such overloadings should only be provided for sensible operations, otherwise there would be little point in creating distinct types. Because parent types and their derived types are related, it is possible to convert values from one type to another related one explicitly. These points will be discussed more fully in 8.4.

If a new type is derived from a subtype, then it inherits the constraints of the subtype as in:

```
type MY_SMALL_METRES is new SMALL_METRES;
```

which inherits the range 0.0..10.0.
It is possible to introduce a new integer type thus:

```
type INT_TYPE is range LO..HI;
```

This is equivalent to the sequence:

```
type ANON is new pre-defined type;    -- e.g. INTEGER
subtype INT_TYPE is ANON range LO..HI;
```

If the parent type is declared in the visible part of a package specification, then any subprograms applicable to the parent type that are also visible in the same package specification are inherited by types derived from the parent. This is illustrated by:

```
package ZOOLOGY is
   type AMPHIBIAN is (EGG, TADPOLE, ADULT);
   procedure METAMORPHOSE(ANIMAL:in out AMPHIBIAN);
      -- advances ANIMAL to next stage of growth
end ZOOLOGY;
```

A user can then say:

```
with ZOOLOGY;
use ZOOLOGY;

procedure MAIN is

    type FROG is new AMPHIBIAN;
    type TOAD is new AMPHIBIAN;
    typc NEWT is new AMPHIBIAN;
    RANA:FROG:=EGG;
    BUFO:TOAD:=EGG;
    TRITURUS:NEWT:=EGG;

    -- ......
end MAIN;
```

METAMORPHOSE is applicable to all three derived types, and may therefore be called with any of the three variables declared above as a parameter. Each call is equivalent to a call of the procedure of the parent type, in which type conversions are effected automatically on the actual parameter.

8.2 Named numbers [LRM 3.2.2]

Objects that will never change value throughout their existence should always be declared as constants, which enhances program readability and enables any attempt to assign a value to be detected. In Chapter 3, it was shown that constants are associated with a particular type. For many situations it is important that typing is as rigorously applied to constants as it is to variables. There are other circumstances, however, where it is inappropriate to associate a constant with a type. We may want to use a constant value with all types of its genre, rather than just one. For this purpose, Ada enables *named numbers* to be declared as either integers or reals. In order that named numbers can remain effectively typeless, they are classified as being of type universal_integer or universal_real, according to the same rules that are applied to the interpretation of numeric literals as integers or reals.

Both universal_integer and universal_real are pre-defined types in an Ada implementation and form the basis for all integer and real types. They are not bounded, nor is their precision restricted by implementation constraints. Although pre-defined, these types are *anonymous*, which means that they cannot be used directly by the programmer. It is not possible, for example, to declare an object explicitly to be of a universal type. However, all numeric literals, as well as named numbers, will belong to the appropriate universal type. As a consequence, literals and named numbers may be used with all pre-defined and programmer-defined numeric types germane to their universal type.

The program extract below illustrates the declaration and use of named numbers and (typed) constants. Note the syntactic distinction: constants are explicitly typed, named numbers are not.

```
-- some declarative part
type MY_REAL is new FLOAT;
type YOUR_REAL is new FLOAT;
PI:constant:=3.14159_26536;
                        -- Universal_real
MY_AREA, MY_CIRC, MY_RAD:MY_REAL;
YOUR_AREA, YOUR_CIRC, YOUR_RAD:YOUR_REAL;
MY_CONST:constant MY_REAL:=2.0*PI;    -- MY_REAL
begin
MY_RAD:=10.0;
                        -- Universal_real literals
YOUR_RAD:=5.0;
                        -- usable with any real type.
MY_AREA:=PI * MY_RAD**2;
                        -- PI is universal_real and
YOUR_AREA:=PI * YOUR_RAD**2;
                        -- usable with any real type.
MY_CIRC:=MY_CONST * MY_RAD;
                        -- Compatible (typed) constant.
YOUR_CIRC:=MY_CONST*YOUR_RAD;   -- INVALID.
                        -- Type conflict.
-- ......
end;
```

Named numbers should often be used in preference to numeric literals, again in the interests of readability and maintainability. In the above example, PI should obviously be a named number. The name used has a well-understood meaning, and the value for the constant only has to be specified once, which reduces the risk of getting it wrong, and makes it more straightforward to change its precision, if required. However, the literal 2, used as an exponent, should not be replaced by a named number.

Universal expressions [LRM 4.10]

In addition to universal numbers, Ada makes provision for universal expressions, which deliver a result of type universal_integer or universal_real. Like named numbers, universal expressions allow accuracy to be maximized and portability to be enhanced, as they are not specific to any particular type. There is an additional advantage to universal expressions that are *static*, i.e. those which only involve literals, named numbers and the pre-defined operators, for they are evaluated at *compile*-time, thus increasing run-time efficiency. In practice, static universal expressions should be constrained within the largest appropriate bounds, such as ten digit reals and 64 bit integers.

The type of a universal expression is inferred from its components. If all operands are of type universal_integer, then the expression will be of the same type, otherwise, it will be a universal_real expression. A certain amount of type mixing is allowed in universal expressions, owing to further overloadings of the multiplication and division operators to include:

```
universal_real * universal_integer
universal_integer * universal_real
universal_real / universal_integer
```

These are provided so that static universal_real expressions may be computed exactly. Examples of universal static expressions in named number declarations:

```
-- some declarative part
PI:constant:=3.14159_26536;        -- universal_real
TWO_PI:constant:=PI * 2;           -- universal_real
KILO:constant:=1000;               -- universal_integer
MEGA:constant:=KILO * KILO;        -- universal_integer
```

Note the distinctions between the following:

```
RATIO_1:constant:=4 /3;        -- universal_integer (=1)
RATIO_2:constant:=4.0 / 3.0;   -- universal_real
RATIO_3:constant:=4.0 / 3;     -- universal_real (better)
```

It should also be noted that it is not possible to mix universal types in ways for which operators are not defined. The expressions PI+1 and 2/PI would both be erroneous for that reason.

Universal expressions may be used in other contexts, such as:

```
    -- some declarative part
    PI:constant:=3.14159_26536;
    E:constant:=2.71828_18285;
    VARIABLE:FLOAT:=E**2;        -- evaluated and converted
                                 -- on compilation
begin
    VARIABLE:=PI/2;              -- evaluated and converted
                                 -- on compilation

    -- ......
end;
```

The universal expressions above are evaluated and then converted to the target type at *compile*-time. Normally, a universal expression would not be used on the right hand side of an assignment statement, as in the last line of the example above. In that context, it is better to use a named number, initialized to the value of the (constant) universal expression.

8.3 Attributes of discrete types [LRM 3.5.5]

Ada provides a number of attributes, through which certain characteristics of types may be accessed. In this section, the attributes of all discrete types are listed in two groups. The first group comprises parameterless attributes, which yield properties of types or subtypes. In the list, T represents a type or subtype identifier.

Attribute	Result type	Comments
T'FIRST	T	Yields the first value of T.
T'LAST	T	Yields the last value of T.
T'WIDTH	universal_integer	Yields the maximum image length over all values of T (see IMAGE).
T'BASE	–	Yields the base type of T; only allowed as a prefix to another attribute.

To illustrate the use of BASE, a valid context would be T'BASE'FIRST, which would give the first value of the *base* type of T, whereas T'FIRST gives the first value of T itself. (If T is not a subtype, then these two uses would give the same result.)

Attributes in the second group require a parameter, referred to below as X. X must be of a certain type, which depends on the attribute in question. The attributes themselves relate to the base type of T.

Attribute	Result type	Parameter type	Comments
T'SUCC(X)	T'BASE	T or T'BASE	Yields the value after X in T'BASE. If X is T'BASE'LAST then CONSTRAINT_ERROR raised.
T'PRED(X)	T'BASE	T or T'BASE	Yields the value before X in T'BASE. If X is T'BASE'FIRST then CONSTRAINT_ERROR raised.
T'POS(X)	universal_integer	T or T'BASE	Yields the position number of the value X in T'BASE. For integers, T'POS(X) equals X.
T'VAL(X)	T'BASE	universal_integer	Inverse of POS, yielding the value in T'BASE which has position X. If there is no such value then CONSTRAINT_ERROR raised.
T'IMAGE(X)	STRING	T or T'BASE	Returns the representation of the value X as a string of characters. No leading or trailing spaces, save for a leading space for positive integers.
T'VALUE(X)	T'BASE	STRING	Inverse of IMAGE. Leading and trailing spaces are ignored. CONSTRAINT_ERROR raised if no value in T'BASE corresponds to X.

There are two other attributes which are applicable to discrete types. Both of them, SIZE and ADDRESS, relate to data representation in a particular implementation.

The following declarations are assumed in the subsequent illustrations of the application of attributes:

```
-- INTEGER assumed to be implemented as
-- -2_147_483_648 .. 2_147_483_647
type DAY is (MON, TUE, WED, THU, FRI, SAT, SUN);
subtype MID_WEEK is DAY range TUE..THU;
type CRAZY is (A, 'A', FUNNY);
```

Now for specific attributes and their results:

Attribute	Result	
DAY'FIRST	MON	
MID_WEEK'FIRST	TUE	
MID_WEEK'BASE'FIRST	MON	
INTEGER'FIRST	−2147483648	
MID_WEEK'LAST	THU	
DAY'WIDTH	3	
INTEGER'WIDTH	11	(no underscores included)
CRAZY'WIDTH	5	
DAY'SUCC(WED)	THU	
MID_WEEK'SUCC(THU)	FRI	(result is base type)
DAY'SUCC(DAY'FIRST)	TUE	
DAY'PRED(FRI)	THU	
MID_WEEK'PRED(WED)	TUE	
DAY'PRED(MON)	CONSTRAINT_ERROR will be raised	
DAY'POS(MON)	0	
DAY'POS(WED)	2	
MID_WEEK'POS(WED)	2	(not 1)
INTEGER'POS(−1234)	−1234	
DAY'VAL(6)	SUN	
MID_WEEK'VAL(5)	SAT	
DAY'IMAGE(FRI)	"FRI"	
CRAZY'IMAGE(A)	"A"	
CRAZY'IMAGE('A')	"'A'"	
CRAZY'VALUE ("A")	A	
CRAZY'VALUE("'A'")	'A'	
DAY'VALUE("SUN")	SUN	
DAY'VALUE("MONDAY")	CONSTRAINT_ERROR will be raised	

8.4 Type conversion [LRM 4.6]

It is worth repeating that automatic type conversion is not a common occurrence in Ada, the only implicit conversions being those from universal_integer to a specific integer type and from universal_real to a particular type of real number representation. This explains the operation of the assignment:

```
VARIABLE:=PI/2;
```

The right hand side expression is of type universal_real, which is then automatically converted to the type of the left hand side variable. For this assignment, the conversion takes place at compile-time, because the expression is static.

Ada allows explicit type conversion between closely related types. There are three classes of explicit type conversion:

(i)   between numeric types, which are always deemed to be related
(ii) between derived types
(iii) between compatible array types

The type conversion of arrays has already been discussed in Chapter 6.

Explicit type conversion is achieved by enclosing an expression of the original type by parentheses, and preceding this by the type identifier of the *target* type. If a real type is converted to an integer one, the result will be rounded to the nearest integer, unless the fractional part is exactly 0.5, in which case an implementation may round either up or down.

```
            -- some declarative part
            type METRES is new FLOAT;
            type M_PER_SEC is new FLOAT;
            type SECONDS is new FLOAT;
            I:INTEGER:=10;
            R_1, R_2:FLOAT:=1.25;
            M:METRES:=1000.0;
            S:SECONDS;
            V:M_PER_SEC;
        begin
            R_1:=FLOAT(I);                          -- 10.0
            I:=INTEGER(R_2 * 7.0);                  -- 8
            I:=INTEGER(R_1 / R_2);                  -- 8
            S:=SECONDS(R_1 * R_2);                  -- 12.5
            V:=M_PER_SEC(M / 12.5);                 -- 80.0
            V:=M_PER_SEC(M / METRES(S));            -- 80.0
            V:=M_PER_SEC(M) / M_PER_SEC(S);         -- 80.0
            -- and so on
        end;
```

The above examples highlight the need for expressions to be constructed correctly, with type uniformity. In the second assignment, for example, the literal has to be a real one to be consistent with the type of R_2, despite the fact that we are converting the result to INTEGER — there is no pre-defined operator for multiplying a FLOAT by an INTEGER. (The additional overloadings of "*" provided for universal expressions are of no help here, as R_2 is a FLOAT object.) An alternative way of writing the assignment would be:

```
        I:=INTEGER(R_2 * FLOAT(7));
```

Note the distinction between this and

     I:=INTEGER(R_2) * 7;

This formulation invokes the INTEGER multiplication operator, with a different result! The three assignments to V in the example are all equivalent. Again, type uniformity is essential, but there are various ways of achieving it. In the case of the last two assignments to V in the extract above, the second of these is preferable — it does not make sense to convert S to METRES as an intermediate step, which the previous statement does.

    Let us briefly return to an idea introduced earlier in this chapter. Here is a function, which provides an additional overloading of "/" for derived types.

```
function "/" (LEFT:in METRES; RIGHT:in SECONDS)
              return M_PER_SEC is
begin
   return M_PER_SEC(LEFT) / M_PER_SEC(RIGHT);
end "/";
```

Although each derived type inherits its own set of operators, they can only be applied to each type alone. The new overloading allows appropriate type mixing, so that it is now possible to say:

    V:=M / S;

without needing explicit type conversion. No other parameter and result type combinations are allowed. The function itself utilizes the "/" operator inherited by the derivation of M_PER_SEC, and explicitly converts both operands to that type first.

    All numeric types in Ada are related via their common bases of universal_integer and universal_real (which are, themselves, related). Consequently, explicit type conversion between numeric types is always possible. This relationship does not apply to other types. With enumeration types, the same literal occurring in more than one type has no significance. For example, the literal 'Y', which appeared in types ANSWERS and ODD_ONE of section 3.8 (as well, of course, as in CHARACTER) has three entirely different meanings. We can qualify an expression containing enumeration literals, as in:

    ANSWERS'('Y') > 'n'

This clarifies the meaning of the literal, but it is *not* possible to convert unrelated types. If CH is of type CHARACTER, and RESPONSE is of type ANSWERS, the following is illegal:

    CH:='Y';
    RESPONSE:=ANSWERS(CH);   -- INVALID

If two or more types are to be related, then this must be done using derived types, as discussed at the beginning of the chapter. So, going back to Nature, the following assignments are all valid:

    RANA:=FROG(BUFO);
    BUFO:=TOAD(TRITURUS);
    TRITURUS:=NEWT(RANA);

Each of these takes the parenthesized value and converts it to the equivalent value in the named target type.

8.5 Real numbers again [LRM 3.5.6]

To complete the account of the scalar types in Ada, we return to real numbers, which were only partly addressed in 3.6, with the introduction of the pre-defined type FLOAT. Before describing the definition and implementation of further floating point types and subtypes, and then treating fixed point types similarly, it is necessary to say a little more about the general nature and use of these two representations of real numbers. Some rather detailed, but important, aspects concerning the implementation of real numbers are presented in Appendix A.

Floating point representation

Real numbers are those which have a fractional part. Of course, all numbers, whatever their nature, are held in computers in a binary form, but to illustrate the essential differences between floating and fixed point numbers, decimal numbers are used here. The base of the numbers does not alter the significance of the discussion. For both representations, the comparison below will assume that there is a total of three decimal digits available, together with a sign for the number.

Floating point numbers are held as two components: a *mantissa*, usually a fraction, and an *exponent*. The fraction is *normalized* (where the exponent permits) so that floating point numbers are held with maximum *precision*, with a non-zero digit always occupying the most significant digit position. In the simple decimal model, two of our three digits are allocated to the mantissa and the third to the exponent. To keep faith with most binary representations of floating point numbers, the ten possible digits of the exponent will be interpreted as the range −5 to +4, which are therefore the exponent limits. The smallest non-zero number is therefore $0.10 * 10^{**}-5$, and the largest in magnitude is $0.99 * 10^{**}4$. Here are some intermediate examples:

Number	Floating point representation	
	Mantissa	Exponent
10.0	0.10	2
1.0	0.10	1 (not .01 2)
2.5	0.25	1
0.25	0.25	0
0.0025	0.25	−2
2500.0	0.25	4
25000.0	UNABLE TO BE REPRESENTED	
0.0000009	0.10	−5 (exponent limit)
1.23	0.12	1 (precision loss)

The last two examples show how accuracy may be lost, if there are too few digits available for the mantissa, as in the last case, or if the negative exponent limit has been reached, which applies to the penultimate number. The advantage of floating point numbers is the wide range of values that they can represent. Even in this very simple model, values in the range $1.0E-6$ to 9900.0 can be expressed, together with zero and the negative numbers of the same magnitude. This gives the total range as −9900.0 to $-1.0E-6$, 0, and $1.0E-6$ to 9900.0. For integers, every possible value within the implementation limits will have an exact representation. The same is clearly not possible for real numbers, which are subject to accuracy constraints imposed by the precision afforded by the implementation. It is worth looking at the effect of this precision. The table below includes selected values from the complete range of non-zero values, which are exactly supported by our model.

Value	Mantissa	Exponent	Difference (absolute)
$1.0E-6$	0.10	−5	
			$0.1E-6$
$1.1E-6$	0.11	−5	
--	--	--	
$9.9E-6$	0.99	−5	
			$0.1E-6$
$1.0E-5$	0.10	−4	
			$0.1E-5$
$1.1E-5$	0.11	−4	
--	--	--	

Value	Mantissa	Exponent	Difference (absolute)
9.9E−5	0.99	−4	
			0.1E−5
1.0E−4	0.10	−3	
			0.1E−4
1.1E−4	0.11	−3	
--	--	--	
990.0	0.99	3	
			10
1000.0	0.10	4	
			100
1100.0	0.11	4	
--	--	--	
9800.0	.98	4	
			100
9900.0	.99	4	

The error bound for a floating point number is half the difference between adjacent representable numbers. From this table, it is obvious that the error bound is *relative* to the value of the exponent, i.e. it is relative to the magnitude of the number. So, crudely, the difference between two exactly represented very small numbers is very small, but between two exactly represented large numbers, the interval is large; however, the *proportion* that the difference represents is the same in both cases.

Fixed point representation

Now it is the turn of fixed point representation. As the name implies, the point, which separate integer and fractional parts of the number occupies the same position, regardless of the magnitude of the number, whereas, as we have seen, the exponent of floating point numbers serves to move (or float) the position of the point. To illustrate fixed point representations, in the interests of fairness, assume that there are three decimal digits available. If the point is fixed before the first digit, then the sequence of values that can be represented is: 0.000, 0.001, 0.002, ..., 0.998, 0.999. Compared to floating point representation with the same number of digits, the range of the available fixed point numbers is very much smaller. In this model, however, the precision is greater than in the fixed point scheme, for the numbers that can be represented, owing to the additional digit for the number itself. For *all* numbers in this fixed point scheme, the error bound is ±0.0005, i.e. the representation accuracy is *absolute*.

If a larger range of numbers is required from the three digits, the point is fixed at a different position, with a concomitant change in absolute accuracy. So we could have, for example: 00.0, 00.1, 00.2, ..., 99.8, 99.9, all of which have an error bound of ±0.05.

Floating point vs. fixed point

For general purpose real numbers, floating point representation should normally be used, owing to the greater range it offers. Many languages only provide floating point real numbers. Wherever absolute precision is important and a restricted range of values is tolerable, then fixed point representation is more appropriate. Fixed point *could* be seen as being suitable for inherently exact data, where integers could and should be used. For example, a sterling currency amount should be represented by integer pounds and integer pence rather than fixed point pounds.

It is in embedded systems that fixed point representation is particularly appropriate. For example, a program may be required to read values from a sensor. Typically, a sensor provides readings over a fixed range, with some absolute precision, such as ± 1mV over −10 to +10 Volts. The fixed point model precisely reflects the characteristics of the data from the sensor and should therefore be used.

There is another property of fixed point numbers that makes them attractive in applications where speed is essential: fixed point arithmetic is faster than floating point arithmetic, as there is no overhead of exponent manipulation. To illustrate this simply, consider adding the numbers 10.0 and 1.0 using the floating point model we saw earlier. The numbers are represented thus:

Number	Mantissa	Exponent
10.0	.10	2
1.0	.10	1

The mantissae cannot be added directly, as the exponents are different, so the smaller number has to be made to conform to the exponent value of the larger:

Number	Mantissa	Exponent
10.0	.10	2
1.0	.01	2
11.0	.11	2

Note also that in shifting the smaller operand, the error bound is reduced to that of the larger operand. The effect of this is revealed by repeating the above process for the addition of 10.0 and 2.5. This is left as an exercise for the reader.

If there is no hardware support for floating point operations, such actions may be unacceptably slow. Even where hardware support is available, fixed point arithmetic is performed more quickly.

Real literals

Real literals are of type universal_real as already discussed, there being no distinction between floating point and fixed point literals. Any conversion to an actual floating or fixed point type is effected at the appropriate time.

8.6 Floating point types [LRM 3.5.7]

All the groundwork regarding declarations of types, subtypes, objects and operations has been laid in Chapter 3, so that it is only necessary here to relate additional points which are specific to all floating point types.

Types and subtypes

A floating point type or subtype declaration must include an indication of relative accuracy, by specifying the required minimum number of significant *decimal* digits. No more accuracy should be requested than is really necessary. The accuracy specification may, optionally, be followed by a range constraint. The application of accuracy and range constraints should always be appropriate to the application. A subtype may have the same precision, or less precision (not more!) than its parent type, and it may incorporate a more restricted range, which must be included in the range of its parent type.

Some examples of floating point declarations:

```
-- some declarative part
type REAL is digits 8;          -- no range constraint
type FRACTION is digits 6 range −1.0..1.0;
subtype ROUGH_REAL is REAL digits 5;
                                -- less accuracy
```

```
subtype POS_REAL is REAL range 0.0..1.0E30;
subtype POS_FRACTION is FRACTION digits 4 range 0.0..1.0;
R:REAL:=0.0;
P:POS_REAL:=1.0;
F:FLOAT;                    -- pre-defined
```

Floating point constraints may be applied to object declarations:

```
SMALL_R:REAL range −100.0..100.0;
ROUGH_R:REAL digits 5;
SQUEEZE:REAL digits 4 range −10.0..10.0;
```

It should be noted that reduced accuracy requirements do not necessarily lead to a different representation. So, the types ROUGH_REAL and REAL above *may* have the same internal representation. The precision specification after **digits** specifies the *minimum* requirement; it is up to the implementation to select an appropriate representation. (See Appendix A for details.) Range constraints do not affect the representation of floating point numbers, they are used to prevent invalid assignments.

Of course, it is possible to derive new floating point types from existing types and subtypes:

```
types MY_REAL is new REAL;
type MY_POS_FRACTION is new POS_FRACTION;
type MY_HALF_FRACTION is new FRACTION digits 5 range
−0.5..0.05;
```

Derived types inherit the attributes of their parent type (as well as any applicable operations and subprograms). Also, as the last example illustrates, additional constraints may be imposed upon the derived type. The declaration of type REAL above is, in fact, equivalent to the sequence:

```
type ANON is new pre-defined type;     -- e.g. FLOAT
subtype REAL is ANON digits 8;
```

The pre-defined type, FLOAT, will have an implementation defined accuracy specification. (It should be assumed that no more than six decimal digits of precision are available over all implementations.) An implementation may (or may not) also support pre-defined types SHORT_FLOAT and LONG_FLOAT, with lower and higher precision respectively. These additional pre-defined types should never be used explicitly, in the interests of portability. (However, an implementation may use LONG_FLOAT in order to create new floating point types.) Each implementation has a maximum number of digits of precision that it can support and from which all floating point types are derived (it is this that could be LONG_FLOAT). SYSTEM.MAX_DIGITS, a named number, gives the implementation limit.

Now, consider how the following type declaration is interpreted:

type REAL is digits D;   -- D is universal_integer

For this declaration to be acceptable, the implementation must support a floating point type of at least D digits of precision. If this is the case, then the minimum number of binary digits (bits) required for the mantissa and, in turn, the range of the exponent are determined. The exact nature of this process (and its implications) are considered in Appendix A.

Floating point operations [LRM 3.5.8]

The arithmetic floating point operators listed in 3.6 for type FLOAT are applicable to all floating point types. The relational operators may be applied to floating point expressions but care is needed, especially with equality and inequality testing. The same test could yield different results on different implementations! (See Appendix A.)

There is also a number of attributes associated with floating point types. Most of these relate to the details of the implementation and are listed in Appendix A. Some are included in the list below, in which T represents a type or subtype identifier:

Attribute	Result type	Comments
T'FIRST	T	Yields the lower bound of T
T'LAST	T	Yields the upper bound of T
T'DIGITS	universal_integer	Yields the number of decimal digits of precision for T.
T'EPSILON	universal_real	Yields the absolute difference between 1.0 and the next representable number in T.
T'BASE	–	Only allowed as a prefix to another attribute, e.g. T'BASE'DIGITS, which gives the number of digits for the base type of T.

The attributes FIRST and LAST should not be used unless the type or subtype concerned has an explicit range constraint, for this could well impair the portability of algorithms. It is acceptable to use them in the following situation:

> subtype POS_FLOAT is FLOAT range 0.0..FLOAT'LAST;

which ensures that the full range of positive floating point numbers of the pre-defined type is used, whatever that range happens to be.

EPSILON, which is explained in more detail in Appendix A, can be useful for testing for convergence in iterative algorithms. To illustrate this, the loop of Unit 4.4 is changed to:

```
while INACCURATE loop
   LAST_ROOT:=ROOT;
   ROOT:=(ARGUMENT/ROOT + ROOT)*HALF;
   INACCURATE:=abs(ROOT-LAST_ROOT)
                   >=ROOT*FLOAT'EPSILON;   -- changed
end loop;
```

The loop will now terminate as soon as no more accuracy can be obtained, on whatever implementation the algorithm is executed.

8.7 Fixed point types [LRM 3.5.9]

There is one pre-defined fixed point type, DURATION, which must be provided by an implementation specifically for representing time values for use with tasking. Any fixed point type will be quite specific to its application, so that a general fixed point type would be inappropriate.

Types and subtypes

As might be expected, a fixed point type declaration must include both an accuracy and a range constraint. A subtype declaration may specify the same precision, or less than that of its base type, and may incorporate a further (non-overlapping) range constraint. Some examples:

```
-- some declarative part
type TEMP_SENSOR is delta 0.1 range 0.0..1000.0;
type GEN_SENSOR is delta 0.01 range -100.0..100.0;
```

```
   subtype POS_SENSOR is
      GEN_SENSOR range 0.0..100.0;   -- delta 0.01
   subtype ROUGH_SENSOR is
      GEN_SENSOR delta 0.5;          -- -100.0..100.0
   subtype CHEAP_SENSOR is GEN_SENSOR delta 1.0
      range -10.0..10.0;
   CELSIUS:TEMP_SENSOR:=0.0;
   ACCELEROMETER:GEN_SENSOR:=0.0;
   SYNCH_TIME:DURATION;             -- pre-defined
```

Objects may be declared with anonymous subtypes, although explicit subtypes are preferable:

```
   SPEEDO:GEN_SENSOR range 0.0..100.0;
```

Fixed point types may be derived, as, for example

```
   type VOLTAGE is new GEN_SENSOR;
   type PRESSURE is new GEN_SENSOR range 0.0..100.0;
   type CURRENT is new GEN_SENSOR delta 0.1
      range -10.0..10.0;
```

All fixed point types are derived from at least one anonymous, implementation-defined fixed point type. From the values specified after delta, the actual (binary) precision of the type is determined, as being the largest power of 2, which does not exceed the specified value. For any subtype, the actual precision is obtainable as the attribute SMALL, while DELTA yields the decimal precision. The table below shows the value of SMALL for some of the fixed point types and subtypes defined above.

Subtype	DELTA	SMALL
TEMP_SENSOR	0.1	0.0625
GEN_SENSOR	0.01	0.0078125
POS_SENSOR	0.01	0.0078125
ROUGH_SENSOR	0.5	0.5
CHEAP_SENSOR	1.0	1.0

In common with the treatment of floating point numbers, further details about the implementation of fixed point numbers are given in Appendix A.

Fixed point operations [LRM 3.5.10]

The arithmetic operators "abs", "+" and "−" (unary and binary) may be applied to all fixed point types. For the binary operators, both operands must be of the same type. The multiplication operators, however, need more explanation. A summary of the pre-defined multiplication operators for fixed point types is given in the following table.

Operator	LEFT operand type	RIGHT operand type	Result type
*	any fixed point	INTEGER	as LEFT
*	INTEGER	any fixed point	as RIGHT
*	any fixed point	any fixed point	universal_fixed
/	any fixed point	INTEGER	as LEFT
/	any fixed point	any fixed point	universal_fixed

A fixed point value may be multiplied or divided by an integer to yield a result of the same fixed point type. If the same operations are required on two fixed point operands (of either the same or *different* types) the exact result is of an anonymous pre-defined type, universal_fixed, which has an arbitrarily small DELTA value. This universal_fixed value *must* be explicitly converted to some numeric type as in:

```
-- some declarative part
type FIXED_1 is delta 0.01 range -100.0..100.0;
type FIXED_2 is delta 0.1 range -1000.0..1000.0;
F_1:FIXED_1:=3.0;
F_2:FIXED_2:=10.0;
begin
F_1:=2 * F_1;                -- 6.0
F_2:=F_2 / 2;                -- 5.0
F_2:=FIXED_2(F_1 * F_2);     -- 30.0
F_1:=FIXED_1(F_2/F_1);       -- 5.0
-- ......
end;
```

The explicit type conversion of the right hand sides of the last two assignments is necessary, as the results of the operations are universal_fixed.

Care needs to be taken concerning the accuracy of fixed point operations, especially if the effects of different implementations are not to have any impact. A precision which requires a representation using more than 32 bits ought not be used, as smaller machines may not be able to support it.

In addition to arithmetic operations, the relational operators may be used with fixed point types with more predictable effects than with floating point types — see Appendix A. There is also a number of attributes, some of which are listed below.

Attribute	Result type	Comments
T'FIRST	T	Yields the lower bound of T
T'LAST	T	Yields the upper bound of T
T'DELTA	Universal_real	Yields the specified delta of T
T'SMALL	Universal_real	Yields the actual incremental delta (precision) of T
T'BASE	—	As in previous uses

Other attributes, which require further understanding of implementation details, are covered in Appendix A.

Practising Ada 8

Rather than set many programming assignments, I suggest that you experiment with some of the ideas discussed in this chapter and bear them in mind when writing future programs. If you are really struggling for inspiration:
1 Find the attributes of FLOAT on your implementation of Ada. Derive other real types and subtypes and ascertain the values of their attributes. Read Appendix A — it not only explains what is happening in more detail, it gives you further opportunity to explore.
2 What is the logical flaw in creating a package that exports derived types for MASS, LENGTH and TIME together with additional overloadings of the operators for all type combinations?
3 Write a package which exports a fixed point type and "*" and "/" operators specifically for that type.
Play with the package. Create subtypes and look at their attributes.
4 When you have read Appendix A, go back to some of your earlier programs, such as the series computations. What can you say about the behaviour of those programs from a portability standpoint? How can you provide some sort of guarantee of behaviour?

Chapter 9

Generics [LRM 12]

The concept of a generally applicable subprogram or package does not accord with the philosophy of a strongly typed language. Nevertheless, it is desirable to have the ability to define a unit in a general way, and then to generate specific units from it, as and when required. This ensures a uniformity of approach over all derivations, while making the life of the programmer somewhat easier.

Ada enables subprograms and packages to be defined as generics, which are templates that are expressed in terms of unspecified types. The generic is then used to *instantiate* an actual subprogram or package associated with specific types — those types are given as parameters. Generic units can only be used for instantiating actual subprograms or packages; a generic subprogram cannot be called, nor can a generic package be used as a normal package. However, subprograms and packages, which have been instantiated from generics, are usable just like any other unit of the same class.

Both generic units and instances of subprograms and packages created from them may be library units. Normally, this is how generics are compiled.

9.1 A simple generic subprogram

Interchanging the values of two objects is a very simple and common operation, which requires the use of a temporary variable. By way of introduction to generics, Unit 9.1 is a generic subprogram that can be used for interchanging values of (almost) any type.

```
generic
   type ITEM is private;
procedure GEN_EXCHANGE(A, B:in out ITEM);
   -- must have a specification and a body

procedure GEN_EXCHANGE(A, B:in out ITEM) is
   TEMP:ITEM:=A;
begin
   A:=B;
   B:=TEMP;
end GEN_EXCHANGE;
```

Unit 9.1 A simple generic subprogram.

The structure of a generic is the same as that of a normal subprogram or package, with a generic formal part preceding its specification. This comprises a listing of the formal parameters of the generic, which follow the reserved word **generic**. Note that a generic subprogram must have a specification and a body.

In the example, there is only one formal parameter, called ITEM. We shall concentrate on the specification (and exact meaning) of generic formal parameters a little later. For now, suffice it to say that specifying ITEM as **private** allows instantiation to take place with virtually any type whatsoever.

On instantiation, the actual type has to be supplied, as in the following excerpt.

```
with GEN_EXCHANGE;
procedure MAIN is
    -- declarations including types PERSON (a record)
    -- and MATRIX (a two-dimensional array)
    procedure INT_EXCHANGE is new GEN_EXCHANGE
        (INTEGER);
    procedure PERSON_EXCHANGE is new GEN_EXCHANGE
        (ITEM=>PERSON);
    procedure MAT_EXCHANGE is new GEN_EXCHANGE
        (MATRIX);
    -- ......
end MAIN;
```

Once an instance has been created during elaboration, it becomes visible and may be used in the normal way. In creating PERSON_EXCHANGE, named notation has been used to associate the actual generic parameter with the formal parameter. Positional and/or named parameter associations may be used in the same way as with subprogram calls.

Unit 9.2 shows the creation of an instance of GEN_EXCHANGE for type FLOAT as a library unit.

```
with GEN_EXCHANGE;
procedure FLOAT_EXCHANGE is new GEN_EXCHANGE(FLOAT);
```

Unit 9.2   An instance as a library unit.

This is all there is to it!

The different types of generic parameter are now discussed in detail. The formal parameters of a generic determine what actual parameters are allowed on instantiation. There are three *classes* of generic formal parameters: types, objects and subprograms. Of these, generic formal types are the most important, so discussion will focus on them. The other two classes will, however, be encountered on the way.

9.2 Generic formal types [LRM 12.1.2]

Generic formal parameters may be one of the kinds listed below. The type of the actual parameter allowed to match each kind of formal parameter is noted alongside each formal parameter.

Generic formal parameter	*Matching actual parameter*
(⟨⟩)	any discrete type
range ⟨⟩	any integer type
delta ⟨⟩	any fixed point type
digits ⟨⟩	any floating point type
access	any access type
private	any type other than limited
limited	any type at all
array(INDEX_TYPE) of SOME_TYPE	any constrained 1−d array
array(INDEX_TYPE range⟨⟩) of SOME_TYPE	any unconstrained 1−d array

Note. Analogous treatment for multi-dimensional arrays.

A generic should always be made as general as possible in order to maximize its utilization potential. On occasions, we can be no more general than specifying that the type must be some integer, for example, because properties uniquely associated with that type are assumed, while at other times, it is possible to specify a match with any type whatsoever.

Let us start with an example in which it is not possible to widen the applicability any further. To do this, some of the geometric types and operations from Unit 6.5 will be taken and housed in a somewhat emasculated generic package in Unit 9.3. The generic will have only one formal parameter, which will be the type of the X and Y co-ordinates for a POINT. This type can only be a floating point one, hence the formal parameter specification reflects this.

```
with TEXT_IO, FLOAT_MATH_LIB;  -- FLOAT_MATH_LIB is non-standard
use  TEXT_IO;
generic
  type REAL_TYPE is digits<>;
package GEOMETRY is
  -- A generic package for exporting some
  -- types and operations for geometric
  -- objects.
  -- No exceptions are handled in this package.
  -- DATA_ERROR could be raised in GET_POINT.
  -- NUMERIC_ERROR could be raised in DISTANCE.
```

```
type POINT is
record
  X,
  Y:REAL_TYPE;
end record;

type LINE is
record
  END_1,
  END_2:POINT;
end record;

procedure GET_POINT(ITEM:out POINT);
-- reads in 2 co-ordinates for a point

function DISTANCE(PT_1, PT_2:in POINT) return REAL_TYPE;
-- returns the distance between two points

package REAL_IO is new FLOAT_IO(REAL_TYPE);

end GEOMETRY;

package body GEOMETRY is         -- a generic package

procedure GET_POINT(ITEM:out POINT) is
begin
  PUT("Type X and Y co-ordinates (real): ");
  REAL_IO.GET(ITEM.X);
  REAL_IO.GET(ITEM.Y);
end GET_POINT;

function DISTANCE(PT_1, PT_2:in POINT) return REAL_TYPE is
begin
  return FLOAT_MATH_LIB.SQRT
        ((PT_1.X - PT_2.X)**2 + (PT_1.Y - PT_2.Y)**2);
end DISTANCE;

end GEOMETRY;
```

Unit 9.3   A generic package of a geometrical nature.

Until now, some of the details of numeric i/o have been hidden by the use of SIMPLE_IO. In fact, TEXT_IO provides generic packages for numeric and enumeration i/o. GEOMETRY needs one of these, FLOAT_IO, in order to instantiate a package for the particular type for which GEOMETRY itself is instantiated. Hence GEOMETRY is dependent on TEXT_IO. (The details of TEXT_IO are now only a chapter away.) The specific i/o package, REAL_IO, is exported by the generic package, so that users always have an i/o package for their own use. They could always, of course, instantiate their own package. As the generic also needs to evaluate a square root, it is also dependent on a (non-standard) library package of mathematical functions. On the system used for testing these programs, FLOAT_MATH_LIB is a pre-defined instantiation of the generic package, MATH_LIB.

To use the generic package, GEOMETRY, we might have:

with GEOMETRY;

procedure MAIN is

    type FEET is new FLOAT;
    type METRES is new FLOAT;
    package IMPERIAL_GEOM is new GEOMETRY(FEET);
    package METRIC_GEOM is new GEOMETRY(METRES);
    IP_1:IMPERIAL_GEOM.POINT;
    MP_1:METRIC_GEOM.POINT;
    -- ......

end MAIN;

Following the instantiations, use clauses could have been placed, but then, a declaration such as:

P:POINT;

would be ambiguous. It is usually better to be specific. Although IMPERIAL_GEOM.GET_POINT and METRIC_GEOM.GET_POINT overload each other, and would not be ambiguous, it is better to be explicit.

GEOMETRY has succeeded in providing (a few) types and subprograms based on a particular floating point type. With the two instantiations shown, two separate packages are created, which maintain the distinction between the two floating point types involved.

Now it is time to bring more of the generic formal types into play. Before doing so, it is worth reflecting on what the different kinds of generic formal types mean as far as writing the generic is concerned. The main point to note is that the operations that the *generic* can perform are determined by the type of the formal parameter. Therefore, if a generic formal type parameter is designated as an integer, only operations that can be applied to integers can be used on objects of that type within the generic. If the type of the generic formal parameter is broadened to become ($\langle \rangle$), then this will allow a match with any discrete type. Consequently, no assumptions can be made about the parameter, other than its being a discrete type, which *may* be an integer, or a character or an enumeration type.

The next example, in Unit 9.4, is a generic procedure to sort a one-dimensional array. Although not written as a function here, the sorting algorithm is the same as the (slow) one used in the function of Unit 6.4. The COMPONENT type of the array itself is specified, as you would

expect, in terms of the INDEX and COMPONENT types. Note that it is
an unconstrained array, which means that it will only match unconstrained
array types on instantiation. As a result, any procedure created from this
template will, itself, have an unconstrained array parameter.

```
generic
  type INDEX is (<>);
  type COMPONENT is (<>);
  type ANY_VEC is array
               (INDEX range <>) of COMPONENT;
procedure GEN_SORT_1(V_IN:in ANY_VEC; V_OUT:out ANY_VEC);

procedure GEN_SORT_1(V_IN:in ANY_VEC; V_OUT:out ANY_VEC) is
  V_WORK:ANY_VEC(V_IN'RANGE):=V_IN;
begin
  for SORT_POS in V_IN'FIRST..INDEX'PRED(V_IN'LAST) loop
     for COMPARISON in INDEX'SUCC(SORT_POS)..V_IN'LAST loop
        if V_WORK(SORT_POS) > V_WORK(COMPARISON) then
           declare
             TEMP:COMPONENT:=V_WORK(SORT_POS);
           begin
             V_WORK(SORT_POS):=V_WORK(COMPARISON);
             V_WORK(COMPARISON):=TEMP;
           end;
        end if;
     end loop;      -- for COMPARISON
  end loop;         -- for SORT_POS
  V_OUT:=V_WORK;
end GEN_SORT_1;
```

Unit 9.4 A generic sort procedure — Mark I.

As there are three generic formal parameters, three actual parameters
must be supplied when the generic is instantiated. Notice that because we
can only assume that INDEX is a discrete type, it is necessary to write
INDEX'PRED(V_IN'LAST) rather than V_IN'LAST-1, which would
only be possible if V_IN were an integer. The following context illustrates
how the generic might be used.

   with GEN_SORT_1;

   procedure MAIN is

      type CH_ARRAY is array(INTEGER range 〈〉) of
        CHARACTER;
      procedure CH_SORT is new GEN_SORT_1
        (INDEX=>INTEGER, COMPONENT=>CHARACATER,
        ANY_VEC=>CH_ARRAY);
      CH_A_1, CH_A_2:CH_ARRAY(1..100);
      CH_A_3, CH_A_4:CH_ARRAY(−10..10);

```
    type COUNT_VEC is array(INTEGER range ⟨⟩) of NATURAL;
    procedure COUNT_SORT is new GEN_SORT_1
        (INTEGER,   NATURAL,   COUNT_VEC);  -- positional
                                             -- association
    CV_1, CV_2:COUNT_VEC(0..31);
    -- . . . . . .
    end MAIN;
```

Once the specific procedures have been instantiated, they can be called just like any other procedure:

```
    CH_SORT(CH_A_1, CH_A_2);
    CH_SORT(V_IN => CH_A_3, V_OUT => CH_A_4);
    COUNT_SORT(CV_1, CV_2);
```

Generic formal private types

Is it possible to make GEN_SORT_1 even more general? The array index type can only be a discrete type, but the component could be any type. The next generic formal type in the generality hierarchy is the private type. The implication of this is exactly the same as that for a type exported by a package, but for a generic, remember, this will restrict what the *generic* can do, rather than what the user can do. Be careful to note this distinction. A package exports, while a generic imports — the restrictions apply to the *im*porter.

So, a private generic formal parameter can only be subjected to assignment, (in)equality testing and subprogram application. Looking at the code of GEN_SORT_1, there is one operation that violates this restriction, and this is the ">" operator. It can not be assumed that this is defined for all possible component types. Fortunately, there is a solution to this problem, which we shall soon discover.

Private generic formal (and therefore actual) parameters may have discriminants, as is allowed for private types in packages.

A limited private generic parameter means that any type at all can be matched as the actual parameter. The drawback, for the generic writer, is that only subprograms passed into the generic can be applied to objects of the limited type. We now look at how this is achieved.

9.3 Generic formal subprograms [LRM 12.1.3]

If a generic has a private formal type parameter, upon which the generic needs to operate using an imported subprogram, then the subprogram is tansmitted to the generic as a subprogram parameter. (Subprograms are not allowed as parameters to other subprograms, remember.)

Our development of a general sorting procedure was halted owing to the inability to apply ">" to a private type. By using a generic formal subprogram parameter, the generic can import the required operator at instantiation — it is up to the instantiator to supply an operator for the actual type on which it is to operate.

To illustrate how this is done, the heading would now become:

```
generic
   type INDEX is (〈〉);
   type COMPONENT is private;
   type ANY_VEC is array
     (INDEX range 〈〉) of COMPONENT;
   with function ">" (LEFT, RIGHT:in COMPONENT)
                      return BOOLEAN;
   procedure GEN_SORT_2(V_IN:in ANY_VEC;
                        V_OUT:out ANY_VEC);
   -- the body would be unchanged
```

The rest of the generic is exactly the same. Consider now the implications for the instantiation of this generic. First, compare how we would use the modified generic to create COUNT_SORT with the equivalent instantiation in the previous section:

```
procedure COUNT_SORT is new GEN_SORT_2
   (INTEGER, NATURAL, COUNT_VEC, ">");
```

The (pre-defined) operator applicable to integers will be used for ">" in the generic. To complete the picture, and show the generality of the generic, assume we want to order an array of records. The relevant declarations are:

```
subtype CH_DIGIT is CHARACTER range '0'..'9';
type WK_TYPE is array(1..6) of CH_DIGIT;
type PERSON is
record
  WORK_NO:WK_TYPE;
  AGE:NATURAL range 0..127;
  -- remaining components are irrelevant
end record;
type PEOPLE is array (POSITIVE range 〈〉) of PERSON;
```

In order to instantiate a generic, we have to supply a function for
">", as there is not one pre-defined for the component type, PERSON.
An obvious requirement is to decide what criterion is to be used in order
to sort the records: is it to be AGE or WORK_NO? We could hedge our
bets and cater for both:

```
function GREATER_AGE(LEFT, RIGHT:in PERSON)
                        return BOOLEAN is
begin
  return LEFT.AGE > RIGHT.AGE;
end GREATER_AGE;

function GREATER_WORK_NO(LEFT, RIGHT:in PERSON)
                        return BOOLEAN is
begin
  return LEFT.WORK_NO > RIGHT.WORK_NO;
end GREATER_WORK_NO;
```

It is not possible to overload ">" with *two* meanings for type PERSON,
hence the use of names for the function designators. The name conveys
more meaning anyway, as it implies the comparison criterion used. The
matching rules require that the formal and actual subprogram parameters
have the same result and parameter profiles and the same parameter
transmission modes.

With two functions at hand, we now have two instantiation possibilities:

```
procedure PERSON_AGE_SORT is new GEN_SORT_2
  (POSITIVE, PERSON, PEOPLE, GREATER_AGE);

procedure PERSON_WORK_NO_SORT is new GEN_SORT_2
  (POSITIVE, PERSON, PEOPLE, GREATER_WORK_NO);
```

One final embellishment is the application of defaults for subprogram
formal parameters. There are two ways of specifying defaults: one is by
naming the default subprogram, the other is to use a box, ⟨ ⟩, to denote a
subprogram with the same name as the formal parameter. If an instantiation
does not supply an actual subprogram parameter, one will be sought
which has either the given default name, or the parameter name, and
which also satisfies the matching criteria.

Unit 9.5 incorporates a default, to complete GEN_SORT_2.

```
generic
  type INDEX is (<>);
  type COMPONENT is private;
  type ANY_VEC is array
               (INDEX range <>) of COMPONENT;
  with function ">"(LEFT, RIGHT:in COMPONENT)
                    return BOOLEAN is <>;
procedure GEN_SORT_2(V_IN:in ANY_VEC; V_OUT:out ANY_VEC);

procedure GEN_SORT_2(V_IN:in ANY_VEC; V_OUT:out ANY_VEC) is
  V_WORK:ANY_VEC(V_IN'RANGE):=V_IN;
begin
  for SORT_POS in V_IN'FIRST..INDEX'PRED(V_IN'LAST) loop
    for COMPARISON in INDEX'SUCC(SORT_POS)..V_IN'LAST loop
      if V_WORK(SORT_POS) > V_WORK(COMPARISON) then
        declare
          TEMP:COMPONENT:=V_WORK(SORT_POS);
        begin
          V_WORK(SORT_POS):=V_WORK(COMPARISON);
          V_WORK(COMPARISON):=TEMP;
        end;
      end if;
    end loop;    -- for COMPARISON
  end loop;      -- for SORT_POS
  V_OUT:=V_WORK;
end GEN_SORT_2;
```

Unit 9.5   A generic sort procedure — Mark II.

The instantiation of COUNT_SORT would not now require the sub-program parameter for ">", as the appropriate pre-defined one will automatically be used. Instantiations for the record type, however, *must* over-ride the default, otherwise, they will fail.

9.4 Generic formal objects [LRM 12.1.1]

Object parameters of generics are either of mode **in**, in which case they act like constants, or of mode **in out**, which makes them variables. If an object parameter has no specified mode, then, as with subprogram parameters, **in** is assumed. An **in** formal parameter is matched by an actual parameter that is an expression of a compatible type.

It is some time since stacks were mentioned, so consider once more CHAR_STACK_2 of Unit 7.5 with a view to making it more general. Obviously, all references to CHARACTER Must be removed and replaced by some unspecified type, such as COMPONENT, which then becomes a formal parameter of the generic. How general can COMPONENT be? To answer that, look at what we want to do with COMPONENTs. We only need to assign them to and from array elements. Therefore, COMPONENT can be a private parameter of the generic.

That change would provide us with a means of instantiating packages for creating and maintaining a stack of any component type (other than a limited one). This is fine, if the only size of stack we ever want is 32. To allow for the creation of stacks of different sizes, STACK_MAX can be made to be a parameter of the generic as a generic formal object (of mode **in**). Default expressions may (and should) be used with **in** mode object parameters. The necessary changes lead to GEN_STACK_1 in Unit 9.6.

```
generic
  STACK_MAX:in POSITIVE:=32;
  type COMPONENT is private;
package GEN_STACK_1 is

  -- Comments omitted: authors'prerogative

  type STACK_TYPE is limited private;
  procedure POP(STACK:in out STACK_TYPE; OBJ:out COMPONENT);
  procedure PUSH(STACK:in out STACK_TYPE; OBJ:in COMPONENT);
  UNDERFLOW, OVERFLOW:exception;
private
  type STACK_ITEMS is array(1..STACK_MAX) of COMPONENT;
  type STACK_TYPE is
  record
    TOP:NATURAL range 0..STACK_MAX:=0;
    ITEM:STACK_ITEMS;
  end record;
end GEN_STACK_1;

package body GEN_STACK_1 is

  procedure POP(STACK:in out STACK_TYPE; OBJ:out COMPONENT) is
  begin
    if STACK.TOP = 0 then
      raise UNDERFLOW;
    end if;
    OBJ:=STACK.ITEM(STACK.TOP);
    STACK.TOP:=STACK.TOP - 1;
  end POP;

  procedure PUSH(STACK:in out STACK_TYPE; OBJ:in COMPONENT) is
  begin
    if STACK.TOP = STACK_MAX then
      raise OVERFLOW;
    end if;
    STACK.TOP:=STACK.TOP + 1;
    STACK.ITEM(STACK.TOP):=OBJ;
  end PUSH;

end GEN_STACK_1;
```

Unit 9.6 A generic package for creating more than one stack.

It is time to reflect once more on what we have created. Using GEN_STACK_1, it is possible to create packages for stacks of any type:

```
with GEN_STACK_1;
procedure MAIN is

   package INT_STACK is new GEN_STACK_1(16, INTEGER);
   package CHAR_STACK is
     new GEN_STACK_1(100, CHARACTER);
   PD_INT:INT_STACK.STACK_TYPE;
   PD_CHAR:CHAR_STACK.STACK_TYPE;
   -- ......
end MAIN;
```

It is possible to include use clauses after the instantiation, to make references shorter, or renaming could be used for the same purpose. However, if we had:

```
use INT_STACK;
use CHAR_STACK;
PD_INT:STACK_TYPE; -- INVALID. which STACK_TYPE?
```

It would fail because STACK_TYPE is ambiguous, being exported by both packages. Calls to PUSH and POP would *not* be ambiguous, as overload resolution rules would identify the correct subprogram from the type of its parameter.

Each package is specific to a type *and* a size. It would be much more useful if we could create a package for any type, which subsequently enabled us to create stacks of any size for that particular type. To achieve this, we transform CHAR_STACK_3 of Unit 7.6 into a generic. The variable size in CHAR_STACK_3, you will recall, results from the use of a discriminant in the definition of the stack type. We simply leave that alone, and only need to replace CHARACTER by the generic formal type parameter, COMPONENT. Unit 9.7 is a listing of GEN_STACK_2.

```
generic
  type COMPONENT is private;
package GEN_STACK_2 is

  -- Documentation here

  type STACK_TYPE(MAX:POSITIVE:=32) is limited private;
  procedure POP(STACK:in out STACK_TYPE; OBJ:out COMPONENT);
  procedure PUSH(STACK:in out STACK_TYPE; OBJ:in COMPONENT);
  UNDERFLOW, OVERFLOW:exception;
private
  type STACK_ITEMS is array(POSITIVE range <>) of COMPONENT;
  type STACK_TYPE(MAX:POSITIVE:=32) is
  record
    TOP:NATURAL:=0;
    ITEM:STACK_ITEMS(1..MAX);
  end record;
end GEN_STACK_2;
```

```
package body GEN_STACK_2 is


   procedure POP(STACK:in out STACK_TYPE; OBJ:out COMPONENT) is
   begin
     if STACK.TOP = 0 then
       raise UNDERFLOW;
     end if;
     OBJ:=STACK.ITEM(STACK.TOP);
     STACK.TOP:=STACK.TOP - 1;
   end POP;

   procedure PUSH(STACK:in out STACK_TYPE; OBJ:in COMPONENT) is
   begin
     if STACK.TOP = STACK.MAX then      -- the only change in the body
       raise OVERFLOW;
     end if;
     STACK.TOP:=STACK.TOP + 1;
     STACK.ITEM(STACK.TOP):=OBJ;
   end PUSH;

end GEN_STACK_2;
```

Unit 9.7   A generic package for creating different size stacks.

Instantiation and use of this package might go:

> with GEN_STACK_2;

> procedure MAIN is

>> package INT_STACK is new GEN_STACK_2(INTEGER);
>> use INT_STACK;
>> BIG_INT_STACK:STACK_TYPE(100);
>> TINY_INT_STACK:STACK_TYPE(4);
>> DEFAULT_INT_STACK:STACK_TYPE;   -- size 32
>> -- ......

> end MAIN;

Formal object parameters of mode **in out** are matched by variables of the same type. The effect is for these actual parameter variables to be renamed as the formal parameters within the generic (which is not the same as the treatment of subprogram parameters of the same mode). This gives the instantiated generic access to the actual parameter variable, which is, in effect, a global variable that is renamed for use within the generic.

Given the outline:

> generic
>> COUNT:in out NATURAL;
>> type ITEM is private;

```
procedure GEN_THING(PARAM:in out ITEM);

procedure GEN_THING(PARAM:in out ITEM) is
begin
   COUNT:=COUNT+1;
   -- the useful part of the procedure
end GEN_THING;
```

we might instantiate:

```
-- some declarative part, with GEN_THING visible
INT_COUNT, DAY_COUNT:NATURAL:=0;

procedure INT_THING is
      new GEN_THING(INT_COUNT, INTEGER);
procedure DAY_THING is
      new GEN_THING(DAY_COUNT, DAY);
```

Each time one of these procedures is called, its own variable, associated at instantiation, is incremented. The same effect could have been achieved by passing the appropriate variable as a parameter to the instantiated procedure rather than to the generic, but this would have to be done at each call. The use of the generic object parameter achieves the effect of binding a different global variable to different instantiations.

(As a reminder, **in out** object parameters cannot have default expressions, as they represent variables.)

9.5 Generic generalities

This section is a pot pourri of remarks about and recommendations for the writing and use of generics.

Points of style

Generics provide a very powerful mechanism for defining general subprograms and packages. It would be easy to obscure the origin of this generality within a program by a poor choice of identifiers. If you are instantiating the same generic for different types, for example, it helps if you reflect the common ancestry by similarly styled names (such as INT_STACK and CHAR_STACK).

If a generic has a subprogram parameter, then all the subprograms that might be passed as an actual parameter should exhibit the same

logical behaviour. So for ">" in Unit 9.5, the association of a pre-defined
">", or of the ones written for type PERSON is quite acceptable;
however, passing a function that does other things, such as input and
validate data en route to delivering the required BOOLEAN result,
should be avoided.

When writing a generic, always endeavour to maintain type independence as far as possible. Using attributes of the discrete types facilitated
the development of the sorting generic of Unit 9.4.

It is a useful reminder, particularly when generic bodies are compiled
separately, to precede the body code by a comment to indicate that the
unit is a generic one.

Parameterless generics

You might well wonder why you should want to have a generic with no
parameters. This can, however, be useful, if you want to create multiple
instances of the same package. CHAR_STACK_1 (Unit 7.1) is a good
example of a package for which you might do this. As a straight package,
CHAR_STACK_1 has a single stack, and cannot be used if more than
one stack is required. So, by preceding the definition of the package by:

```
generic
  -- no parameters
package CHAR_STACK_1_G is
-- and so on, with no other changes
-- except to the name
```

the user can now create as many stacks (packages) as are required:

```
with CHAR_STACK_1_G;   -- (generic version)

procedure MAIN is

  package EXP_STACK is new CHAR_STACK_1_G;
  package POST_STACK is new CHAR_STACK_1_G;
  -- ......
end MAIN;
```

Elaboration issues

What we have seen about elaboration order strongly suggests that you
should *not* instantiate a generic in the same compilation unit that contains

its specification. If an attempt is made to use the instantiation before the generic body has been elaborated, PROGRAM_ERROR will be raised.

It is normal practice to implement generics as library units, anyway, which circumvents this problem, as long as specifications and bodies are kept together, otherwise the pragma ELABORATE may be required, as shown in Chapter 7.

Generics and recursion

Generic subprograms may be recursive, i.e. they may *call* themselves, as in:

```
generic
  type DISC is (⟨⟩);
procedure RECURSE(D:in DISC);

procedure RECURSE(D:in DISC) is
begin
  if D=DISC'FIRST then
    -- do something
  else
    RECURSE(DISC'PRED(D));
  end if;
end RECURSE;
```

However, a generic is *not* allowed to contain an *instantiation* of itself, so that, immediately before the **begin** above, we could not have:

```
procedure CORKSCREW is new RECURSE;   -- INVALID in
                                      -- RECURSE
```

By the same token, it is not possible to have an instantiation of some other generic unit within RECURSE that would lead to an eventual instantiation of RECURSE.

Exceptions in generics

In Chapter 5, we saw that an exception declared in a recursive subprogram is the *same* exception for all calls of that subprogram. If an exception is declared within a generic, then each instantiation creates a *different* exception, although each exception has the same name. So a generic with the outline:

```
generic
package GP is
   OUCH:exception;
   -- other things here, presumably
end GP;
```

could be instantiated:

```
package P_1 is new GP;
package P_2 is new GP;
```

Within each package, OUCH will refer to the exception that is local to that particular package. Outside the package, though, in order to distinguish between the exceptions, selection will be required to select P_1.OUCH or P_2.OUCH.

9.6 Final example

To bring together many of the facets of generics introduced in this chapter, Unit 9.8 develops the facilities of Unit 6.6 to produce a generic package for maintaining an ordered list for any type of object (other than a limited one).

The package itself will own, hide and maintain the list. The interface with the user are the procedures INSERT, REMOVE and PRINT_LIST. The list contains objects of type OBJ_TYPE, and is ordered on some key of type KEY_TYPE. INSERT places the given OBJECT into the correct position in the list, while REMOVE deletes the first object from the list that has a given KEY (if there is such an object).

INSERT needs to establish the correct position for an object in the list, and REMOVE needs to know where it is in the list while it is traversing it. Equality and a relational operator, "<", are sufficient for this, and assignment is required to place OBJECT in the list in INSERT. Because OBJ_TYPE is a private parameter of the generic, of these operations, only "<" needs to be provided as a subprogram parameter.

Some other ramifications of privatization may not be quite so obvious. The ordering is being performed according to the comparison of keys. REMOVE involves the comparison of the given KEY with the keys of the objects in the list. Therefore, it is necessary that the instantiator provide the generic with the means of finding the KEY_OF an object — the generic can assume nothing about the properties of objects.

The procedure PRINT_LIST writes out every object in the list. In order for it to do this, it must be given the ability to write out a single OBJ_TYPE object. This explains the presence of the generic subprogram parameter PRINT_OBJECT.

```
with SIMPLE_IO, UNCHECKED_DEALLOCATION;
use  SIMPLE_IO;
generic
  type OBJ_TYPE is private;
  type KEY_TYPE is private;
  with function KEY_OF(OBJECT:in OBJ_TYPE) return KEY_TYPE;
  with function "<"(LEFT, RIGHT:in KEY_TYPE) return BOOLEAN;
  with procedure PRINT_OBJECT(OBJECT:in OBJ_TYPE);
package LIST_MANAGER is

  -- Provides a set of routines for inserting,
  -- removing and printing items in an ordered
  -- list hidden within the package body.
  -- An attempt to REMOVE an object with
  -- a non-existent key will cause NOT_FOUND
  -- to be raised. The caller must handle this.

  NOT_FOUND:exception;

  procedure INSERT(OBJECT:in OBJ_TYPE);
    -- inserts OBJECT into the correct position
    -- in the ordered list.

  procedure REMOVE(KEY:in KEY_TYPE);
    -- removes the first object (if any) with
    -- key = KEY from the list.
    -- NOT_FOUND raised if not present.

  procedure PRINT_LIST;
    -- prints all the members of the list.

end LIST_MANAGER;

-- generic
package body LIST_MANAGER is

  type NODE;
  type POINTER is access NODE;
  type NODE is
  record
    OBJ:OBJ_TYPE;
    NEXT:POINTER:=null;
  end record;

  HEAD:POINTER:=null;                        -- points to head of list
```

```
   procedure INSERT(OBJECT:in OBJ_TYPE) is
     HERE:POINTER;
     OBJ_KEY:KEY_TYPE:=KEY_OF(OBJECT);
   begin
     if HEAD = null or else OBJ_KEY < KEY_OF(HEAD.OBJ) then
       HEAD:=new NODE'(OBJECT, HEAD);
     else
       HERE:=HEAD;
     while HERE.NEXT /= null and KEY_OF(HERE.OBJ) < OBJ_KEY loop
       HERE:=HERE.NEXT;
     end loop;
     if OBJ_KEY = KEY_OF(HERE.OBJ) then
       PRINT_OBJECT(OBJECT);
       PUT(" is already in the list.");
       NEW_LINE;
     elsif OBJ_KEY < KEY_OF(HERE.OBJ) then      -- insert before HERE
       HERE.NEXT:=new NODE'(HERE.all);
       HERE.OBJ:=OBJECT;
     else                                       -- insert after HERE
       HERE.NEXT:=new NODE'(OBJECT, HERE.NEXT);
     end if;
   end if;
end INSERT;

procedure REMOVE(KEY:in KEY_TYPE) is

   procedure DISPOSE_NODE is new
             UNCHECKED_DEALLOCATION(NODE, POINTER);

   DEL_NODE, PRE_NODE:POINTER;
begin
   if HEAD = null then
     PUT("List empty.");
     raise NOT_FOUND;
   end if;
   -- list is not empty if we get here
   DEL_NODE:=HEAD;
   if KEY = KEY_OF(HEAD.OBJ) then
     HEAD:=HEAD.NEXT;
   elsif KEY < KEY_OF(HEAD.OBJ) then
     raise NOT_FOUND;
   else
     while KEY /= KEY_OF(DEL_NODE.OBJ) and DEL_NODE.NEXT/=null loop
       PRE_NODE:=DEL_NODE;
       DEL_NODE:=DEL_NODE.NEXT;
     end loop;
     if KEY /= KEY_OF(DEL_NODE.OBJ) then
       raise NOT_FOUND;
     end if;
     PRE_NODE.NEXT:=DEL_NODE.NEXT;              -- bypass the node
   end if;
   DISPOSE_NODE(DEL_NODE);
end REMOVE;
```

```
procedure PRINT_LIST is
  THIS:POINTER:=HEAD;
begin
  if HEAD = null then
    PUT("The list is empty.");
    NEW_LINE;
  else
    PUT("The list is:");
    NEW_LINE;
    while THIS /= null loop
        PRINT_OBJECT(THIS.OBJ);
        NEW_LINE;
        THIS:=THIS.NEXT;
      end loop;
    end if;
  end PRINT_LIST;

end LIST_MANAGER;
```

Unit 9.8   A generic package for maintaining an ordered list.

Practising Ada 9

Re-assess some of the programs you have already written — can you
generalize them; if so, how? Some instantiated ideas:

1 Write a generic function which returns the largest value in *any* one-
dimensional array of a discrete type. Extend this for a one-dimensional
array of *any* type.

2 Develop a generic package of matrix manipulation routines (addition,
multiplication, transposition for example) for any two-dimensional array
of a floating point type. (Could you extend this to encompass fixed point
types?)

3 Generalize your set package (or mine) for sets of any discrete type.
When would "yours" be more applicable and when would "mine" — in
other words, when should you use a BOOLEAN array and when should
you use a list? Could you automate the choice?

4 Write a generic procedure to print out any two-dimensional array.

Chapter 10

Input and output [LRM 14]

Throughout this book, use has been made of the i/o packages TEXT_IO and SIMPLE_IO. TEXT_IO is pre-defined for all implementations, while SIMPLE_IO is the creation of a user. In fact, every Ada implementation must provide three packages for general i/o operations: TEXT_IO is for character-based i/o, which is used for all communication readable by humans; SEQUENTIAL_IO and DIRECT_IO are generic packages for i/o handling with files of component types that are defined on instantiation. The specifications of all three packages are defined in the LRM and are reproduced in this chapter. Each of them uses exceptions that are defined in another pre-defined package, IO_EXCEPTIONS.

Another package for direct interaction with physical devices must be provided by an implementation. LOW_LEVEL_IO is not intended for general purpose use and will receive scant attention in this book. Most of the discussion in this chapter will focus on TEXT_IO, owing to its general importance. In addition to looking at the file processing packages and taking a cursory look at LOW_LEVEL_IO, a listing and commentary on the non-standard package, SIMPLE_IO is given, for much use of it has been made throughout the examples.

Before looking at packages in detail, it is logical to say something about files in general and then introduce the exceptions defined in IO_EXCEPTIONS.

10.1 External files and file objects [LRM 14.1]

In an Ada program, all input and output operations are specified to act upon objects of some particular file type, which are *logical* files. To get these i/o operations to be executed on a particular physical or *external* file or device, an association has to be made between the external file and the file object. This is done when the file is opened.

The three pre-defined i/o packages provide two subprograms for opening files: CREATE is used to create a *new* file in some MODE and open it. (The default mode depends on the package, but it will not be for reading, as there will be nothing to read!); OPEN is used to open an *existing* file, in the mode specified at the call. Both of these subprograms

219

associate the physical and logical files using the actual parameters. The
specification of OPEN in the three high level packages is:

```
procedure OPEN   (FILE:in out FILE_TYPE;
                  MODE:in FILE_MODE;
                  NAME:in STRING;
                  FORM:in STRING:="");
```

FORM may be used by an implementation but it is often ignored; it
depends on the file attribute conventions of the host operating system.
With a null string as the default, we can ignore this parameter.

If we have an external file called ADA_BOOK.TEXT, which we
want to read within an Ada program, first, there has to be a declaration
of a file object, the logical name, followed by a call of OPEN:

```
    IN_TEXT:FILE_TYPE;
    -- other declarations may go here
begin
    -- some other statements, perhaps
    OPEN(IN_TEXT, IN_FILE, "ADA_BOOK.TEXT");
    -- ......
end;
```

Subsequently, any operation on IN_TEXT will be performed on the
actual external file specified, viz. ADA_BOOK.TEXT. The NAME
parameter of OPEN must, obviously, be a string which conforms to the
file naming convention of the environment (operating system) in which
Ada is running, and the file must already exist, otherwise NAME_ERROR
will be raised (see 10.2).

If no NAME is provided for a call of CREATE, then the default null
string applies and an anonymous file will be used, i.e. a temporary file is
created, which will not exist after the end of the execution of the program.
A null NAME cannot, of course, be used with OPEN.

Further discussion and examples will be given in subsequent sections,
which will also cover other aspects of file management, such as closing
files.

10.2 IO_EXCEPTIONS [LRM 14.4, 14.5]

This package exports the exceptions that may raised by any of the three
pre-defined high level i/o packages. As you will see, each of these packages is dependent on IO_EXCEPTIONS and makes the exceptions directly
visible to users by renaming them.

There are eight pre-defined i/o exceptions, each of which is briefly explained here. More specific information on some of them is given during the explanation of the i/o packages themselves. Consult the LRM for a full account of the conditions under which they are raised.

STATUS_ERROR is raised when an attempt is made to operate on a file that is not open, or if an attempt is made to open a file that is already open.

MODE_ERROR is raised when an attempt is made to perform an operation, which is inappropriate to the current mode of the file, such as trying to read from a file that is open only for writing.

NAME_ERROR is raised when an attempt is made to open a file for which the given internal file name is incorrect, for some reason.

USE_ERROR is raised if an operation is attempted that is not possible, owing to the characteristics of the file, such as invalid access priveleges.

DEVICE_ERROR is raised, if there is a malfunction in the i/o subsystem during an attempted i/o operation.

END_ERROR is raised on an attempt to read past the end of a file.

DATA_ERROR, is (frequently) raised when an input operation does not find a value of the expected type.

LAYOUT_ERROR is raised (when using TEXT_IO only), if any page layout parameters exceed their limits, or if an attempt is made to write too many characters to a string. Different external files may be associated with the same logical file at different times.

10.3 TEXT_IO [LRM 14.3]

This package provides the means for interfacing Ada programs with humans. TEXT_IO input and output operations involve the reading and writing of sequences of characters, which may be formatted into lines and pages. The i/o may take place via external files, or via the standard i/o devices, such as keyboard and screen. Because TEXT_IO is character based, compatible files may be created and processed by any system utilities, such as editors and printers, which utilize the same character set.

The specification of TEXT_IO has the structure:

```
with IO_EXCEPTIONS;
package TEXT_IO is
    -- File and layout type declarations
    -- File management subprograms
    -- Default file control
    -- Line and page length specification
    -- Column, line and page control
    -- CHARACTER i/o procedures
    -- STRING i/o procedures
    -- generic package INTEGER_IO
    -- generic package FLOAT_IO
    -- generic package FIXED_IO
    -- generic package ENUMERATION_IO
    -- Renaming of i/o exceptions
private
    -- implementation-dependent
end TEXT_IO;
```

Space is too limited to allow a description of all the features of TEXT_IO in detail, however, sufficient information is given to enable you to use the package effectively.

There now follows a complete listing of the visible specification of TEXT_IO, a section at a time.

File and layout type declarations

```
type FILE_TYPE is limited private;

type FILE_MODE is (IN_FILE, OUT_FILE);

type COUNT is range 0..implementation_defined;
subtype POSITIVE_COUNT is COUNT range 1..COUNT'LAST;
UNBOUNDED:constant COUNT:=0;

subtype FIELD is INTEGER range 0..implementation_defined;
subtype NUMBER_BASE is INTEGER range 2..16;

type TYPE_SET is (LOWER_CASE, UPPER_CASE);
```

FILE_TYPE enables (logical) file objects to be declared — the details of the type are implementation dependent. Text files may be of mode IN_FILE or OUT_FILE, as defined by the type FILE_MODE.

COUNT and POSITIVE_COUNT are integer subtypes that are used for layout control object declarations. The zero value of COUNT is used to denote unbounded formats, and is represented by the constant UNBOUNDED.

FIELD is a subtype that is concerned with controlling the input and output of formatted items, which applies to the numeric and enumeration types. NUMBER_BASE is used for setting the default base used by INTEGER_IO.

Finally, TYPE_SET is used by ENUMERATION_IO to determine the default case for the i/o of enumeration literal identifiers.

File management and default file control

These two sections are taken together, as there is some interdependence.

```
-- file management subprograms

procedure CREATE (FILE:in out FILE_TYPE;
                  MODE:in FILE_MODE:=OUT_FILE;
                  NAME:in STRING:="";
                  FORM:in STRING:="");

procedure OPEN (FILE:in out FILE_TYPE;
                MODE:in FILE_MODE;
                NAME:in STRING;
                FORM:in STRING:="");

procedure CLOSE (FILE:in out FILE_TYPE);
procedure DELETE (FILE:in out FILE_TYPE);
procedure RESET (FILE:in out FILE_TYPE;
                 MODE:in FILE_MODE);
procedure RESET (FILE:in out FILE_TYPE);

function MODE (FILE:in FILE_TYPE) return FILE_MODE;
function NAME (FILE:in FILE_TYPE) return STRING;
function FORM (FILE:in FILE_TYPE) return STRING;

function IS_OPEN (FILE:in FILE_TYPE) return BOOLEAN;

-- default file control

procedure SET_INPUT (FILE:in FILE_TYPE);
procedure SET_OUTPUT (FILE:in FILE_TYPE);
```

```
function STANDARD_INPUT return FILE_TYPE;
function STANDARD_OUTPUT return FILE_TYPE;

function CURRENT_INPUT return FILE_TYPE;
function CURRENT_OUTPUT return FILE_TYPE:
```

When program execution begins, default input and output files are automatically opened in modes IN_FILE and OUT_FILE respectively. These files will initially be the standard input and standard output files of the system, which would normally be the terminal keyboard and screen. The significance of the default files is that there are two forms of all GET and PUT procedures, as well as for the formatting subprograms. Each has a long form which includes a file name, FILE, and a short form which has no FILE parameter. The short form uses the current default input or output file, as appropriate. The means of over-riding the defaults will be revealed shortly.

For i/o using files other than standard input and output, an external file association has to be made using CREATE or OPEN, as described in 10.1. There is little to add to what was said there, other than remarking that the default mode for CREATE is OUT_FILE. A file object must always be associated with an external file. When it is required to terminate that association, CLOSE may be called. DELETE goes one step further by also physically deleting the external file. Note that the effect of not closing files before program termination is not defined by the language. Files may be closed automatically for you — there is no reason why this should happen, though!

RESET resets the given file object (which must already be open) for reading or writing. There are two versions of this procedure. The first enables the mode to be changed by the second parameter, while the second form resets the file in its current mode. *Note* that the standard i/o files cannot be passed to OPEN, CLOSE, DELETE or RESET.

Four functions, namely MODE, NAME, FORM and IS_OPEN, are provided to enable the status of a given FILE to be interrogated. Their use is self-explanatory.

For over-riding the default files for TEXT_IO, SET_INPUT makes the given file, FILE (which must be of mode IN_FILE, otherwise MODE_ERROR will be raised), the default input file, and SET_OUTPUT sets its given FILE as the default for output (and this must be of mode OUT_FILE). The standard input and output files of the system are returned by the functions STANDARD_INPUT and STANDARD_

OUTPUT respectively, while CURRENT_INPUT and CURRENT_OUTPUT do the same for the *current* default files. All four of these functions return, of course, the *logical* file names, and not the external names.

It is not a good idea to over-ride default files, as this can lead to confusion. CURRENT_INPUT and CURRENT_OUTPUT can be changed dynamically, remember, whereas STANDARD_INPUT and STANDARD_OUTPUT *always* refer to the same, standard i/o files. If you always want i/o to take place via the standard files, whatever the default files are, the long form of i/o subprograms should be used, with STANDARD_INPUT or STANDARD_OUTPUT as the actual parameter for FILE.

Consider the following skeleton, in which it is assumed that the screen is the standard output file:

```
    -- some declarative part
    OUTPUT:FILE_TYPE;
begin
    CREATE(OUTPUT, OUT_FILE, "results");
    SET_OUTPUT(OUTPUT);       -- Change the default.
    PUT(STANDARD_OUTPUT, "Error message.");
                              -- Always to screen.
    PUT("Some other message.");   -- To file "results".
    -- . . . . . .
end;
```

The output from the second PUT will be sent to whatever the current default output file happens to be (in this case it is the external file "results"), while the first PUT will always be directed to the screen.

An example will be given later, which will illustrate the use of some of the other subprograms in this portion of TEXT_IO.

Line and page length specification

```
    procedure SET_LINE_LENGTH (FILE:in FILE_TYPE;
                               TO:in COUNT);
    procedure SET_LINE_LENGTH (TO:in COUNT);

    procedure SET_PAGE_LENGTH (FILE:in FILE_TYPE;
                               TO:in COUNT);
    procedure SET_PAGE_LENGTH (TO:in COUNT);
```

```
function LINE_LENGTH (FILE:in FILE_TYPE)
                     return COUNT;
function LINE_LENGTH return COUNT;

function PAGE_LENGTH (FILE:in FILE_TYPE)
                     return COUNT;
function PAGE_LENGTH return COUNT;
```

A text file is a collection of characters, which can be structured into lines and pages. A line ends in a *line terminator* and a page is terminated by a line terminator immediately followed by a *page terminator*. The file itself is terminated by the sequence: line terminator, page terminator, *file terminator*. These terminators are generated automatically as a file is written. Their nature is implementation dependent, therefore no assumption should be made about the characters used to represent them, or indeed that they are characters at all. You may only assume that the subprograms of TEXT_IO will correctly generate and recognize them, as appropriate. For this reason, you should always use NEW_LINE to generate a new line rather than say:

PUT(ASCII.CR & ASCII.LF);   -- implementation-dependent

Similarly, END_OF_LINE should be used, rather than testing for some character(s) you assume might be correct.

Characters in a line are numbered as their *column number*. The first character in a line has column number 1. A line terminator has a column number, which is one greater than the number of characters in the line. The lines of a page and the pages of a file are numbered in the same way. The current state of a file, i.e. the current column, line and page numbers, may be easily obtained from functions. These values may be changed explicitly by procedure calls, or implicitly by the use of GET and PUT operations.

It is possible to specify maximum line and page lengths for files of mode OUT_FILE. These will over-ride the default UNBOUNDED configuration. If a maximum line length is specified, a line terminator will be generated automatically when a value to be PUT cannot be accommodated on the current line. The same logic applies to page length and automatic page termination.

SET_LINE_LENGTH and SET_PAGE_LENGTH set the length parameters of the specified FILE to the given value, TO. A value of zero indicates an unbounded length. The short forms of these procedures apply to the current output file. LINE_LENGTH and PAGE_LENGTH return the current settings for the named (or current) output file.

Column, line and page control

```
procedure NEW_LINE (FILE:in FILE_TYPE;
                     SPACING:in POSITIVE_COUNT:=1);
procedure NEW_LINE (SPACING:in POSITIVE_COUNT:=1);

procedure SKIP_LINE(FILE:in FILE_TYPE;
                     SPACING:in POSITIVE_COUNT:=1);
procedure SKIP_LINE(SPACING:in POSITIVE_COUNT:=1);

function END_OF_LINE (FILE:in FILE_TYPE)
                     return BOOLEAN;
function END_OF_LINE return BOOLEAN;

procedure NEW_PAGE (FILE:in FILE_TYPE);
procedure NEW_PAGE;

procedure SKIP_PAGE (FILE:in FILE_TYPE);
procedure SKIP_PAGE;

function END_OF_PAGE (FILE:in FILE_TYPE)
                     return BOOLEAN;
function END_OF_PAGE return BOOLEAN;

function END_OF_FILE (FILE: in FILE_TYPE)
                     return BOOLEAN;
function END_OF_FILE return BOOLEAN;

procedure SET_COL (FILE: in FILE_TYPE;
                   TO:in POSITIVE_COUNT);
procedure SET_COL (TO:in POSITIVE_COUNT);

procedure SET_LINE (FILE: in FILE_TYPE;
                    TO:in POSITIVE_COUNT);
procedure SET_LINE (TO:in POSITIVE_COUNT);

function COL (FILE: in FILE_TYPE)
             return POSITIVE_COUNT;
function COL return POSITIVE_COUNT;

function LINE (FILE: in FILE_TYPE)
             return POSITIVE_COUNT;
function LINE return POSITIVE_COUNT;

function PAGE (FILE: in FILE_TYPE)
             return POSITIVE_COUNT;
function PAGE return POSITIVE_COUNT;
```

The above subprograms enable the current position in a text file to be controlled explicitly. NEW_LINE outputs a line terminator, incrementing the current line number by one and setting the current column number to 1. If the default for the parameter, SPACING, is over-ridden, then this process will be repeated SPACING times. A new page will be generated automatically if the file has a page size limit to which the current line number is set when NEW_LINE is called.

SKIP_LINE is to IN_FILEs what NEW_LINE is to OUT_FILEs. For a (default) SPACING of one, all remaining input on the current line is discarded, and the next line terminator is read. The file then becomes set for reading at the beginning of the next line. For a SPACING of more than one, this process is repeated the requisite number of times. If the skipping embraces a page boundary, then it automatically moves to the first line of the next page. Any attempt to skip beyond the end of a file will cause END_ERROR to be raised.

END_OF_LINE returns TRUE, if a line (or file) terminator is next, otherwise it returns FALSE.

NEW_PAGE, SKIP_PAGE and END_OF_PAGE behave analogously to their line based counterparts. END_OF_FILE returns TRUE, if a file, or page, or line terminator is next to be read.

The final group of procedures in this section may be used to control the current column and line positions in IN_FILE or OUT_FILE files. The default file for the short forms is the current *output* file. For output files, if the TO parameter is greater than LINE_LENGTH, then LAYOUT_ERROR will be raised (unless LINE_LENGTH is zero, i.e. unbounded). The effect of the call will depend on the value of the TO parameter compared with the current column number. If they are the same, the subprogram has no effect. If the specified value exceeds the current column number, then spaces are written until the current column is that specified. However, if the specified value is less than the current column, a line terminator is output followed by spaces (one fewer than TO) on the *next* line. A page terminator will be output if, during this operation, a bounded page is filled.

For an input file, if the specified column is the same as the current column, there is no effect, as for an output file, otherwise all input will be skipped until a character is found in the column specified by TO. Such a column will be on the current line if the current column is less than TO, or on the next line with a character in the specified column. A call of SET_COL which results in an attempt to read past the end of a file will cause END_ERROR to be raised.

SET_LINE operates in a similar way to SET_COL but, obviously, for lines rather than columns.

The current column, line and page numbers of the specified FILE (or CURRENT_OUTPUT for the short forms) are returned by COL, LINE and PAGE respectively. LAYOUT_ERROR will be raised, if an attempt is made to return a number greater than TEXT_IO.COUNT'LAST (although surprisingly, perhaps, the column, line and page numbers themselves *may* exceed this value, without the raising of any exception).

All GET and PUT procedures, as well as GET_LINE and PUT_LINE, will update the current file position for the file on which they are operating, at the end of the operation.

GET will always skip line and page terminators until a character is found but an attempt to skip past the end of a file will cause END_ERROR to be raised.

CHARACTER i/o procedures

```
procedure GET (FILE:in FILE_TYPE;
                    ITEM:out CHARACTER);
procedure GET (ITEM:out CHARACTER);

procedure PUT (FILE:in FILE_TYPE; ITEM:in CHARACTER);
procedure PUT (ITEM:in CHARACTER);
```

Some of the above procedures should be like old friends by now! There are, of course, two forms of these (and all other) GET and PUT procedures.

GET will read the next character from the specified FILE (or from CURRENT_INPUT) skipping any line terminators and page terminators that occur between the current position and the next character. END_ERROR will be raised, if no character is found before the end of the file is reached — the correct use of END_OF_LINE should prevent this from happening.

PUT will output the given character to the specified FILE (or to CURRENT_OUTPUT). If the file is bounded, and the current column is at LINE_LENGTH, then a line terminator will be output before the character (and a page terminator will be output, if required).

Note that these GET procedures do not require input characters to be quoted, nor will these PUT procedures enclose output characters by quotes.

STRING i/o procedures

```
procedure GET (FILE:in FILE_TYPE; ITEM:out STRING);
```

```
procedure GET (ITEM:out STRING);

procedure PUT (FILE:in FILE_TYPE; ITEM:in STRING);
procedure PUT (ITEM:in STRING);

procedure GET_LINE (FILE:in FILE_TYPE;
                    ITEM:out STRING;
                    LAST:out NATURAL);
procedure GET_LINE (ITEM:out STRING;
                    LAST:out NATURAL);

procedure PUT_LINE (FILE:in FILE_TYPE; ITEM:in STRING);
procedure PUT_LINE (ITEM:in STRING);
```

String data for a string input procedure does not require enclosing string parentheses, nor will output strings be quoted. If you do wish to output a string quote, as part of a string literal, remember that you require two of them together (within string quotes), so that:

```
PUT("This is a""".");
```

will ouptut the string:

This is a ".

A GET for strings is effectively equivalent to repeated calling of the corresponding GET for characters, once for each character of the string. So, the long form of GET can be thought of as:

```
procedure GET(FILE:in FILE_TYPE; ITEM:out STRING) is
begin
  for CH in ITEM'RANGE loop
    GET(FILE, ITEM(CH));
  end loop;
end GET;
```

This equivalence reinforces the fact that a string may be spread over a number of lines. In a bounded text file, line (and page) terminators will be skipped as required, until sufficient characters have been read to fill the string. These terminators will not form part of the string itself.

PUT is also equivalent to repeated calls of the corresponding procedure for character output. Line (and page) teminators will automatically be output for a bounded file.

GET and PUT have no effect if the string parameter is null.

GET_LINE is a very useful procedure, which reads in a number of characters into a string until either a line terminator is met, or the actual string parameter for ITEM is full. In the former case, the line terminator causes the GET_LINE to terminate as if SKIP_LINE had been called at that point — any characters of the string that are not assigned values in the input operation will be undefined. The parameter, LAST, gives the index (position) of the last character actually read into the string. This makes the procedure applicable to the input of variable length strings. If no characters are read, there being no characters between the current column and the line terminator, the value of LAST will be (ITEM'FIRST−1).

PUT_LINE has the same effect as a call of PUT to write a string, followed by a call of NEW_LINE. This is another useful procedure. (Additional line terminators will be generated automatically, if the file is bounded and the format requires them.)

Unit 10.1 illustrates the use of many of the TEXT_IO subprograms. It is written as a library procedure that would be called by a user program. The procedure checks the validity of editing the file, the external name of which is supplied by the user. If the file is already open, control is passed out of the procedure. Other error conditions are handled within the procedure itself. Similar action is taken with output file validity checking.

```
with TEXT_IO;
use  TEXT_IO;
procedure EDIT is

   SPACE:constant CHARACTER:=' ';
   NAME_LENGTH:constant INTEGER:=32;
   subtype NAME_TYPE is STRING(1..NAME_LENGTH);
   INPUT_NAME:NAME_TYPE;
   IN_LENGTH:NATURAL range 0..NAME_LENGTH;
   INPUT, OUTPUT, WORK_FILE:FILE_TYPE;
   ESCAPE:exception;

   procedure GET_INPUT_NAME is
   begin
     loop
       begin
         PUT("Name of file to be edited (<CR> to quit)? ");
         GET_LINE(INPUT_NAME, IN_LENGTH);
         if IN_LENGTH = 0 then
           raise ESCAPE;              -- to escape from editor
         end if;
         OPEN(INPUT, IN_FILE, INPUT_NAME(1..IN_LENGTH));
         exit;
       exception
         when STATUS_ERROR=>
           PUT_LINE("File already open. Close it before editing.");
           PUT_LINE("Edit abandoned.");
           raise ESCAPE;
         when NAME_ERROR=>
           PUT_LINE("No file with this name exists.");
           PUT_LINE("Try again.");
         when USE_ERROR=>
           PUT_LINE("File cannot be opened for reading.");
```

```
            PUT_LINE("Check name and re-try.");
      end;
    end loop;
end GET_INPUT_NAME;

procedure COPY(FROM, TO:in out FILE_TYPE) is
  CH:CHARACTER;
begin
  RESET(FROM, IN_FILE);
  RESET(TO, OUT_FILE);
  -- copy the structure
  SET_LINE_LENGTH(TO, LINE_LENGTH(FROM));
  SET_PAGE_LENGTH(TO, PAGE_LENGTH(FROM));
  -- copy the contents
  while not END_OF_FILE(FROM) loop
    if END_OF_PAGE(FROM) then
      NEW_PAGE(TO);
    elsif END_OF_LINE(FROM) then
      NEW_LINE(TO);
    else
      GET(TO, CH);
      PUT(FROM, CH);
    end if;
  end loop;
end COPY;

procedure DO_EDIT is
begin
  null; -- editing operations on WORK_FILE
end DO_EDIT;

procedure ABANDON is
-- Saves WORK_FILE before quitting.
  PANIC_FILE:FILE_TYPE;
  PANIC_NAME:constant STRING:="ZZZEDIT";
begin
  CREATE(PANIC_FILE, NAME => PANIC_NAME);
  RESET(WORK_FILE, IN_FILE);
  COPY(WORK_FILE, PANIC_FILE);
  CLOSE(PANIC_FILE);
  PUT_LINE("Edit abandoned.");
  PUT_LINE("Work file saved in " & PANIC_NAME);
  raise ESCAPE;
end ABANDON;

procedure GET_OUTPUT_NAME is
  OUTPUT_NAME:NAME_TYPE;
  OUT_LENGTH:NATURAL range 0..NAME_LENGTH;
  CH:CHARACTER;
begin
  loop
    PUT("Output file name ? ");
    GET_LINE(OUTPUT_NAME, OUT_LENGTH);
    if OUT_LENGTH = IN_LENGTH and then
       OUTPUT_NAME(1..OUT_LENGTH) =
       INPUT_NAME(1..IN_LENGTH)
    then
      PUT("Overwrite original file (y/n) ? ");
      GET(CH);
      if CH = 'y' or CH = 'Y' then
        if IS_OPEN(INPUT) then
          CLOSE(INPUT);
```

```
          end if;
        OPEN(OUTPUT, OUT_FILE, OUTPUT_NAME(1..OUT_LENGTH));
          return;
        end if;
      else      -- different file names
        exit;
      end if;
    end loop;
    CREATE(OUTPUT, NAME => OUTPUT_NAME(1..OUT_LENGTH));
  exception
    when STATUS_ERROR =>
      PUT_LINE("File already open.");
      ABANDON;
    when USE_ERROR=>
      PUT_LINE("File cannot be opened for writing.");
        ABANDON;
    end GET_OUTPUT_NAME;

begin     -- EDIT
  GET_INPUT_NAME;
  CREATE(WORK_FILE);
  COPY(INPUT, WORK_FILE);
  RESET(WORK_FILE, IN_FILE);
  DO_EDIT;
  GET_OUTPUT_NAME;
  COPY(WORK_FILE, OUTPUT);
  if IS_OPEN(INPUT) then
    CLOSE(INPUT);
  end if;
  CLOSE(OUTPUT);
  CLOSE(WORK_FILE);
exception
  when ESCAPE=>
    if IS_OPEN(INPUT) then
      CLOSE(INPUT);
    end if;
    if IS_OPEN(WORK_FILE) then
      CLOSE(WORK_FILE);
    end if;
end EDIT;
```

Unit 10.1 A text file editor, in outline.

Procedure COPY is first called to create a working copy of the original file. The copy will have exactly the same format as the original. After the editing operations, which have been omitted from the example, owing to space restrictions, the destination file name is obtained, and the work file is then copied into it.

Generic package INTEGER_IO

```
generic
  type NUM is range ⟨⟩;
package INTEGER_IO is
```

```
DEFAULT_WIDTH:FIELD:=NUM'WIDTH;
DEFAULT_BASE:NUMBER_BASE:=10;

procedure GET (FILE:in FILE_TYPE;
               ITEM:out NUM;
               WIDTH:in FIELD:=0);
procedure GET (ITEM:out NUM; WIDTH:in FIELD:=0);

procedure PUT (FILE:in FILE_TYPE;
               ITEM:in NUM;
               WIDTH:in FIELD:=DEFAULT_WIDTH;
               BASE:in NUMBER_BASE:=DEFAULT_BASE);
procedure PUT (ITEM:in NUM;
               WIDTH:in FIELD:=DEFAULT_WIDTH;
               BASE:in    NUMBER_BASE:=DEFAULT_BASE);

procedure GET (FROM:in STRING;
               ITEM:out NUM;
               LAST:out POSITIVE);
procedure PUT (TO:out STRING;
               ITEM:in NUM;
               BASE:in NUMBER_BASE:=DEFAULT_BASE);
end INTEGER_IO;
```

INTEGER_IO has to be instantiated for each integer type for which i/o
is required, passing that type to the generic formal parameter, NUM.
Each instantiation will have its own DEFAULT_WIDTH and DEFAULT_
BASE, which are used by the PUT procedures. DEFAULT_WIDTH is
automatically initialised to the WIDTH of the actual type for which the
package is instantiated. In Chapter 8, we saw that the attribute WIDTH
yields the total number of characters required to represent the longest
value of a discrete type in textual form. The DEFAULT_BASE is initialized to decimal.

    The GET procedures read an integer from the specified FILE, or
CURRENT_INPUT. If the WIDTH parameter has the value zero (its
default), then this signifies free format input, which means that any
leading banks and/or line and page terminators will be skipped. Having
skipped over blanks and terminators a GET will attempt to read an
integer literal, which must conform to the rules for constructing integer
literals but may be preceded by a sign. If a non-zero value is supplied for

WIDTH, then exactly WIDTH characters will be read from the current line (blanks are included in the count) unless a line terminator is encountered, which will terminate the GET. If, after all this, the characters that are read are not an integer literal, or are not in the range of the actual generic parameter, then DATA_ERROR will be raised.

The corresponding PUT procedures output an integer value, without leading zeros, underscores or exponent. If the integer is negative, it will be immediately preceded by a minus sign. If the number of characters to be output (including any necessary minus sign) is fewer than WIDTH, then leading blanks will be used to right justify the value. Should more characters be required than are specified by WIDTH, the necessary length will be used. If the BASE is one other than decimal, then the rules for forming based integer literals will be used with any letters in upper case.

As you will have noticed, there is another GET and another PUT to be accounted for. These are used for reading integers from and writing them to strings, rather than files. The GET reads an integer from the beginning of the given string, FROM, setting LAST to be the index of the last character used for forming the integer ITEM. This GET behaves similarly to the file-based ones, with DATA_ERROR being raised under the same circumstances. The corresponding PUT procedure outputs the given integer value to the named string variable, TO, using TO'LENGTH as the WIDTH. LAYOUT_ERROR will be raised if this value is too small.

The following extract shows two instantiations of INTEGER_IO and some uses of them.

```
with TEXT_IO;
use TEXT_IO;

procedure MAIN is
  type ONE_BYTE is new INTEGER range -128..127;

  type TWO_BYTE is new INTEGER range -16_384..16_383;

  BYTE:ONE_BYTE;
  WORD:TWO_BYTE;

  STR_MAX:constant:=4;
  subtype STR_RANGE is INTEGER range 1..STR_MAX;
  STRING_VAL:STRING(STR_RANGE):="1234";
  LAST_CH:STR_RANGE;
```

```
      package ONE_BYTE_IO is new INTEGER_IO(ONE_BYTE);
         -- DEFAULT_WIDTH=4       DEFAULT_BASE=10

      package TWO_BYTE_IO is new INTEGER_IO(TWO_BYTE);
         -- DEFAULT_WIDTH=6       DEFAULT_BASE=10

      use ONE_BYTE_IO;
      use TWO_BYTE_IO;

   begin
      GET(BYTE);              -- Free format: skips blanks etc.
      GET(WORD, 8);           -- Reads next 8 chars, this line
      GET(STRING_VAL, WORD, LAST_CH);
                              -- WORD:=1234; (LAST_CH=4)
      PUT(STRING_VAL, ONE_BYTE'(-32));
                              -- STRING_VAL:="  -32";
      PUT(ONE_BYTE' (10));   -- Outputs "     10" (no quotes)
      PUT(TWO_BYTE' (10));   -- Outputs "        10" (no quotes)
      BYTE:=63;
      PUT(BYTE, 6);           -- Outputs "        63" (no quotes)
      PUT(BYTE, 1);           -- Outputs "   63" (no quotes)
                              -- over-riding WIDTH of 1.

      PUT(ITEM=>BYTE,
          WIDTH=>10,
          BASE=>2);           -- Outputs "  2#111111#"
                              -- (no quotes)

      -- ......
      end MAIN;
```

Note that, in the above context, the following are all erroneous:

```
      PUT(10);                        -- ILLEGAL. Ambiguous.
      PUT(STRING_VAL, 12345);         -- ILLEGAL. Amgibuous.
      GET("1234", BYTE, LAST_CH);     -- DATA_ERROR raised.
                                      -- Too large.
```

Generic package FLOAT_IO

```
      generic
        type NUM is digits ⟨⟩;
      package FLOAT_IO is
```

```
DEFAULT_FORE:FIELD:=2;
DEFAULT_AFT:FIELD:=NUM'DIGITS-1;
DEFAULT_EXP:FIELD:=3;

procedure GET   (FILE:in FILE_TYPE;
                 ITEM:out NUM;
                 WIDTH:in FIELD:=0);
procedure GET   (ITEM:out NUM:
                 WIDTH:in FIELD:=0);

procedure PUT   (FILE:in FILE_TYPE;
                 ITEM:in NUM;
                 FORE:in FIELD:=DEFAULT_FORE;
                 AFT:in FIELD:=DEFAULT_AFT;
                 EXP:in FIELD:=DEFAULT_EXP);
procedure PUT   (ITEM:in NUM;
                 FORE:in FIELD:=DEFAULT_FORE;
                 AFT:in FIELD:=DEFAULT_AFT;
                 EXP:in FIELD:=DEFAULT_EXP);

procedure GET   (FROM:in STRING;
                 ITEM:out NUM;
                 LAST:out POSITIVE);
procedure PUT   (TO:out STRING;
                 ITEM:in NUM;
                 AFT:in FIELD:=DEFAULT_AFT;
                 EXP:in FIELD:=DEFAULT_EXP);

    end FLOAT_IO;
```

The output format for real numbers (both floating and fixed point) is
determined by the values of FORE, AFT and EXP. FORE and AFT
specify the number of characters before and after the decimal point,
respectively, and have no nautical connection here. FORE may include
leading blanks and a minus sign, while AFT comprises only digits (which
may include trailing zeros). If EXP is zero, there is no exponent, otherwise the AFT field will be followed by an E and as many characters for
the exponent as specified by the value of EXP. These characters include
the sign (+ or −) and, possibly, leading zeros. Only decimal values are
written. The default values for PUT procedures are established as shown.

The GET procedures, including the one for string input, operate in
the same way as those in INTEGER_IO, so little further need be said.

Obviously, they do expect to find a real literal (and not an integer one) otherwise DATA_ERROR will be raised. The PUT procedures require a little more explanation.

Both file-based PUT procedures have parameters FORE, AFT and EXP, which have the default values of the instantiated package. If EXP is zero, then the integer part of the number will occupy as many character positions as necessary, which may cause FORE to be over-ridden. If there is no integer part, a single zero will be output before the decimal point. If EXP is greater than zero, the integer part will comprise a single digit which will be non-zero, unless the value of ITEM is 0.0. Leading blanks will precede the integer part, if it requires fewer than FORE characters.

The fractional part is rounded to the nearest value with AFT digits in the fraction. (A value of *exactly* half the last fractional digit position may be rounded up or down.)

PUT for the output of floating point numbers to a string is similar to the file-based procedure. The value of FORE will be made sufficiently large, so that the number exactly fills the string, TO. As with the INTEGER_IO counterpart, leading spaces will be used to right justify the characters.

The program in Unit 10.2 gives some examples of output formats for floating point numbers.

```
with TEXT_IO;
procedure MAIN is
   type MY_REAL is digits 6;
   package MY_REAL_IO is new TEXT_IO.FLOAT_IO(MY_REAL);
      -- defaults will be FORE=2  AFT=5  EXP=3
   use MY_REAL_IO;

   POS_NUM:MY_REAL:=123.456;
   NEG_NUM:MY_REAL:=-POS_NUM;
   MY_ZERO:constant MY_REAL:=0.0;

   procedure PUT_LINE(ITEM:in MY_REAL;
                      FORE:in TEXT_IO.FIELD:=DEFAULT_FORE;
                      AFT:in TEXT_IO.FIELD:=DEFAULT_AFT;
                      EXP:in TEXT_IO.FIELD:=DEFAULT_EXP) is
   begin
      PUT(ITEM, FORE, AFT, EXP);
      TEXT_IO.NEW_LINE;
   end PUT_LINE;

begin
   PUT_LINE(POS_NUM);              -- default   " 1.23456E+02"
   PUT_LINE(NEG_NUM);              -- default   "-1.23456E+02"
   PUT_LINE(POS_NUM*100.0);        -- default   " 1.23456E+04"
   PUT_LINE(MY_ZERO);              -- default   " 0.00000E+00"
```

```
PUT_LINE(POS_NUM,
         FORE=>3, AFT=>3, EXP=>2); --            "    1.235E+2"
PUT_LINE(NEG_NUM, 3, 3, 2);       --            "   -1.235E+2"
PUT_LINE(NEG_NUM, 1, 3, 2);       --            "-1.235E+2"
                                  -- FORE too small. Over-ridden.
PUT_LINE(NEG_NUM, 2, 3, 2);       --            "-1.235E+2"
PUT_LINE(POS_NUM, 3, 7, 4);       --            "  1.2345600E+002"
PUT_LINE(POS_NUM, 6, 2, 0);       --            "    123.46"
PUT_LINE(NEG_NUM, 6, 2, 0);       --            "   -123.46"
PUT_LINE(POS_NUM, 1, 2, 0);       --            "123.46"
                                  -- FORE too small. Over-ridden.
   end MAIN;
```

Unit 10.2 Illustration of floating point output.

Generic package FIXED_IO

generic
   type NUM is delta $\langle\rangle$;
package FIXED_IO is

  DEFAULT_FORE:FIELD:=NUM'FORE;
  DEFAULT_AFT:FIELD:=NUM'AFT;
  DEFAULT_EXP:FIELD:=0;

  procedure GET (FILE:in FILE_TYPE;
                ITEM:out NUM;
                WIDTH:in FIELD:=0);
  procedure GET (ITEM:out NUM;
                WIDTH:in FIELD:=0);

  procedure PUT (FILE:in FILE_TYPE;
                ITEM:in NUM;
                FORE:in FIELD:=DEFAULT_FORE;
                AFT:in FIELD:=DEFAULT_AFT;
                EXP:in FIELD:=DEFAULT_EXP);
  procedure PUT (ITEM:in NUM;
                FORE:in FIELD:=DEFAULT_FORE;
                AFT:in FIELD:=DEFAULT_AFT;
                EXP:in FIELD:=DEFAULT_EXP);

  procedure GET (FROM:in STRING;
                ITEM:out NUM;
                LAST:out POSITIVE);
  procedure PUT (TO:out STRING;
                ITEM:in NUM;

```
                    AFT:in FIELD:=DEFAULT_AFT;
                    EXP:in FIELD:=DEFAULT_EXP);

    end FIXED_IO;
```

As you can see, this package is almost identical to FLOAT_IO. The main difference is the initialization of the format defaults, which, sensibly, are performed to match the integer and fractional component sizes of the type for which the package is instantiated. If the default settings are used, there will be no exponent field for fixed point number output.

Generic package ENUMERATION_IO

```
generic
   type ENUM is (⟨⟩);
package ENUMERATION_IO is

  DEFAULT_WIDTH:FIELD:=0;
  DEFAULT_SETTING:TYPE_SET:=UPPER_CASE;

  procedure GET   (FILE:in FILE_TYPE; ITEM:out ENUM);
  procedure GET   (ITEM:out ENUM);

  procedure PUT   (FILE:in FILE_TYPE;
                   ITEM:in ENUM;
                   WIDTH:in FIELD:=DEFAULT_WIDTH;
                   SET:in TYPE_SET:=DEFAULT_SETTING);
  procedure PUT   (ITEM:in ENUM;
                   WIDTH:in FIELD:=DEFAULT_WIDTH;
                   SET:in TYPE_SET:=DEFAULT_SETTING);

  procedure GET   (FROM:in STRING;
                   ITEM:out ENUM;
                   LAST:out POSITIVE);
  procedure PUT   (TO:out STRING;
                   ITEM:in ENUM;
                   SET:in TYPE_SET:=DEFAULT_SETTING);

end ENUMERATION_IO;
```

This package is used to instantiate i/o packages for enumeration types (other than CHARACTER). The default WIDTH for PUT procedures is zero, which means an output value will occupy exactly as many character positions as it requires. The default style for the output of enumeration value identifiers is upper case.

The file-based GET procedures skip any leading blanks and terminators before reading an identifier or character literal of the instantiated type. Character literals must be enclosed by character quotes (a single character quote is represented by '''). DATA_ERROR is raised if the syntax is incorrect, or if the item read is not a value of the enumeration type.

The corresponding PUT procedures output the value ITEM as an enumeration literal. If it is a character, then character quotes will embrace it. The default for WIDTH may be over-ridden by supplying an actual parameter for it. If the value output has fewer than WIDTH characters, the value will be *left* justified by the appending of trailing blanks. The parameter SET may be used to control the case of the letters used for the output of enumeration value identifiers.

GET and PUT for string-based i/o of enumeration literals operates in a similar way to the file-based procedures, with the same additional comments that were made for the string-based procedures of the other generic packages.

Theoretically, it is possible to instantiate ENUMERATION_IO for integer types; however, the effect of so doing is undefined. It is possible to instantiate this generic for CHARACTER, but so doing would require all input characters to be quoted and all output characters would appear between quotes.

Renaming of i/o exceptions

```
STATUS_ERROR  :exception renames
              IO_EXCEPTIONS.STATUS_ERROR;
MODE_ERROR    :exception renames
              IO_EXCEPTIONS.MODE_ERROR;
NAME_ERROR    :exception renames
              IO_EXCEPTIONS.NAME_ERROR;
USE_ERROR     :exception renames
              IO_EXCEPTIONS.USE_ERROR;
DEVICE_ERROR  :exception renames
              IO_EXCEPTIONS.DEVICE_ERROR;
```

```
END_ERROR        :exception renames
                 IO_EXCEPTIONS.END_ERROR;
DATA_ERROR       :exception renames
                 IO_EXCEPTIONS.DATA_ERROR;
LAYOUT_ERROR:exception renames
                 IO_EXCEPTIONS.LAYOUT_ERROR;
```

The final visible part of the specification of TEXT_IO is the renaming of the exceptions exported by IO_EXCEPTIONS. This has the effect of making TEXT_IO itself export these exceptions (using the same names). User programs do not therefore have to include IO_EXCEPTIONS in a context clause for the exceptions to be visible.

10.4 SIMPLE_IO

Little needs to be said about the facilities provided by SIMPLE_IO, because it is simply a subset of TEXT_IO, together with instantiations of INTEGER_IO, FLOAT_IO and ENUMERATION_IO for the pre-defined types INTEGER, FLOAT and BOOLEAN, respectively. All the facilities exported by SIMPLE_IO are renamings of TEXT_IO sub-programs, or subprograms of the instantiated packages. Relevant i/o exceptions are also renamed for re-export (remember that they were originally renamed in TEXT_IO itself).

You can add whatever routines you want to the package and, of course, you can remove any superfluous subprograms, thereby creating a single i/o package to suit your everyday requirements. If you do augment SIMPLE_IO, take care to ensure that any renamed subprograms match the originals in TEXT_IO (or some other source package). Also note that you have to be careful about naming the origin of types and defaults, distinguishing between what is exported by TEXT_IO, such as FIELD, and what is exported by an instantiation, as is the case with INT_IO.DEFAULT_WIDTH, for example).

```
with TEXT_IO;
use  TEXT_IO;
package SIMPLE_IO is

   -- line control

   procedure NEW_LINE (SPACING:in POSITIVE_COUNT:=1)
                       renames TEXT_IO.NEW_LINE;

   procedure SKIP_LINE (SPACING:in POSITIVE_COUNT:=1)
                        renames TEXT_IO.SKIP_LINE;
```

```
function END_OF_LINE return BOOLEAN
                    renames TEXT_IO.END_OF_LINE;

-- CHARACTER i/o

procedure GET (ITEM:out CHARACTER)
            renames TEXT_IO.GET;

procedure PUT (ITEM:in CHARACTER)
            renames TEXT_IO.PUT;

-- STRING i/o

procedure GET (ITEM:out STRING)
            renames TEXT_IO.GET;

procedure PUT (ITEM:in STRING)
            renames TEXT_IO.PUT;

procedure GET_LINE (ITEM:out STRING; LAST:out NATURAL)
                    renames TEXT_IO.GET_LINE;

procedure PUT_LINE (ITEM:in STRING)
                    renames TEXT_IO.PUT_LINE;

-- INTEGER i/o

package INT_IO is new INTEGER_IO(INTEGER);

procedure GET (ITEM:out INTEGER; WIDTH:in FIELD:=0)
            renames INT_IO.GET;

procedure PUT (ITEM :in INTEGER;
               WIDTH:in FIELD:=INT_IO.DEFAULT_WIDTH;
               BASE :in NUMBER_BASE:=INT_IO.DEFAULT_BASE)
            renames INT_IO.PUT;

-- FLOAT i/o

package REAL_IO is new FLOAT_IO(FLOAT);

procedure GET (ITEM:out FLOAT; WIDTH:in FIELD:=0)
            renames REAL_IO.GET;

procedure PUT (ITEM:in FLOAT;
               FORE:in FIELD:=REAL_IO.DEFAULT_FORE;
               AFT :in FIELD:=REAL_IO.DEFAULT_AFT;
               EXP :in FIELD:=REAL_IO.DEFAULT_EXP)
            renames REAL_IO.PUT;

-- BOOLEAN i/o

package BOOLEAN_IO is new ENUMERATION_IO(BOOLEAN);

procedure GET (ITEM:out BOOLEAN)
            renames BOOLEAN_IO.GET;

procedure PUT (ITEM :in BOOLEAN;
               WIDTH:in FIELD:=BOOLEAN_IO.DEFAULT_WIDTH;
               SET  :in TYPE_SET:=BOOLEAN_IO.DEFAULT_SETTING)
            renames BOOLEAN_IO.PUT;
```

```
-- i/o exceptions

DEVICE_ERROR   :exception renames TEXT_IO.DEVICE_ERROR;
END_ERROR      :exception renames TEXT_IO.END_ERROR;
DATA_ERROR     :exception renames TEXT_IO.DATA_ERROR;
end SIMPLE_IO;
```

Unit 10.3   The non-standard package, SIMPLE_IO.

10.5 File processing [LRM 14.2]

Having discussed TEXT_IO at some length, we now look at the two pre-defined generic packages for processing binary files, i.e. files that are not held as (readable) characters but as memory images, or bit patterns. These files may only be read and written by Ada programs — it cannot be assumed that any other software or human can read or create them. Because they are not text files, binary files have no line or page structure. Whichever generic package is used, it has to be instantiated for the component type in question. First, consider the package for sequential files.

Generic package SEQUENTIAL_IO

Sequential files are files of components that can only be processed in sequence. Therefore, when writing to a sequential file, the first value is written at the start, the second follows immediately, and so on. On reading such a file, the elements are input in the same sequence, from first component to last.

As you will see from the listing of the specification below, its beginning and end are almost identical to the equivalent parts of TEXT_IO. CREATE, OPEN and so on, are the same, and all the exceptions (except LAYOUT_ERROR, which is only relevant to text files) are renamed at the end of the specification. The only items requiring explanation are the subprograms READ, WRITE and END_OF_FILE.

```
with IO_EXCEPTIONS;
generic
   type ELEMENT_TYPE is private;
package SEQUENTIAL_IO is

   type FILE_TYPE is limited private;

   type FILE_MODE is (IN_FILE, OUT_FILE);
```

-- File management

```
procedure CREATE    (FILE:in out FILE_TYPE;
                     MODE:in FILE_MODE:=OUT_FILE;
                     NAME:in STRING:="";
                     FORM:in STRING:="");
procedure OPEN      (FILE:in out FILE_TYPE;
                     MODE:in FILE_MODE;
                     NAME:in STRING;
                     FORM:in STRING:="");

procedure CLOSE     (FILE:in out FILE_TYPE);
procedure DELETE    (FILE:in out FILE_TYPE);
procedure RESET     (FILE:in out FILE_TYPE;
                     MODE:in FILE_MODE);
procedure RESET     (FILE:in out FILE_TYPE);

function MODE    (FILE:in FILE_TYPE) return FILE_MODE;
function NAME    (FILE:in FILE_TYPE) return STRING;
function FORM    (FILE:in FILE_TYPE) return STRING;
function IS_OPEN (FILE:in FILE_TYPE) return BOOLEAN;
```

-- Input and output operations

```
procedure READ     (FILE:in FILE_TYPE;
                    ITEM:out ELEMENT_TYPE);
procedure WRITE    (FILE:in FILE_TYPE;
                    ITEM:in ELEMENT_TYPE);

function END_OF_FILE (FILE:in FILE_TYPE)
                    return BOOLEAN;
```

-- Exceptions

```
STATUS_ERROR:exception renames
             IO_EXCEPTIONS.STATUS_ERROR;
MODE_ERROR  :exception renames
             IO_EXCEPTIONS.MODE_ERROR;
NAME_ERROR  :exception renames
             IO_EXCEPTIONS.NAME_ERROR;
USE_ERROR   :exception renames
             IO_EXCEPTIONS.USE_ERROR;
DEVICE_ERROR:exception renames
             IO_EXCEPTIONS.DEVICE_ERROR;
```

```
END_ERROR      :exception renames
                IO_EXCEPTIONS.END_ERROR;
DATA_ERROR     :exception renames
                IO_EXCEPTIONS.DATA_ERROR;

private
   -- implementation-dependent
end SEQUENTIAL_IO;
```

READ simply reads the next ITEM from the file, FILE. If there are no more items to be read, then END_ERROR will be raised. WRITE writes ITEM to the file, immediately after the last component written. The function END_OF_FILE enables an input file to be tested to see if there are more components to be read, as with the equivalent function in TEXT_IO.

Sequential file processing operates in the same manner as the text file processing in procedure EDIT. Text files are, after all, sequences of characters. Updating a sequential file, then requires copying the existing file up to the amendment point, making the amendment, then copying the remainder of the original file. The new file is then copied back to the original, if required. Direct files are not so cumbersome to use.

Generic package DIRECT_IO

Direct files are the disk equivalent of arrays in memory, being a collection of components, any one of which may be accessed *directly* using some index. The first component has an index of one. Each open file has a current index associated with it. Much of the specification of this package is similar to that of SEQUENTIAL_IO.

```
with IO_EXCEPTIONS;
generic
   type ELEMENT_TYPE is private;
package DIRECT_IO is

   type FILE_TYPE is limited private;

   type FILE_MODE is (IN_FILE, INOUT_FILE, OUT_FILE);
   type COUNT is range 0..implementation_defined;
   subtype POSITIVE_COUNT is COUNT
         range 1..COUNT'LAST;
```

-- File management

```
procedure CREATE   (FILE:in out FILE_TYPE;
                    MODE:in FILE_MODE:=INOUT_FILE;
                    NAME:in STRING:="";
                    FORM:in STRING:="");
procedure OPEN      (FILE:in out FILE_TYPE;
                    MODE:in FILE_MODE;
                    NAME:in STRING;
                    FORM:in STRING:="");

procedure CLOSE     (FILE:in out FILE_TYPE);
procedure DELETE    (FILE:in out FILE_TYPE);
procedure RESET     FILE:in out FILE_TYPE;
                    MODE:in FILE_MODE);
procedure RESET     (FILE:in out FILE_TYPE);

function MODE   (FILE:in FILE_TYPE) return FILE_MODE;
function NAME   (FILE:in FILE_TYPE) return STRING;
function FORM   (FILE:in FILE_TYPE) return STRING;

function IS_OPEN  (FILE:in FILE_TYPE)
                  return BOOLEAN;
```

-- Input and output operations

```
procedure READ      (FILE:in FILE_TYPE;
                    ITEM:out ELEMENT_TYPE;
                    FROM:in POSITIVE_COUNT);
procedure READ      (FILE:in FILE_TYPE;
                    ITEM:out ELEMENT_TYPE);

procedure WRITE     (FILE:in FILE_TYPE;
                    ITEM:in ELEMENT_TYPE;
                    TO:in POSITIVE_COUNT);
procedure WRITE     (FILE:in FILE_TYPE;
                    ITEM:in ELEMENT_TYPE;

procedure SET_INDEX  (FILE:in FILE_TYPE;
                     TO: in POSITIVE_COUNT);

function INDEX (FILE:in FILE_TYPE)
               return POSITIVE_COUNT;
function SIZE   (FILE:in FILE_TYPE) return COUNT;
```

```
function END_OF_FILE (FILE:in FILE_TYPE)
                    return BOOLEAN;

-- Exceptions
STATUS_ERROR:exception renames
                    IO_EXCEPTIONS.STATUS_ERROR;
MODE_ERROR   :exception renames
                    IO_EXCEPTIONS.MODE_ERROR;
NAME_ERROR   :exception renames
                    IO_EXCEPTIONS.NAME_ERROR;
USE_ERROR    :exception renames
                    IO_EXCEPTIONS.USE_ERROR;
DEVICE_ERROR:exception renames
                    IO_EXCEPTIONS.DEVICE_ERROR;
END_ERROR    :exception renames
                    IO_EXCEPTIONS.END_ERROR;
DATA_ERROR   :exception renames
                    IO_EXCEPTIONS.DATA_ERROR;

private
   -- implementation-dependent
end DIRECT_IO;
```

The first thing to note is that there is an additional file mode, IN-OUT_FILE. This mode reflects the fact that direct files may be open for reading *and* writing. The package introduces COUNT as a non-negative integer type which defines the values of the file index. CREATE differs from its namesake in SEQUENTIAL_IO in that the default mode is INOUT_FILE. The other file management subprogram specifications are the same.

In DIRECT_IO, there are two versions of the READ and WRITE procedures. The READ procedures operate on files of mode IN_FILE or INOUT_FILE. The first form has a parameter FORM, which is used to set the current index of the file before reading. READ returns the ITEM at the position in the file that is specified by the current index, and then causes that index to be increased by one. END_ERROR is raised, if the specified index is beyond the size of the external file. An implementation is not obliged to check that ITEM is a valid value of ELEMENT_TYPE, as this could be quite an involved process.

The two forms of the WRITE procedure mirror those of READ. The first sets the current index to the value of TO before writing. When the ITEM has been written to the current index position, the index is incremented.

SET_INDEX sets the current index of a file of any mode to the actual parameter provided for TO. (This may exceed the current size of the file.) The function INDEX returns the current index of a file, and SIZE returns the current size of the external file currently associated with the given file. END_OF_FILE operates as it does in its other incarnations.

Direct files are much more convenient than sequential ones, from the programmer's point of view. If they are actually implemented as direct access files, processing individual file components can be executed relatively quickly.

It is possible to set the index of a direct access file well beyond the size of the current file (as long as the external file is large enough). If an attempt is made to READ from that position, END_ERROR will be raised. However, it is possible to write to that position. Any intervening components, holes, if you like, will be undefined.

To include a complete, realistic direct file processing package would be too lengthy. The following is therefore only an outline of a package, which manages a file of bank accounts. The given details concentrate on the file operations. Use clauses have been omitted, so that the origin of all items exported by i/o packages is obvious.

```
with DIRECT_IO, TEXT_IO;
package ACCOUNT_MANAGER is

   type ACC_NUM is private;
   procedure OPEN_ACCOUNT(ACC:out ACC_NUM);
   procedure PUT_BALANCE(ACC:in ACC_NUM);
   procedure UPDATE_ACCOUNT(ACC:in ACC_NUM);
   procedure PUT_ALL_ACCOUNTS;
   procedure START_UP;
   procedure SHUT_DOWN;

private
   subtype DIGIT is CHARACTER range '0'..'9';
   type ACC_NUM is array (1..8) of DIGIT;
end ACCOUNT_MANAGER;

package body ACCOUNT_MANAGER is

   type MONEY is new INTEGER;
   subtype POUNDS_PART is MONEY range 0..9_999;
   subtype PENCE_PART is MONEY range 0..99;
   type RED_OR_BLACK is (DEBIT, CREDIT);

   type AMOUNT is
   record
     STATUS:RED_OR_BLACK:=CREDIT;
     POUNDS:POUNDS_PART:=0;
     PENCE:PENCE_PART:=0;
   end record;
```

```
type ACCOUNT is
record
  -- information fields
  BALANCE:AMOUNT;
end record;

package MONEY_IO is new TEXT_IO.INTEGER_IO(MONEY);

package ACCOUNT_IO is new DIRECT_IO(ACCOUNT);

ACCOUNT_FILE:ACCOUNT_IO.FILE_TYPE;
NEXT:ACCOUNT_IO.COUNT:=0;

function ACC_TO_INDEX(ACC:in ACC_NUM)
                      return ACCOUNT_IO.COUNT is
  -- returns conversion of account num to file index
begin
  return 12345678;        -- for compilation
end ACC_TO_INDEX;

function INDEX_TO_ACC(INDEX:in ACCOUNT_IO.COUNT)
                      return ACC_NUM is
  -- returns conversion of file index to account num
begin
  return "12345678";      -- for compilation
end INDEX_TO_ACC;

procedure OPEN_ACCOUNT(ACC:out ACC_NUM) is
  ACC_DETAILS:ACCOUNT;
begin
  NEXT:=ACCOUNT_IO.COUNT'SUCC(ACCOUNT_IO.SIZE(ACCOUNT_FILE));
  -- Fill in account details. Balance will be (CREDIT, 0, 0)
  ACCOUNT_IO.WRITE(ACCOUNT_FILE, ACC_DETAILS, NEXT);
  ACC:=INDEX_TO_ACC(NEXT);
exception
  when ACCOUNT_IO.USE_ERROR=>
    TEXT_IO.PUT_LINE("File capacity exceeded.");
end OPEN_ACCOUNT;

procedure PUT_BALANCE(ACC:in ACC_NUM) is
  INDX:ACCOUNT_IO.COUNT:=ACC_TO_INDEX(ACC);
  THIS_ACC:ACCOUNT;
begin
  ACCOUNT_IO.READ(ACCOUNT_FILE, THIS_ACC, INDX);
  -- use TEXT_IO for output of details
  -- use MONEY_IO for output of BALANCE
end PUT_BALANCE;

procedure UPDATE_ACCOUNT(ACC:in ACC_NUM) is
  INDX:ACCOUNT_IO.COUNT:=ACC_TO_INDEX(ACC);
  THIS_ACC:ACCOUNT;
begin
  ACCOUNT_IO.READ(ACCOUNT_FILE, THIS_ACC, INDX);
  -- use TEXT_IO and MONEY_IO to read credit/debit amount
  -- update THIS_ACC.BALANCE accordingly
  ACCOUNT_IO.WRITE(ACCOUNT_FILE, THIS_ACC, INDX);
end UPDATE_ACCOUNT;

procedure PUT_ALL_ACCOUNTS is
  THIS_ACC:ACCOUNT;
begin
  -- use TEXT_IO to write headings
```

```
    ACCOUNT_IO.SET_INDEX(ACCOUNT_FILE,1);
    while not ACCOUNT_IO.END_OF_FILE(ACCOUNT_FILE) loop
      ACCOUNT_IO.READ(ACCOUNT_FILE, THIS_ACC);
      -- use TEXT_IO and MONEY_IO to write details
      -- (or use a subprogram also common to PUT_BALANCE)
    end loop;
  end PUT_ALL_ACCOUNTS;

  procedure START_UP is
  -- Used to initialise file, or restart after a crash.
    FILE_NAME:STRING(1..16);
    FILE_EXISTS:BOOLEAN;
  begin
    -- use TEXT_IO to ask user for external file name
    -- and if the FILE_EXISTS
    if FILE_EXISTS then
      ACCOUNT_IO.OPEN(ACCOUNT_FILE,
                      ACCOUNT_IO.INOUT_FILE, FILE_NAME);
    else
      ACCOUNT_IO.CREATE(ACCOUNT_FILE, NAME=>FILE_NAME);
        -- INOUT_FILE by default
    end if;
  end START_UP;

  procedure SHUT_DOWN is
  begin
    ACCOUNT_IO.CLOSE(ACCOUNT_FILE);
  end SHUT_DOWN;

begin
  START_UP;
end ACCOUNT_MANAGER;
```

Unit 10.4   A package for processing files of records, in outline.

10.6 LOW_LEVEL_IO [LRM 14.6]

This package is provided, not for general use, but for applications where direct interaction with the i/o devices is required. Consequently, the package will be highly implementation dependent. It would be normal to perform such low-level device control using tasks, so that correct synchronization can be obtained. Obviously, where portability is important, this package should not be used. However, a desire to communicate directly with the i/o hardware would normally indicate a system-specific application, anyway.

Not all implementations do, in fact, provide LOW_LEVEL_IO, for the running environment does not always allow direct communication with the i/o hardware. Instead, i/o packages that interface with operating system i/o routines may be provided, which keeps the operating system in control of the i/o devices.

10.7 Ins and outs

Whatever further i/o facilities are required, these should always be provided by additional packages, inside which all unnecessary details should be hidden. You may well find that your implementation already provides i/o packages over and above those required by the LRM.

It is more important to provide a clear, consistent interface (friendly, if you like) for the user, rather than concentrate on efficiency. (Efficiency here relates more to execution efficiency than programmer efficiency.) So, in an environment for inexperienced programmers, for example, it would be useful to provide a package, SAFE_TEXT_IO, perhaps, which would export many of the features of TEXT_IO, but be more robust. Most exceptions would be handled by the subprograms of SAFE_TEXT_IO, so that if DATA_ERROR were to occur during a GET, an error message would be issued and the user re-prompted for input (with some convenient means of escape). Germs of these ideas are contained in procedure EDIT in Unit 10.1. It makes sense to use exceptions to handle invalid input but it is not always convenient for the end user to have to handle them.

There are portability questions about the i/o packages which may not be immediately apparent. Typically, file naming conventions differ from system to system. Therefore, any programs for which portability is important should not contain external file name literals. It is better to read file names as strings at run-time or, at least, collect them as string constants in a package of implementation dependent entities. The use of the FORM parameter has already been cited as a feature that is implementation specific.

Different environments may impose different file size limitations, which could lead to behavioural variations. There is no easy general solution to this problem.

Finally, you should, by now, be fully aware that the representation of numeric types may differ from one implementation to the next. If portability is important, then you should not leave formatting to the mercy of the defaults of a particular system, but exercise your own control. For example, you might carry the following package around with you.

```
with TEXT_IO;
package MY_REAL_STUFF is
  type MY_REAL is digits 6;
  package MY_REAL_IO is new
         TEXT_IO.FLOAT_IO(MY_REAL);
end MY_REAL_STUFF;
```

This has two advantages. The first is that MY_REAL will always have the same precision, whereas FLOAT will not. Also, MY_REAL_IO will always use the same formatting parameters, whereas instantiation of FLOAT_IO for FLOAT on different systems would not.

Practising Ada 10

Make sure you understand TEXT_IO and SIMPLE_IO. Try any features you haven't yet used. Get as much experience of using files as you can. If you can't think of anything better:

1 Complete the editor of Unit 10.1. Build up the editing facilities slowly, adding one feature at a time. Base it on a line editor with which you are familiar.

2 Define a generic package that exports a floating point type of decimal digit precision specified by the instantiator, together with an i/o package for that type.

3 Develop the account manager package of Unit 10.4 into a complete system.

4 If you have not already done so, create your own i/o package which meets your everyday programming requirements.

Chapter 11

Tasks [LRM 9]

This book cannot devote sufficient space to tasks to cover all aspects of their nature and use. Tasking is a specialized subject, which requires additional programming skills and experience in order to effect correct solutions. Tasks are the major *active* components of an embedded system program, so that it is usually imperative that such programs be correct.

In this chapter, most of the features of tasks are introduced, but not with lengthy discussions as to how they should all be used. If you are going to be programming embedded systems using Ada, it is first of all most important that you become *au fait* with the other elements of the language. Once you are at home with Ada, turn your attention to tasking and, before writing the code for an autopilot, or nuclear power plant controller, consult more specialized texts, such as [1, 2, 6].

11.1 The nature of tasks

In a sequential Ada program, i.e. one without tasks, there is a single thread of control throughout program execution, which starts at the beginning of the code for the main program and terminates on completion of the main program. This single thread of control may involve the temporary transfer of control to subprograms, which may be deeply nested, but the essential characteristic is that, at any time, there is only one statement that can execute and you can determine which will be the next to execute, knowing the current statement.

Tasks are *concurrent* units of Ada programs. Each task will have its own thread of control, which reflects the fact that each one has an independent execution path. (There may be times when these paths need to meet, as you will see, but essentially, tasks are independent, active program units.)

To illustrate this, consider some events in a day in the life of a family:

- 07.00   All get up.
- 07.30   Have breakfast.
- 08.15   Paul takes Ellen and Beth to school.
- 08.30   Ellen and Beth start school.
- 08.35   Christine takes Anna to playschool.

254

08.45 Paul starts work. Anna starts playschool.
09.00 Christine starts class.
10.15 Christine goes to library.
11.30 Christine leaves to collect Anna.
11.45 Anna goes home with Christine.
12.00 Ellen and Beth have lunch at school.
12.15 Christine and Anna have lunch.
12.30 Paul has lunch at work.
14.15 Christine and Anna go to meet Ellen and Beth.
14.30 Ellen and Beth finish school and go home.
14.45 Ellen, Beth and Anna play.
15.40 Christine cooks.
17.00 Paul leaves work.
17.15 Paul arrives home. All eat dinner.

and so their day continues. The way these activities have been expressed is as a single "program", or schedule. However, this does not constitute a very natural representation, because each member of the family has a different role to act out even though, at times, these roles interact. A more faithful description would be to have the five life histories expressed as independent units as in:

Anna (A)		Christine (C)	
07.00	Get up.	07.00	Get up.
07.30	Have breakfast.	07.30	Have breakfast.
08.35	Go to playschool with C.	08.35	Take A to playschool.
08.45	Start playschool.	09.00	Start class.
11.45	Go home with C.	10.15	Go to library.
12.15	Have lunch.	11.30	Leave to collect A.
14.15	Go to meet E and B.	11.45	Collect A and go home.
14.30	Meet E and B and go home.	12.15	Have lunch
14.45	Play.	14.15	Go to meet E and B.
17.15	Eat dinner.	14.30	Meet E and B and go home.
		15.40	Cook.
		17.15	Eat dinner.

These two outlines are sufficient to convey the idea. Ellen and Beth will have identical "scripts" but, nevertheless, each has her own independent thread of control. Although each member of the family has this independence, there are many occasions when the life histories come together. This is typical in concurrent situations. Here we have five concurrent people. If we want to express this concurrency in an Ada program, then this can be done using tasks, one for each person. Should a sixth person need to be added to the drama, this would only necessitate the addition of a sixth task, rather than a manual threading of the additional life history into the global (sequential) picture.

The reasons for wanting to express concurrency are usually because it reflects the nature of the problem being programmed and not because we want to execute the concurrent units in parallel. We will turn to execution considerations in a moment.

There are three main uses of tasks:

(i) as modelling agents, like in the family life histories, where it is desirable to reflect the concurrency in the application by the structure of the program.

(ii) as resource and process controllers, to control access to shared resources by concurrent tasks, and to control external processes (as in a typical embedded system).

(iii) for expressing concurrent algorithms, where there are advantages to implementing an algorithm as a number of concurrent elements, each of which handles a subset of the overall problem.

It was clear from the family example that concurrent tasks often require synchronization. In general, this might be because tasks need to communicate by exchanging information, or it might be that certain actions have to be performed simultaneously. Alternatively, simultaneity might be the one thing you want to avoid, if you are trying to ensure mutually exclusive access to some critical, unshareable resource.

Now, back to concurrency and execution considerations. Assume that you have five tasks, one for each family member, but, as is usually the case, there is only one central processor to execute them all. The five tasks then have to share the single processor by *interleaved execution*. First, one task will execute for a short time, then another, and so on. The overall effect is one of *apparent concurrency*.

If you are very lucky and have five processors at your disposal, then it is possible to allocate one task to each processor. You then have *true concurrency*, as each task is able to execute in parallel.

Whether or not true concurrency is possible, the *logic* of concurrent programs should not be dependent on the number of processors available. We want concurrency, remember, because it matches the nature of the application. Indeed, the Ada scheme for synchronizing and controlling tasks is designed to work in the same way on any number and any configuration of processors. So, the *effect* of concurrent programs should not change with a different processor configuration although, obviously, the execution time could alter drastically.

11.2 Packages are passive

It is useful to compare tasks with packages, as they share certain similarities but are, nevertheless, fundamentally different.

Packages, as we have seen, are important units for the modular construction of (large) programs, which can exercise a certain degree of control over the way they are used. For example, exported types may be private, and critical information may be hidden from users. It is an inescapable fact, though, that packages are *passive* objects, which are not able to control how their subprograms are called. In a sequential program, this does not present a problem but in a concurrent environment, it is not acceptable.

To illustrate this, consider the outline in Unit 11.1, in which there are two tasks, a producer and a consumer, which have their production and consumption recorded by an integer hidden within the package HIDDEN_TALLY.

```
-- with relevant library units
procedure MAIN is

    package HIDDEN_TALLY is
       procedure INCREMENT;
       procedure DECREMENT;
    end HIDDEN_TALLY;

    task PRODUCER;

    task CONSUMER;

    package body HIDDEN_TALLY is
       COUNT:NATURAL:=0;

       procedure INCREMENT is
       begin
          COUNT:=COUNT + 1;
       end INCREMENT;

       procedure DECREMENT is
       begin
          COUNT:=COUNT - 1;
       end DECREMENT;

    end HIDDEN_TALLY;

    task body PRODUCER is
    begin
      loop
        -- produce something
        HIDDEN_TALLY.INCREMENT;
      end loop;
    end PRODUCER;
```

```
task body CONSUMER is
begin
  loop
    HIDDEN_TALLY.DECREMENT;
    -- consume something
  end loop;
end CONSUMER;

begin
  -- main program statements
  null;      -- for compilation
end MAIN;
```

Unit 11.1   An insecure package.

Because there are two concurrent elements which call the package procedures, the package cannot guard against:
(i) simultaneous calls during parallel execution;
(ii) apparently simultaneous calls during interleaved execution, in which case, one call might be interrupted while the other is processed. These are really the same situation under different execution circumstances. They could both lead to the corruption of the value of COUNT, i.e. it could have an incorrect value. Satisfy yourself about exactly what could go wrong, and how it could come about.

Really, COUNT is a (hidden) resource, which is shared by the two tasks. For correct behaviour, however many processors are available for execution, mutually exclusive access to COUNT must be ensured. This can only be done by using a third task as a resource controller, as we shall see. The role of this particular resource controller is to ensure that once an INCREMENT or DECREMENT starts, it must complete before another INCREMENT or DECREMENT is allowed to start.

11.3 Task syntax and activation

Tasks comprise a specification and a body. The specification must always be present, even if it only consists of a heading, as was the case for PRODUCER and CONSUMER. All task specifications should be placed before any task bodies in some declarative part, which ensures that all specifications are visible to all bodies. It is usually better to make the task bodies separate, particularly if they are complex. Tasks themselves cannot be library units but they can be declared in a package, subprogram or generic, which may form a library unit. More will be said about this later.

A task specification may only include *entry* declarations, which, syntactically, look very much like procedure declarations in a package specification. Like procedures, entries may have parameters. The entry of a task is its interface with other tasks — it is, effectively, a synchronization point that is callable by other tasks. You will discover how this synchronization works in the next section.

The body of a task has the same structure as any other program unit body in Ada: a declarative part, a sequence of statements and an (optional) exception handler.

Task Activation

Execution of a task begins when all items in the declarative part that contains it have been elaborated. If there is more than one task in a declarative part, then the order of activation is not defined by the language — no particular activation sequence should be assumed. If a certain activation order is required, this must be realized by explicit synchronizations. A task declared in a package specification is activated when the declarative part of the package body has been elaborated.

All tasks have a *master* (or more than one), which is normally the program unit or block statement that contains its declaration. A package cannot be a master, unless it is a library unit, for packages are passive objects. A master cannot *terminate* until all its dependent tasks have terminated. We shall return to termination later. A task that depends on a block statement or subprogram may also indirectly depend on the executor of the block or subprogram, if it is another master.

11.4 Task synchronization — the rendezvous

The synchronization of tasks in Ada is achieved by the *rendezvous*, in which one task (the slave) calls an entry of another (the controller). Hence, the rendezvous is an asymmetric relationship. The controller task, i.e. the one whose entry is called, decides whether or not to *accept* an entry call — it controls the rendezvous. A simple example will show the nature of the rendezvous.

Assume that there are two tasks, a PUTTER and a GETTER. The GETTER reads a character and passes it to the PUTTER, which then writes it out, while the GETTER is free to read another character. In order to synchronize their activities, the GETTER calls an entry of the PUTTER, which has the effect of letting the called task know that there is a task waiting on the entry. The controller, PUTTER, executes an accept statement for an entry, when it is in a position to rendezvous. The code for the tasks is shown in Unit 11.2.

```
with TEXT_IO;
use  TEXT_IO;
procedure MAIN is

  TERMINATOR:constant CHARACTER:='?';

  task GETTER;

  task PUTTER is
    entry MEET(CH:in CHARACTER);
  end PUTTER;

  task body GETTER is
    CHAR:CHARACTER;
  begin
    loop
      GET(CHAR);
      PUTTER.MEET(CHAR);
      exit when CHAR = TERMINATOR;
    end loop;
  end GETTER;

  task body PUTTER is
    CHAR:CHARACTER;
  begin
    loop
      accept MEET(CH:in CHARACTER) do
        CHAR:=CH;          -- copy parameter
      end MEET;
      PUT(CHAR);
      exit when CHAR = TERMINATOR;
    end loop;
  end PUTTER;

begin
  null;                    -- no actions
end MAIN;
```

Unit 11.2   A simple rendezvous.

Once activated, both tasks cycle through their actions until the designated character, TERMINATOR, has been processed by each of them.

The order of activation of the tasks is of no consequence, as the
synchronization of the rendezvous ensures correctness. Let us now see
how this rendezvous works.

When GETTER calls PUTTER.MEET, it declares its desire to rendezvous with PUTTER. Rendezvous can only take place, however, when
both tasks are ready, which, here, requires that the called task execute an
accept statement for the called entry, MEET. If PUTTER reaches the
accept statement before GETTER has called the entry, then PUTTER
will wait for the call. GETTER must also wait if it calls MEET before
PUTTER has reached the accept statement. On rendezvous, the accept
statement is executed with both tasks effectively locked together, the

called task being in control. During rendezvous, information is exchanged via the parameter(s) of the entry. The rendezvous should always be kept as short as possible in order to maximize the independence of the participating tasks.

MAIN is the master of both tasks and, as such, cannot terminate until they, themselves, have terminated, even though MAIN has no statements to be executed.

Entries and accept statements in general

All entries (if any) must be declared in the specification of the task that owns and controls them, otherwise they are not visible to would-be callers. If a task is not to be called at all, it will not require any entries. For every entry in a task specification, there must be at least one accept statement in the body, otherwise you will have a (dissatisfied) caller that might never terminate.

Entries may have any number of parameters with the same syntax, transmission modes and meaning as subprogram parameters. The parameters in the corresponding accept statement(s) must conform to those in the entry declaration in the same way that subprogram declaration and body headings must conform.

The syntax of the accept statement is either:

    accept E;

where E is the name of the entry, or:

    accept E(⟨PARAMETERS⟩) do
       ⟨SEQUENCE_OF_STATEMENTS⟩
    end E;

In both forms, the entry may, or may not, have parameters. However, in the first form, there would be no point in having parameters, for there are no statements within the accept statement to use them. In the second outline, it is normal for the entry to have parameters, because the sequence of statements will largely be concerned with using them to exchange information with its companion. It is not mandatory, but desirable, that the entry name be repeated after the **end** of the accept statement.

Typically, the sequence of statements of an accept statement is used to transfer information via the parameters, which cannot be done outside the accept statement. This sequence of statements can include another accept statement, which would effect a rendezvous between three tasks. The first (parameterless) form of the accept statement above is used for situations where two tasks need to synchronize briefly, without exchanging information. This is illustrated by the simple resource controller that was used as the task example of Chapter 2, p. 20.

This controller regulates access to a single resource for any number of calling tasks. It does this by enforcing the sequence ACQUIRE; RELEASE; ACQUIRE; RELEASE; and so on. Each entry has its own first-in first-out (FIFO) queue of calling tasks. When an entry is accepted by the controller, the first task (if any) that is waiting on that entry, is taken for rendezvous. In this example, the first task waiting on the *other* entry will then be the next candidate for rendezvous, owing to the enforced alternation.

The calling protocol for a slave task will be:

        CONTROLLER.ACQUIRE;
          -- use the resource
        CONTROLLER.RELEASE;

(By changing ACQUIRE to WAIT, or P, and changing RELEASE to SIGNAL, or V, we have a task, which more clearly simulates a binary semaphore. Semaphores are software primitives that were designed for synchronizing concurrent processes. Semaphores are described in most books on operating systems.)

Communication between two tasks is often best achieved by the use of an intermediary task, which acts as a buffer. Unit 11.3 shows such a task, albeit a very simple one.

```
task BUFFER is
  entry PLACE(ITEM:in SOME_TYPE);
  entry TAKE(ITEM:out SOME_TYPE);
end BUFFER;

task body BUFFER is
  BUFFER:SOME_TYPE;
begin
  loop
    accept PLACE(ITEM:in SOME_TYPE) do
      BUFFER:=ITEM;
    end PLACE;
    accept TAKE(ITEM:out SOME_TYPE) do
      ITEM:=BUFFER;
    end TAKE;
  end loop;
end BUFFER;
```

Unit 11.3   A single item buffer. Not a library unit.

As you can see, the structure of BUFFER_1 is exactly the same as that of CONTROLLER. The only difference is that PLACE has a parameter for the item to be placed into the buffer and TAKE has a parameter for returning the item removed from the buffer. As with many tasks, BUFFER includes an indefinite loop. A task like this could be used as a buffer between the PUTTER and GETTER of Unit 11.2. This change is implemented in the program of Unit 11.4.

```
with TEXT_IO;
use  TEXT_IO;
procedure MAIN is

   TERMINATOR:constant CHARACTER:='?';

   task BUFFER_1 is
      entry PLACE(ITEM:in CHARACTER);
      entry TAKE(ITEM:out CHARACTER);
   end BUFFER_1;

   task GETTER;

   task PUTTER;

   task body BUFFER_1 is
      BUFFER:CHARACTER;
   begin
      loop
         accept PLACE(ITEM:in CHARACTER) do
            BUFFER:=ITEM;
         end PLACE;
         accept TAKE(ITEM:out CHARACTER) do
            ITEM:=BUFFER;
         end TAKE;
      end loop;
   end BUFFER_1;

   task body GETTER is
      CHAR:CHARACTER;
   begin
      loop
         GET(CHAR);
         BUFFER_1.PLACE(CHAR);
         exit when CHAR = TERMINATOR;
      end loop;
   end GETTER;

   task body PUTTER is
      CHAR:CHARACTER;
   begin
      loop
         BUFFER_1.TAKE(CHAR);
         PUT(CHAR);
         exit when CHAR = TERMINATOR;
      end loop;
   end PUTTER;

begin
   null;
end MAIN;
```

Unit 11.4 Using a single item buffer.

In Unit 11.4, GETTER and PUTTER terminate but BUFFER_1 (and therefore MAIN) do not. One of the aims of buffering is to allow the buffered tasks more freedom to get on with their own lives, independently of the other tasks. A single item buffer, like the one that has been used so far, enforces a lock-step synchronization of PLACE; TAKE; PLACE; TAKE; and so on, like CONTROLLER. To overcome this restriction, we need more flexibility in the controller task. This is obtained by the use of *selective waits*.

11.5 The selective wait [LRM 9.7.1]

It is in the area of tasking that Ada is at its worst for the multiple uses of reserved words. In particular, **select** and **delay** have different meanings, which can be rather confusing.

There are three forms of the select statement, each having its own syntax. The first form is the selective wait, which is used by a controller (called) task to select from calls on a number of entries. The second and third forms are the *conditional entry call* and the *timed entry call*, which, as the names imply, are used by calling tasks. The subject of this section is the first of these, the selective wait. The other forms are discussed in 11.8.

The selective wait has a variable structure which, using the BNF notations introduced earlier in the book, can be expressed as:

```
select
    ⟨SELECT_ALTERNATIVE⟩
{or
    ⟨SELECT_ALTERNATIVE⟩}
[else
    ⟨SEQUENCE_OF_STATEMENTS⟩]
end select;
```

The curly brackets indicate that there may be any number (including none) of occurrences of alternatives after an **or**, while the square brackets denote that the else part is optional.

There are three kinds of select alternative possible:

(i) *accept alternative* — an accept statement followed by an optional sequence of statements. A selective wait must have at least one of these.

(ii) *delay alternative* — a delay statement followed by an optional sequence of statements.

(iii) *terminate alternative* — just the word **terminate**.

There are additional restrictions on the structure of a selective wait, such that the presence of one component mutually excludes another. A selective wait may have:

one else part
OR
one terminate alternative
OR
one or more delay alternatives

There is an additional feature of select alternatives, the guard, that will be revealed after seeing how the basic selective wait operates. Its various facets will be introduced, one by one.

The accept alternative

Ignoring guards, the accept alternative has the structure of an accept statement followed by an optional sequence of statements:

```
accept E;
[⟨SEQUENCE_OF_STATEMENTS⟩]
```

or:

```
accept E(⟨PARAMETERS⟩) do
    ⟨SEQUENCE_OF_STATEMENTS⟩
end E;
[⟨SEQUENCE_OF_STATEMENTS⟩]
```

The optional sequence of statements (if used) in both of the above forms, is executed *after* the rendezvous of the preceding accept statement. To see how this accept alternative might be used, we go back to the buffer of Unit 11.4 and attempt to make it more useful. The first step is to increase the capacity of the buffer by having an array of buffer elements. This will be superfluous, if the lock-step synchronisation remains in force, so more flexibility is needed in the controller task. This is gained by using a selective wait with the following structure:

```
select
    accept PLACE(...) ...
or
    accept TAKE(...) ...
end select;
```

What this states is that, each time the select is executed, the buffer will accept a rendezvous with either a caller of PLACE, or a caller of TAKE. (The exact operation of the selective wait will be explained a little later.) This, then, results in the program of Unit 11.5.

```
task BUFFER_2 is
  entry PLACE(ITEM:in CHARACTER);
  entry TAKE(ITEM:out CHARACTER);
end BUFFER_2;
-- task specification as in BUFFER_1

task body BUFFER_2 is
  SIZE:constant INTEGER:=32;
  subtype BUFF_RANGE is NATURAL range 0..SIZE - 1;
  NEXT_IN, NEXT_OUT:BUFF_RANGE:=0;
  BUFFER:array (BUFF_RANGE) of CHARACTER;
begin
  loop
    select
      accept PLACE(ITEM:in CHARACTER) do
        BUFFER(NEXT_IN):=ITEM;
      end PLACE;
      NEXT_IN:=(NEXT_IN + 1) mod SIZE;
    or
      accept TAKE(ITEM:out CHARACTER) do
        ITEM:=BUFFER(NEXT_OUT);
      end TAKE;
      NEXT_OUT:=(NEXT_OUT + 1) mod SIZE;
    end select;
  end loop;
end BUFFER_2;
```

Unit 11.5   An unreliable bounded Buffer. Not a library unit.

This version of the buffer is, indeed, more flexible. However, it is a little *too* flexible, for it imposes no constraints on the acceptance of calls of PLACE and TAKE. In particular, it does not prevent rendezvous with a caller of TAKE when there are no items in the buffer, nor does it prevent rendezvous with a caller of PLACE, when the buffer is full. So, we need to add some conditions to the accept alternatives.

Guards

A guard is a conditional expression that precedes a wait alternative thus:

    when ⟨CONDITION⟩ =>
        ⟨SELECT_ALTERNATIVE⟩

So, now we have the means to make the buffer reliable. Basically, we want to prevent a TAKE from being successful, if the buffer is empty, and to prevent a PLACE from being allowed when the buffer is full. The variable ITEMS is introduced, so that the buffer can keep track of the number of (unread) items it currently contains. The necessary changes are incorporated into Unit 11.6.

```
task BUFFER_3 is
   entry PLACE(ITEM:in CHARACTER);
   entry TAKE(ITEM:out CHARACTER);
end BUFFER_3;
-- task specification as in BUFFER_1

task body BUFFER_3 is
  SIZE:constant INTEGER:=32;
  subtype BUFF_RANGE is NATURAL range 0..SIZE - 1;
  NEXT_IN, NEXT_OUT:BUFF_RANGE:=0;
  BUFFER:array (BUFF_RANGE) of CHARACTER;
  ITEMS:NATURAL range 0..SIZE:=0;
begin
  loop
    select
      when ITEMS < SIZE =>
        accept PLACE(ITEM:in CHARACTER) do
          BUFFER(NEXT_IN):=ITEM;
        end PLACE;
        NEXT_IN:=(NEXT_IN + 1) mod SIZE;
        ITEMS:=ITEMS + 1;
    or
      when ITEMS > 0 =>
        accept TAKE(ITEM:out CHARACTER) do
          ITEM:=BUFFER(NEXT_OUT);
        end TAKE;
        NEXT_OUT:=(NEXT_OUT + 1) mod SIZE;
        ITEMS:=ITEMS - 1;
    end select;
  end loop;
end BUFFER_3;
```

Unit 11.6 A bounded buffer. Not a library unit.

Remember that the rendezvous itself must always be kept as short as possible, hence the accept statements in the buffer controller only include what has to be done during the rendezvous, viz. transfer information between the buffer and the calling task. All internal housekeeping is performed outside the rendezvous.

Execution of a selective wait

The execution of a selective wait is rather intricate, and it is important, in a tasking environment, that it be correctly understood. The first thing to realize is that any guards are only evaluated once for any execution of a selective wait, and that this evaluation takes place when the **select** is executed. A select alternative that has no guard, or has a guard that has evaluated to TRUE, is called an *open* alternative. An alternative with a guard that has evaluated to FALSE is a *closed* alternative, which can play no part in the *current* execution of the select statement.

The logic of the operation of each execution of a selective wait can be expressed as follows, with if statements to highlight the decision making that is involved:

```
(i)  evaluate all guards
(ii) if ALL GUARDS CLOSED then
         if THERE IS AN else PART then
           EXECUTE else PART;
         else
           PROGRAM_ERROR raised;
         end if;
     elsif THERE IS A TASK WAITING ON AN
             OPEN accept ALTERNATIVE then
         ACCEPT RENDEZVOUS; -- if more than one, choice
                            -- is undefined
     elsif THERE IS AN else PART then
         EXECUTE else PART;
     else  -- there are open alternatives, but no callers yet
         WAIT FOR FIRST CALL TO AN OPEN ALTERNATIVE;
     end if;
```

The else part of the selective wait is an escape clause for the controller task, which enables it to avoid being committed to rendezvous, if there are no open alternatives, or if no tasks are waiting on open alternatives. In other words, if *immediate* rendezvous is not possible, the else part will take the controller out of the selective wait.

If there is more than one open alternative, which has a task already waiting, then the language does not define which of the open alternatives will be selected. The only thing that you can safely assume is that rendezvous will take place with the first task waiting in the queue of *one* of the open entries. It is to be hoped that the selection process will not lead to the undue favouring of any particular entry, and will approximate to random selection.

Because guards are only evaluated at the beginning of the execution of a selective wait, these conditions will remain in force, however long the controller has to wait for rendezvous. This is one reason why guards should not (normally) utilize global variables; it could lead to misunderstandings on the part of the programmer. To illustrate the danger, assume that GLOBAL is a variable which is global to some controller task and that the controller, in outline is:

```
select
  when GLOBAL > CUT_OFF=>
    accept E1;
or
  when GLOBAL <= CUT_OFF=>
    accept E2;
end select;
```

The guards are evaluated on entry to the select statement and will therefore reflect the value of GLOBAL at that time. If there is no task waiting on the open entry (only one of the entries can be open at a time, as the guards are mutually exclusive) then the controller task waits. Meanwhile, GLOBAL may be changed — it is beyond the control of the waiting task. This *could* result in a rendezvous with an inappropriate task, if the programmer intended that the guards represent the conditions obtaining at the time of rendezvous. If that were the programmer's intention, then an else part would provide a means of escape for the controller, which could be made to wait for a while and then loop round for another attempt at rendezvous. We now look at how such a wait can be expressed in Ada.

11.6   Delay statements and alternatives [LRM 9.6]

The multiple uses of **delay** have already been mentioned. In fact, this reserved word can be used in three contexts:
(i) as a stand-alone statement
(ii) as part of a delay alternative
(iii) for timed entry calls
The first two of these are considered in this section. Timed entry calls are discussed in 11.8. Before talking about delays of any kind, it is necessary to consider the general question of *time* in Ada programs.

TIME and DURATION

The package STANDARD includes the one pre-defined fixed point type in Ada, DURATION. Although implementation dependent, DURATION must always represent a value in seconds, up to at least one day (86_400.000 seconds), with a precision of at least 20 milliseconds. The full range of fixed point operators is applicable to objects of type DURATION.

Ada implementations must also provide a package, CALENDAR, which exports a (private) type, TIME. Subprograms and subtypes are provided to facilitate conversion between TIME values and YEAR, MONTH, DAY and SECONDS, the latter being a positive subtype of DURATION. Additional overloadings of "+" and "−" are provided for adding and subtracting types as summarized in the table:

LEFT type	Operator	RIGHT type	Result type
TIME	+	DURATION	TIME
DURATION	+	TIME	TIME
TIME	−	DURATION	TIME
TIME	−	TIME	DURATION

The function, CLOCK, returns the current value of TIME, however that value happens to be determined by the implementation. It should therefore be used with caution.

The delay statement

This statement may appear anywhere within the body of a task. It comprises the reserved word **delay** followed by an expression of type DURATION. The effect is to suspend execution of the task for *at least* the period of time specified by the expression. Of course, the actual time at which a task executes again depends on the number of processors available for execution, together with the task scheduling algorithm that is used to allocate tasks to them. Consequently, the delay statement should not be regarded as a precise task scheduling mechanism: all delays are subject to some *local drift*.

If a task has a certain action to perform at regular intervals, care must be taken to eliminate *cumulative drift*, caused by repeated occurrences of local drift. To illustrate this, consider an alarm clock task, which has to wake up every hour, on the hour and, say, ring a bell. We could have:

```
task ALARM_1;

task body ALARM_1 is
   ONE_HOUR:constant DURATION:=60.0 * 60.0;
begin
```

```
    loop
       delay ONE_HOUR;
       -- ring the bell
    end loop;
  end ALARM_1;
```

Because of local drift, each re-awakening will be a little slow. If, on average, this local drift is 5 seconds, then, over the course of a day, the error could lead to a cumulative error of two minutes. To overcome this, we need to relate the next waking up time to the real time, and not the time of the last awakening. This may be done as follows:

```
  task ALARM_2;
```

```
  task body ALARM_2 is
     ONE_HOUR:constant DURATION:=60.0 * 60.0;
     WAKE_UP_TIME:TIME:=CLOCK + ONE_HOUR;
                                      -- an hour from now
  begin
     loop
        delay WAKE_UP_TIME — CLOCK;  -- type DURATION
        -- ring the bell
        WAKE_UP_TIME:=WAKE_UP_TIME + ONE_HOUR;
                                      -- relative to last
                                      -- scheduled time
```

```
     end loop;
  end ALARM_2;
```

Note the use of the overloadings of "+" and "−" provided by CALENDAR. Each bell ringing will still be subject to local error, but not a cumulative one. A loop like this is sometimes called a regular loop.

If the expression following **delay** is negative, this has the same effect as "delay 0.0;". This does *not* necessarily mean that there will be no delay. The task is still likely to be re-scheduled for the processor(s), possibly behind any other tasks already waiting to execute.

The delay alternative

This is the second of the possible alternatives of the selective wait. The form of the delay alternative is:

```
  [when ⟨CONDITION⟩ =>]
     delay ⟨SIMPLE_EXPRESSION⟩;
  [⟨SEQUENCE_OF_STATEMENTS⟩]
```

As an alternative in a selective wait, **delay** cannot be used, if there is an else part (or a terminate alternative), owing to their being mutually exclusive. When a selective wait is executed, any open delay alternatives form the escape routes for the controller task. The delay alternative comes into play, if there are no tasks waiting on open accept alternatives. The time after **delay** specifies how long the (controller) task is prepared to wait for a call to be made to an open accept alternative. If there is no such call within that time, the sequence of statements following **delay** is executed (if any statements are present) and execution of the select statement terminates.

If there is more than one open delay alternative, the one with the smallest time will be used. The language does not define which open delay alternative should be chosen, if more than one has the same delay period.

To illustrate the use of the delay alternative, imagine a deadlock detection task, which might form part of an operating system. Every minute (or so), it has to wake up and check for deadlock. If deadlock is detected, the operator is informed. Should the operator not acknowledge the notice within ten seconds, the task, being of simple mind, initiates a restart of the system.

```
task DEADLOCK_DETECTOR is
  entry OPERATOR_ACTION;
end DEADLOCK_DETECTOR;

task body DEADLOCK_DETECTOR is
  TEST_INTERVAL:constant DURATION:=60.0;
  WAIT_TIME:constant DURATION:=10.0;
  NEXT_TEST:TIME:=CLOCK + TEST_INTERVAL;
  DEADLOCKED:BOOLEAN:=FALSE;
begin
  loop
    delay NEXT_TEST — CLOCK;   -- delay statement
      -- test for deadlock
    if DEADLOCKED then INFORM_OPERATOR (DEADLOCK);
      -- operating system procedure
      select
        accept OPERATOR_ACTION;
      or
        delay WAIT_TIME;
```

```
        SYSTEM_REBOOT;
           -- operating system procedure
        end select;
     end if;
        NEXT_TEST:=NEXT_TEST + TEST_INTERVAL;
     end loop;
  end DEADLOCK_DETECTOR;
```

Often the action to be taken when a delay alternative is executed will include raising an exception, for it is probably an exceptional occurrence that has caused the delay alternative to be selected. It is natural to use exceptions for such cases.

To illustrate the distinction between various forms of the select alternative and the use of **delay**, compare the following extracts.

```
-- Version 1          -- Version 2          -- Version 3
select                select                select
   accept E;             accept E;             accept E;
or                    else                  or
   delay 1.0;            delay 1.0;            delay 0.5;
end select;           end select;              delay 0.5;
                                            end select;
```

For each version, consider its behaviour, when the select statement is executed and there are no tasks waiting on E. In version 1, the controller task will wait for up to one second for another task to call E, during which time, any such call will be accepted for rendezvous.

Version 2 is not as patient. The else part will be entered immediately and the delay *statement* will be executed. No calls to E will be accepted during the delay, after which time the select statement terminates. Finally, in the third version, the controller task is prepared to wait for half a second for another task to call E. If no call is made during the wait, feeling rather peeved, it turns a deaf ear to callers for (at least) another half a second. The select then terminates.

The above extracts serve to highlight the problem of overloading reserved words with different meanings.

11.7 Task termination [LRM 9.4]

Task termination is not a trivial topic and all the nuances cannot be

included here. The concept of termination has already been introduced. However, there is a distinction to be drawn between tasks that have terminated and those that have completed. A completed task is one that has no more actions to perform and is waiting to terminate. A task may complete for one of the following reasons:
(i) it has finished executing its body statements
(ii) an exception was raised during its activation (when its body was elaborated)
(iii) an exception was raised, but not handled, within the task body
(iv) an exception was raised, but handled at the outermost level of the body (exceptions are not propagated out of tasks)

If a completed task has no dependent tasks, then it becomes terminated, and so will it remain. However, the task will stay as a completed task all the time that any dependent tasks have not terminated. This argument also applies to task masters. So, if we have a procedure that contains a task (and little else):

```
procedure P;
   task T;
   task body T is separate;
begin
   null;
end P;
```

A call of P will complete immediately, but P cannot terminate until T has terminated.

If an attempt is made to rendezvous with a completed or terminated task, then the pre-defined exception, TASKING_ERROR will be raised in the calling task. This also applies if the called task completes while the caller is waiting. If an exception is raised during a rendezvous between two active, normal tasks and is not handled within the accept statement, the rendezvous is abandoned and the exception is propagated in both the called and calling tasks.

The terminate alternative

Of the three alternatives, this one has the simplest syntax:

```
[when ⟨CONDITION⟩ =>]
   terminate;
```

When a selective wait is executed, an open terminate alternative will be selected, if and only if:

(i) the master of the task has completed (remember that the master cannot terminate before this dependent task)

(ii) each task dependent on the master (directly or indirectly) has terminated, or is also waiting on an open terminate alternative

These rules ensure that there can be no tasks waiting on any entries of a task so terminated (whether or not the accepts for these entries are open, or whether or not these entries are even included in the current selective wait).

The terminate alternative is very useful as a means of getting a tasking program to close down in a controlled manner. For example, a terminate alternative could be added to the select statement of BUFFER_3:

```
select
    when ...
        accept ...
        ...
or
    when ...
        accept ...
        ...
or
    terminate;
end select;
```

This enables the buffer to terminate when its master is ready to close *and* when there is no outstanding work for it. To ensure that the buffer is empty, just to make doubly sure that the buffer doesn't shut down prematurely, a guard could be added to the terminate alternative:

```
    ..
or
    when ITEMS = 0 =>
        terminate;
end select;
```

11.8 Conditional and timed entry calls

These have a similar syntactic structure, being rather restricted forms of the select statement to provide the *calling* task with a means of escaping from a commitment to a rendezvous.

Conditional entry calls [LRM 9.7.2]

This has the structure:

```
select
  ⟨ENTRY_CALL_STATEMENT⟩
  [⟨SEQUENCE_OF_STATEMENTS⟩]
else
  ⟨SEQUENCE_OF_STATEMENTS⟩
end select;
```

If the called task is in a position to rendezvous *immediately*, then rendezvous proceeds, followed by execution of the optional sequence of statements, which follows the entry call. Otherwise, if the called task is not in the required position, the rendezvous is avoided and the else part is executed.

Imagine a task for routing messages to their ultimate destination via one of two exchanges. EXCHANGE_1 is to be tried first. If that cannot immediately accept the call, then EXCHANGE_2 is tried. If that, too, is busy, then the attempt at routing is repeated. The code for the routing task has a conditional entry call nested within the else part of another one. We ignore details concerning how the messages get to ROUTER in the first place.

```
task ROUTER;

task body ROUTER is
  -- possibly some local declarations
begin
  -- somehow the calls have to get into ROUTER
  loop               -- the routing algorithm
    select
      EXCHANGE_1.CALL(...);
      PUT_LINE("Call taken by Exchange 1.");
      exit;
    else
      select
        EXCHANGE_2.CALL(...);
        PUT_LINE("Call taken by Exchange 2.");
        exit;
      else
        PUT_LINE("Call failed. Trying again.");
      end select;
```

```
      end select;
    end loop;
    -- presumably loops back for another call
  end ROUTER;
```

As a general rule, it is better to avoid "busy waits" like this, in which a task continues looping until some condition is satisfied. They are very wasteful of processor time. So, we might want to find an alternative solution.

Timed entry calls [LRM 9.7.3]

These have an equally simple structure, adding a *single* delay alternative to the entry call, which yields the third and final form of the select statement:

```
select
  ⟨ENTRY_CALL_STATEMENT⟩
  [⟨SEQUENCE_OF_STATEMENTS⟩]
or
  ⟨DELAY_ALTERNATIVE⟩
end select;
```

The delay alternative has an identical structure to that used in selective waits and its behaviour is somewhat analogous. Now, the meaning is such that, if the called task is not in a position to rendezvous immediately, then the calling task will wait for the specified time for rendezvous to *commence*. If rendezvous has not been initiated by that time, the rendezvous is cancelled and any statements after the delay are executed.

We could now change the body of ROUTER, making use of timed entry calls in place of the conditional entry calls.

```
task body ROUTER is
  -- same declarations (if any)
begin
  -- same pre-amble
  loop              -- the routing algorithm
    select
      EXCHANGE_1.CALL(...);
      PUT_LINE("Call taken by Exchange 1.");
      exit;
```

```
        or
          delay 1.0;
          select
            EXCHANGE_2.CALL(...);
            PUT_LINE("Call taken by Exchange 2.");
            exit;
          or
            delay 1.0;
            PUT_LINE("Call failed. Re-trying.");
          end select;
        end select;
      end loop;
      -- same post amble
    end ROUTER;
```

In this solution, ROUTER is prepared to wait one second for EXCHANGE_1 to respond, before moving on to try EXCHANGE_2 (the first exchange might be swamped with traffic, or out of service). ROUTER is prepared to wait for up to a second to be accepted by EXCHANGE_2. If this also fails, it will repeat the process. Although not ideal, this is a more efficient solution than the previous one.

Rather than have a task re-testing for rendezvous, as is the case with both versions of ROUTER, it is better to have it issue a request to the controlling task (e.g. EXCHANGE_1) and then be woken up as soon as, and precisely when that request can be satisfied. There is no room to elaborate, unfortunately.

11.9 Task types [LRM 9.2]

All the tasks given so far have been task *objects* — each task has been declared with a name to identify it uniquely. If we want to create a number of identical tasks, then it is more appropriate to use a task type. Doing just that for the resource controller simply involves the addition of **type** before the name in the specification. The name has been changed to avoid confusion.

```
    task type RESOURCE is
      entry ACQUIRE;
      entry RELEASE;
    end RESOURCE;
```

```
task body RESOURCE is
begin
  loop
    accept ACQUIRE;
    accept RELEASE;
  end loop;
end RESOURCE;
```

Task types are limited types, therefore assignment and equality testing cannot be performed on them. However, like limited private types, it is possible to pass tasks as parameters of mode **in** or **in out** to subprograms, as in the heading:

```
procedure SERVICE(RES:in RESOURCE);
```

The task type is used to create task objects by simply declaring the objects just as is done with any other type, or, access types can be used.

```
DISK:RESOURCE;
type RES_PTR is access RESOURCE;
PRINTER:RES_PTR:=new RESOURCE;
RES_LIST:array(0..15) of RESOURCE;
```

These declarations show that task types can be very flexible. If access types are used for task objects, then the allocator **new** is used in the same way as for dynamic variables.

Sometimes, tasks need to be referred to by a permanent name but on other occasions, it is sufficient to be able to locate a task, when required, using some temporary name. This is the situation, if a linked list of tasks is created, as in a pool of buffers, for example.

If access types are used for tasks, there are a few additional points that need to be noted. First, the master of a task created by an allocator is the master that contains the corresponding access type definition, which is not necessarily the creating task. Secondly, a task that is created by the evaluation of an allocator, is activated by that evaluation. One final point is that the use of access types enables aliases for tasks to be established, because pointers to tasks may be copied, whereas tasks themselves cannot be assigned, as they are a limited private type. Task aliases should be avoided. Also, by making a new assignment to a task pointer variable, the previous task object, to which that variable pointed, could become anonymous, and unable to be referenced. In a critical tasking environment, such a situation could be disastrous. These points are illustrated by the following skeleton code.

```
procedure MAIN is
   task type TT;
   type TT_PTR is access TT;
   ST_1:TT;                      -- Static, MAIN is master.
   task body TT is
      -- body goes here
   end TT;

   procedure P is
      ST_2:TT;                   -- Static, P is master.
      DT_1:TT_PTR:=new TT;  -- Dynamic, MAIN is master,
                               -- activated here.
      DT_2:TT_PTR:=new TT;  -- Same comments as DT_1.
      DT_3:TT_PTR;           -- No task object yet.
   begin                       -- ST_2 activated here (each call).
      DT_3:=DT_1;            -- Introduces an alias for DT_1.all,
      DT_2:=DT_1;            -- the task referenced by DT_1.
                               -- Old DT_2.all is now anonymous
                               -- and unable to be referenced.

   end P;

begin
                               -- ST_1 activated here.
   -- some useful statements
end MAIN;
```

11.10 Rendezvous and scheduling priorities

There are two aspects to priority that are quite distinct. The first relates
to the allocation of different priorities to tasks waiting for rendezvous.
The other is concerned with the execution of a tasking program —
specifically, the scheduling of tasks to be run on the available processor(s).

Rendezvous priority [LRM 9.5]

The queue of tasks waiting on any entry is always FIFO. However, Ada
provides for a *family* of distinct entries to be created, which may be
thought of as an array of entries with a discrete index. This index is used
to distinguish between the individual members of the family. An entry
family enables the owning task to apply some selection strategy to rendezvous with the task it prefers.

Using operating systems again as the background for an example, consider the role of a dispatcher, which allocates the processor to the process with highest priority. There are two global declarations, for process priority and some process identification:

```
type PROCESS_PRIORITY is (BACKGROUND,
    FOREGROUND, EXEC, INTERRUPT);
type PID_TYPE is new INTEGER range 0..9999;
```

There are four priorities. Background jobs have the lowest priority, with foreground jobs next, then the operating system routines, except interrupt handlers, which have the highest priority. The code for the dispatcher could go something like:

```
task DISPATCHER is
  entry CONTEXT_SWITCH;
  entry RUN (PROCESS_PRIORITY)
          (PROCESS_ID:in PID_TYPE);
end DISPATCHER;

task body DISPATCHER is
  THIS_PROCESS:PID_TYPE;
begin
  loop
    accept CONTEXT_SWITCH;
    for P_P in reverse PROCESS_PRIORITY loop
      select
        accept RUN (P_P) (PROCESS_ID:in PID_TYPE) do
          THIS_PROCESS:=PROCESS_ID;
        end RUN;
        -- allocate THIS_PROCESS to processor
        exit;
      else
        null;
      end select;
    end loop;
  end loop;
end DISPATCHER;
```

(Of course, the dispatcher itself will have the highest priority of all, for it must always be running, concurrently with the other processes. Because it is special, the dispatcher does not have to run itself.)

The dispatcher itself is not always actually running and consuming the very resource it allocates. It waits on the entry CONTEXT_SWITCH, which we only need assume is called by some other task of the operating system as a new process (also a task, of course) enters the queue by calling the entry RUN. To make this call, the process task has to supply a value for the index, so it would look like:

        DISPATCHER.RUN (MY_PRIORITY)(MY_ID);

Each of the four members of the entry family has its own FIFO queue of calling tasks. The way the DISPATCHER examines these different queues is controlled by the for loop, which ensures that, each time the DISPATCHER is woken up, the queue for RUN(INTERRUPT) is looked at first.

If there is nothing waiting, then the else part takes it out of the select and on to the next iteration of the for loop, with the next (lower) priority level, and so on. As soon as a waiting process is found, it is allocated and the DISPATCHER exits the for loop, subsequently looping back to the beginning of its life history, waiting on CONTEXT_SWITCH.

When CONTEXT_SWITCH is called, it is assumed that the running process has to stand down and rejoin the queue for the processor. To actually achieve that synchronization in Ada is very difficult. The solution does not belong here. See [1] for ideas.

Scheduling priorities [LRM 9.8]

As pointed out earlier, scheduling priority is unrelated to entry priority. PRIORITY is a pre-defined pragma, which may be used to associate an integer priority with a task. This priority is intended for use by the Ada run-time system to help determine which task to allocate to the available processor(s), from the queue of those tasks in an executable state. (This is the same problem that faced the DISPATCHER! Here, though, the focus of attention is not on how Ada tasks are used, but on how they are actually implemented.) An implementation is not obliged to provide more than one priority level, consequently, the use of PRIORITY will result in a highly implementation-specific program. PRIORITY can be useful for *local* optimization of task scheduling to suit a particular application and system. It should always be used with care.

11.11 A tasking miscellany

This section introduces more aspects of tasking and illustrates their use by examples. Before that, there is a brief discussion about the writing and portability of tasking programs.

Task writing

Tasks should not be used unnecessarily, as they may introduce time-dependent errors into a program, impair readability and greatly reduce run-time efficiency. Their use, then, should be restricted to the type of applications mentioned earlier: where concurrency is relevant to the problem, either to model some real world situation, or to interact and synchronize with some external, physical system. When used correctly, tasks improve program comprehension (but do not necessarily enhance execution speed).

Now some points on writing the code for tasks. As a general rule, tasks should either be controller tasks, with entries that may be called by other tasks and with no calls to entries to other tasks, or, they should be calling tasks, which do not themselves possess any entries. Adherence to these rules helps to obviate the possibility of tasks entering *deadlock* in which, for example, T_1 calls an entry of T_2 while T_2 has called an entry of T_1. Each task is then obliged to wait for the other — indefinitely. Occasionally it is necessary to violate the rule; correct sequencing of entry calls and accept statements can help, but you can never be entirely sure in a concurrent environment. The use of additional, intermediate controller or agent tasks can often solve the problem and can actually help to clarify the code.

The problems of task communication by shared variables were mentioned earlier. It is not always possible to avoid accessing shared variables. Some control of such accesses is possible in Ada, by means of a pragma for their synchronization [LRM 9.11]. Synchronization doesn't always matter but when it does, an additional task may be used to control access to the shared data which is, after all, a resource requiring mutually exclusive access.

Portability problems should be expected in tasking programs. Different program execution speeds are inevitable: all systems will not use the same scheduling algorithm for processor allocation and execution is dependent on the software and hardware environments. However, the overall behaviour of a tasking program should remain the same as long as you don't (deliberately or unwittingly) utilize any implementation-specific features. For example, no particular task activation sequence should be assumed, nor should any assumption be made about the order of processing entry calls *vis-à-vis* the calling sequence. DURATION is, of course, a more obvious implementation-dependent feature.

Additional problems will arise for tasking programs implemented on distributed systems. Specifically, a rendezvous involving tasks on different processors should be expected to take longer than one between tasks on the same processor. The degree of independence in a distributed system can also create problems for task synchronization.

Readers and Writers

The "Readers and Writers" problem is a well-worn favourite of courses and texts on operating systems, for it involves the correct synchronization of a number of concurrent readers and writers. The problem is usually stated in terms of controlling access to a file, such that any number of readers may read from the file simultaneously, whereas a writer requires sole access to the file while updates are made. Unit 11.7 incorporates a task to control file access accordingly. A reader process would call START_READ in order to gain permission to read from the file and will call END_READ to indicate that it has finished reading. Writers follow a similar protocol.

```
-- with relevant i/o packages
procedure MAIN is

    -- some declarations

    task FILE_CONTROL_1 is
      entry START_READ;
      entry END_READ;
      entry START_WRITE;
      entry END_WRITE;
    end FILE_CONTROL_1;

    -- specification of reader and writer tasks

    task body FILE_CONTROL_1 is
      READERS:NATURAL:=0;
    begin
      loop
        select
          accept START_READ;
          READERS:=READERS + 1;
        or
          accept END_READ;
          READERS:=READERS - 1;
        or
          when READERS = 0 =>
            accept START_WRITE;
          accept END_WRITE;
        or
          terminate;
        end select;
      end loop;
    end FILE_CONTROL_1;
```

```
   -- some other bodies

begin
   -- main program statements
end MAIN;
```

Unit 11.7 File controller 1.

From the select statement, you can see that the task will always consider accepting calls of START_READ and END_READ and, when there are no READERS of the file, and only then, it will accept a call of START_WRITE. If a caller of this last entry is selected for rendezvous, then the writer will be allowed exclusive access to the file, as the controlling task waits for the writer to call END_WRITE before looping back to the select statement once more. Note that the accept statement for END_WRITE is one of the statements in the sequence of statements that follows the accept alternative for START_WRITE and, as such, is not an alternative of the select statement. The terminate alternative will enable the task to terminate when there is no more work to do.

This solution would be criticized in a discussion about concurrent programming, because it discriminates against writers, which are only allowed to proceed if there are no readers waiting to access the file. So in concurrent programming terminology, writers can be indefinitely postponed, which is not a good characteristic. This solution can, then, be improved. These improvements are made, not because the problem itself is important here, but because it does enable further features of tasking to be introduced.

Task and entry attributes [LRM 9.9]

Three attributes are provided for use in conjunction with tasks. However, they should only be used in exceptional circumstances. T'CALLABLE yields TRUE if task T may be called, thus enabling a rendezvous with a completed or terminated task to be avoided. T'TERMINATED yields TRUE, if T has terminated. The third attribute may be applied to entries. E'COUNT gives the number of entry calls currently queued on the entry E.

The danger with all of these is that they are evaluated when called, and do not necessarily represent the state of affairs that obtains at the time that some decision is made on the basis of their value. For example, E'COUNT will be incremented for each new entry call, and it will also be decremented for each acceptance of E *and*, if a task is removed from the queue, owing to a timed or conditional entry call. So, a statement like:

```
        if E'COUNT > 0 then
           accept E;
        end if;
```

does *not* guarantee immediate rendezvous. One or more tasks might disappear from the queue for E between the evaluation of E'COUNT and the execution of the accept statement. Remember that this is a concurrent environment in which things can happen (apparently or truly) simultaneously.

Notwithstanding the warning, Unit 11.8 is an attempt at a fairer solution to the readers and writers problem, which uses the COUNT attribute.

```
        task FILE_CONTROL_2 is
          entry START_READ;
          entry END_READ;
          entry START_WRITE;
          entry END_WRITE;
        end FILE_CONTROL_2;

        task body FILE_CONTROL_2 is
          READERS:NATURAL:=0;
        begin
          loop
            select
              when START_WRITE'COUNT = 0 => -- this is not good practice
                accept START_READ;
                READERS:=READERS + 1;
            or
                accept END_READ;
                READERS:=READERS - 1;
            or
              when READERS = 0 =>
                accept START_WRITE;
                accept END_WRITE;
                loop
                  select
                    accept START_READ;
                    READERS:=READERS + 1;
                  else
                    exit;
                  end select;
                end loop;
            or
                terminate;
            end select;
          end loop;
        end FILE_CONTROL_2;
```

Unit 11.8   File controller 2. Not a library unit.

Now, readers are only allowed access all the time that no writers are waiting for access. When the first writer joins the queue, it has to wait for all readers to call END_READ before being allowed to access the file.

After it has modified the file, all readers currently waiting are allowed into the file, before the same strategy is re-applied. This, clearly, is a fairer solution (as long as it works).

The rationale for using COUNT was that the file controller needs to know if there are any writers waiting. Another way of establishing this is to get prospective writers to call an additional entry of the file controller (WANT_TO_WRITE), which will then only rendezvous with writers that really do (still) want to write, and not attempt to rendezvous with long-gone ghosts, as could happen using COUNT. The new controller now becomes Unit 11.9.

```
task FILE_CONTROL_3 is
  entry START_READ;
  entry END_READ;
  entry WANT_TO_WRITE;
  entry START_WRITE;
  entry END_WRITE;
end FILE_CONTROL_3;

task body FILE_CONTROL_3 is
  READERS:NATURAL:=0;
  WRITER_WAITING:BOOLEAN:=FALSE;
begin
  loop
    select
      when not WRITER_WAITING =>
        accept START_READ;
      READERS:=READERS + 1;
    or
      accept END_READ;
      READERS:=READERS - 1;
    or
      when not WRITER_WAITING =>
        accept WANT_TO_WRITE;
      WRITER_WAITING:=TRUE;
    or
      when READERS = 0 =>
        accept START_WRITE;
    or
      accept END_WRITE;
      WRITER_WAITING:=FALSE;
    or
      terminate;
    end select;
  end loop;
end FILE_CONTROL_3;
```

Unit 11.9   File controller 3. Not a library unit.

Tasks in library units

Tasks are program units, but they are not compilation units, therefore they cannot be library units. This may appear to be rather restricting, particularly if you are going to need the same resource controller in a number of programs, or if you would like a generic buffer task, say, for creating buffers for any type. The usual solution to this problem is to put the task in a package, which gives a number of other advantages, in that a simpler interface can be provided for the user by utilizing the information hiding capability of packages.

To show how this may be done, consider putting the file controller of Unit 11.9 into a package, together with the direct i/o file to be controlled. It would be possible to put the task specification in the package specification, so that the package would export all the entries of the task. Often, though, it is more desirable to hide some, or even all of the task entries, by hiding the task specification in the package body and providing a number of visible subprograms which, themselves, synchronize via the entries of the task they can see, but the package user can't.

For this particular example, it will be much more convenient for users, if they only have to call a single procedure when they want to READ or WRITE an ITEM of information, rather than have to use the correct entry calling sequence. (With the earlier file controllers, correct operation is dependent on the correct entry call sequences by the readers and writers themselves.) It is no more trouble to make the package a generic one, which can be used for controlling access to a direct file of any component type. The culmination of all this is the generic file control package of Unit 11.10.

```
with DIRECT_IO, TEXT_IO;
generic
  type COMPONENT is private;
package CONTROLLED_FILE is
  procedure SAFE_READ(COMP_NUM:in POSITIVE;
                      ITEM:out COMPONENT);
  procedure SAFE_WRITE(COMP_NUM:in POSITIVE;
                       ITEM:in COMPONENT);
end CONTROLLED_FILE;

package body CONTROLLED_FILE is

  package COMPONENT_DIRECT_IO is new DIRECT_IO(COMPONENT);
  use COMPONENT_DIRECT_IO;
  SAFE_FILE:FILE_TYPE;

  task CONTROLLER is
    entry START_READ;
    entry END_READ;
    entry WANT_TO_WRITE;
    entry START_WRITE;
    entry END_WRITE;
  end CONTROLLER;
```

```
      procedure SAFE_READ(COMP_NUM:in POSITIVE;
                           ITEM:out COMPONENT) is
      begin
        if COMP_NUM > INTEGER(SIZE(SAFE_FILE)) then
          TEXT_IO.PUT_LINE("Component number too large.");
        else
          CONTROLLER.START_READ;
          READ(SAFE_FILE, ITEM, COUNT(COMP_NUM));
          CONTROLLER.END_READ;
        end if;
      end SAFE_READ;

      procedure SAFE_WRITE(COMP_NUM:in POSITIVE;
                           ITEM:in COMPONENT) is
      begin
        CONTROLLER.WANT_TO_WRITE;
        CONTROLLER.START_WRITE;
        WRITE(SAFE_FILE, ITEM, COUNT(COMP_NUM));
        CONTROLLER.END_WRITE;
      end SAFE_WRITE;

      task body CONTROLLER is
        READERS:NATURAL:=0;
        WRITER_WAITING:BOOLEAN:=FALSE;
      begin
        loop
          select
            when not WRITER_WAITING =>
              accept START_READ;
            READERS:=READERS + 1;
          or
            accept END_READ;
            READERS:=READERS - 1;
          or
            when not WRITER_WAITING =>
              accept WANT_TO_WRITE;
            WRITER_WAITING:=TRUE;
          or
            when READERS = 0 =>
              accept START_WRITE;
          or
            accept END_WRITE;
            WRITER_WAITING:=FALSE;
          or
            terminate;
          end select;
        end loop;
      end CONTROLLER;

    begin
      CREATE(SAFE_FILE);
    end CONTROLLED_FILE;
```

Unit 11.10   A generic file control package.

As you can see, the task itself is unchanged from that in Unit 11.9.

Two things should be noted about this approach. One is that, because user tasks are no longer directly calling task entries, but calling package procedures instead, conditional and timed entry calls cannot be used by the readers and writers. (It would be possible for the package to export procedures which could issue delayed entry calls on behalf of the procedure caller.) Also, it has already been stated that packages can only be masters of tasks if they are library units. However, there is something of a problem here, for the language does not specify whether or not tasks in library units have to terminate before program execution can terminate. Consequently, it is possible, unless specific precautions are taken, for a program to terminate while tasks are still working. If this worries you, consult a specialist text.

Abortion

This is as controversial in tasking as it is in gynaecology. Tasks in Ada may be aborted by the execution of an abort statement. The result of taking such drastic action may be unpredictable. Consequently, it should only be used if the situation is really desperate. If things really are that bad, though, it indicates poor program design.

11.2 Embedded systems programming [LRM 13]

In addition to the use of tasks for synchronization and clarity, there are other requirements for embedded systems programming. Some of these requirements are discussed in this section.

   In any embedded application, the program has to interact with some hardware, which may be the computer system, or external devices, or both. Therefore, the program has to be able to refer to specific hardware elements.

   Ada allows the programmer to have some control over how certain data structures (records and enumeration types) are stored, where data and code is stored, and how much space is to be associated with a type. These features should only be used where absolutely necessary, which is the case with embedded systems. An example will illustrate the use of some of the *representation clauses* of the language.

An example

Assume that you are writing a control program for the master processor in a multi-processor system. When a slave processor wants to communicate with the master, it generates an interrupt, and a specific memory location is loaded with the identification of the processor and the interrupt.

First, the necessary objects and types are declared, followed by the representation clauses which define how and where the objects are to be represented. The type and object declarations are:

```
PROCESSOR_MAX:constant:=64;
type INTERRUPT_TYPE is
  (IDLE, MESSAGE, IO_REQUEST, DEV_FAIL);
type PROCESSOR_RANGE is
  new INTEGER range 0..PROCESSOR_MAX;

type INTERRUPT_DATA is
record
  CPU:PROCESSOR_RANGE;
  KIND:INTERRUPT_TYPE;
end record;
```

Now, the representation of these types must be specified, for we have to describe exactly how the hardware represents them. Normally, enumerated type values are held as the integer value that results from the application of the attribute POS to them. For this example, the hardware indicates an INTERRUPT_TYPE by setting a unique bit that is associated with it, and setting all other bits to zero. So, we have to express this:

```
for INTERRUPT_TYPE use
  (IDLE=>1, MESSAGE=>2, IO_REQUEST=>4,
    DEV_FAIL=>8);
```

Note that in assigning the representation values, the representation order must be the same as the declaration order, so that, for example, MESSAGE must have a greater value than IDLE. The values of the attributes (including POS) are *not* affected by a change of representation.

All INTERRUPT_DATA has to be held in a specific format; again, this is dictated by the hardware. The format to be used is to have two contiguous bytes, at an even address, with CPU in the lower byte and KIND in the higher one. This is stated as:

```
for INTERRUPT_DATA use
record at mod 2;              -- even byte boundary
  CPU at 0 range 0..7;
  KIND at 1 range 0..3;
end record;

for INTERRUPT_DATA'SIZE
  use 2*SYSTEM.STORAGE_UNIT;  -- 2 byte limit
```

We have now specified the data both logically and physically. It has been assumed that the standard storage unit for this implementation is a byte — this is made available as SYSTEM.STORAGE_UNIT. The record representation, then, means that CPU is at bits 0 to 7 of byte 0, while KIND occupies bits 0 to 3 of byte 1. The length specification for the whole record is needed to ensure that only 2 bytes are used for the type, otherwise, the compiler could allocate more memory. This is known as a length clause, in which a size is specified in bits [LRM 13.2].

To declare a variable object for holding interrupt data, we need to say where that object is located in memory, using an *address clause*:

```
INTERRUPT_INFO:INTERRUPT_DATA;
for INTERRUPT_INFO use at 16#000F#;
```

The final aspect of the example is the interrupt handler itself. Remember that this is to be invoked by the occurrence of an external hardware interrupt. It is possible to associate a task entry with a hardware address, thereby creating an *interrupt entry* for some external task (i.e. the hardware) to call. This external task is given a higher priority than any internal task. So, in outline, the interrupt handler task will be:

```
task INTERRUPT_HANDLER is
  entry EXTERNAL_INTERRUPT;
  for EXTERNAL_INTERRUPT use at 16#0010#;
end INTERRUPT_HANDLER;

task body INTERRUPT_HANDLER is
  INT_KIND:INTERRUPT_TYPE;
  INT_CPU:PROCESSOR_RANGE;
begin
  loop
    accept EXTERNAL_INTERRUPT do
      INT_KIND:=INTERRUPT_INFO.KIND;
      INT_CPU:=INTERRUPT_INFO.CPU;
    end EXTERNAL_INTERRUPT;
    -- invoke the specific handler —
    -- e.g. case INT_KIND is ....
  end loop;
end INTERRUPT_HANDLER;
```

If you feel like trying out some of these ideas for yourself, you may well be disappointed. Running Ada under a multi-user operating system is not the same as running it on a dedicated machine. The operating system may well impose impenetrable barriers to your experiments, so that you can do no harm.

Representation attributes [LRM 13.7]

Attributes are provided to enable you to ascertain where an object, program unit, or entry is placed in memory, as well as the number of bits used to represent a type or an object. These, and other representation attributes are explained in the LRM.

In-line expansion [LRM 6.3.2]

In an embedded system, speed may be rather crucial. Subprograms, although desirable from the software engineering point of view, do incur an execution overhead at run-time. Usually, this overhead is of no concern, but in a real time control system, things could be different. The LRM specifies a pragma, INLINE, which may be used to request that the named subprogram(s) be subjected to in-line expansion during compilation, which means that calls to them should be replaced by code for the subprogram itself. This treats subprograms as macros rather than subroutines. Unfortunately, INLINE, like other pragmas, is open to liberal interpretation by the implementors and/or the compiler. A compiler is under no obligation to comply with the request.

If you must

Occasionally, it is possible to justify incorporating machine code, or calls to subprograms written in other languages, into an Ada program. The language designers have made it possible to express both of these intentions in an Ada program. See 13.8 and 13.9 of the LRM for details.

In section 13.10.2 of the LRM, you can discover that it is possible to convert quite freely from one type to another, quite unrelated type. This is achieved by a generic function, which enables a bit pattern (of some type) to be re-interpreted as a value of some target type. The use of this facility undermines all the advantages of using a strongly typed language, so it should not be resorted to as a means of writing untyped C programs in Ada!

Practising Ada 11

There is a lot of scope for having fun here. The (serious) object is to be able to write concurrent code and explain all that happens at run-time. Don't be too ambitious to start with. Gradually introduce the features discussed in the text. Some specific tasks:

1 Run Unit 11.1 in a modified form: limit PRODUCER and CONSUMER to ten iterations of their loops; add statements to write the value of COUNT in INCREMENT and DECREMENT. Run the program several times. Can you explain all that happens? Modify the program to ensure correct operation.

2 Using a sort routine as a basis (e.g. Unit 6.4) write a program which sorts a vector of N integers, using three tasks:

(i) LOW_SORT sorts half the vector

(ii) HIGH_SORT sorts the other half

(iii) MERGE merges the two half arrays, *after* they have been sorted.

How can this be more efficient than simply sorting the whole vector in one go? (Hint, this sort involves $0(N^{**}2)$ comparisons.)

3 Create a linked list of single item buffer tasks. Modify Unit 11.4 so that a call of PLACE gets a free buffer (if there is one) and deposits ITEM and then puts the buffer in a queue of full buffers. TAKE removes the first buffer from the queue (if it is not empty), removes its contents and replaces it in the pool of empty buffers.

4 Write a task that will "bleep" (ASCII.BEL) every ten seconds. Modify it to also ring an alarm (multiple bleeps) at a specified time. Then modify it so that the program will automatically terminate, if you do not respond to a bleep within two seconds. (WARNING. This program has been known to annoy adjacent users!)

Chapter 12

Ada in perspective

The best programming language in the world tends to be the one with which you are most familiar. It is interesting that, if anybody has an opinion about Ada, it is likely to be a very strong one. Ada has succeeded in dividing programmers into two camps, the glassy-eyed fanatics on the one hand, and the vehement detractors on the other. It is no good sitting in either camp with your eyes closed, which is, unfortunately, often the case. Ada is not perfect but, despite its faults, it has a number of commendable features. In this final chapter, I shall attempt to put the language in context, as objectively as possible.

Programming language developments

Traditional programming languages can be divided into two (more or less) disjoint classes: procedural languages and declarative languages. In a procedural language, such as FORTRAN, COBOL, BASIC or Pascal, the programmer lists the required sequence of steps (the procedure to be followed) to solve a particular problem. Using a declarative language, of which LISP and PROLOG are (different) kinds, the exact process to be followed is not specified, rather a set of rules is given, together with data on which they operate. Consider a simple problem, which illustrates the differences in approach:

I have a set of grades for each student in my class. What I want to know is those students who are 'clever', which, for this example, means those who attained a grade of A. If I were to write a program for this in a procedural language, I would have to define the searching process. In a declarative language, however, I can be less explicit, as the problem can be specified in a more general way, such as:

> Form a list of STUDENT-GRADE pairs
> State that CLEVER means GRADE=A
> Ask to find all STUDENTs who are CLEVER

From these descriptions, the language would apply reasoning to solve the problem. This logical power makes declarative languages very attractive for artificial intelligence (AI) applications.

295

The procedural languages are well-suited to the traditional (von Neumann) computer architecture, in which there is a single processor, with a memory for instructions and data. All instructions are sequenced through this single processor, which imposes a limit on execution speed.

Many manufacturers are now actively pursuing the design and production of computers that perform parallel processing, in some shape or form. The problem then arises: how do we utilize that parallelism effectively? The onus is back on the software. It is not generally sufficient to have a language with concurrent features, such as tasking. Communication between parallel components must be very efficient, if the advantages of having parallel hardware are not to be lost.

One interesting concept is the transputer, developed by INMOS Ltd [9]. This device is a complete processor on a chip, which also accommodates local memory and four high speed links that can be connected to other transputers. Consequently, transputers can be used effectively in an infinite variety of configurations. The transputer is programmed in a special purpose (procedural) language, occam, which enables the programmer to define all the parallelism in a program and to map truly parallel processes onto different transputers.

For most users, the additional burden of programming specifically for a parallel machine will be too much (and too risky, as it is so easy to make mistakes in such an environment). The mapping of the source code, procedural or declarative, onto target code for the parallel hardware should be performed automatically.

Ada's place in Babel

Well, where does Ada fit into the scheme of things? Clearly, it is a procedural language, and one with a very long pedigree. Its detractors call it an evolutionary dead-end. In some respects they are right, but you could use the same argument against all languages, if you believe that our massively parallel wrist computers will ultimately be driven by natural language! Until that time, software tools will be needed to fulfil current requirements.

Ada's development was briefly traced in Chapter 1. It evolved at a time when software engineering methodologies were becoming established and their advantages appreciated. It is as a vehicle for implementing these methodologies that the language must be judged.

Ada should not be used for many AI applications, because it is simply not appropriate. This, however, is of little concern, given that by far the greatest programming effort currently goes into the production of procedural code for von Neumann machines. A shift in emphasis may eventually come, as extremely powerful software packages are developed using whichever language class is appropriate. Meanwhile, despite the increased development and use of languages of a radically different nature, Ada is, and will continue to be, appropriate for the majority of programming projects.

The strengths of Ada

Ada gains its strength from two sources: a coherent design, which embodies support for software engineering practices and the rigorous management of Ada by the Ada Joint Program Office (AJPO), which has a number of advantages.

The support that Ada provides for data abstraction, information hiding, modularity, readability, strong typing, portability and so on, should be readily apparent. In practice, Ada has been successfully employed for the completion of a number of large programming projects. See the articles by Sammet and Lieblein [5,7] for approbationary appraisals of Ada.

As noted in Chapter 1, Ada was standarized in 1983, before it was widely used — compilers were a little thin on the ground in those days. No dialects are recognized. AJPO acts as a centralized collection point and dissemination source for matters relating to the language, its implementation and its use. Current official information on Ada is released by the Ada Information Clearing house (address supplied at the end of this book). A compiler receives a validation certificate only when it has passed the 2500 or so tests of the Ada Compiler Validation Capability (ACVC), which is (now) updated every year. At the time of writing, over sixty Ada compilers have current validation certificates. Target machines range from large mainframes to personal computers. Many other compilers are in development.

SIGAda is a special interest group of the Association for Computing Machinery. This group publishes "Ada Letters", a bi-monthly collection of announcements and articles, which is a very useful source of information on Ada and a forum for comment, praise and condemnation. Local, national and international conferences are organized under the auspices of SIGAda. AdaUK and AdaEurope cater for the interests of users within their compass. (Relevant addresses may be found at the end of this book.)

Disadvantages of Ada

.. And now for the bad news. It would be unreasonable to expect Ada to
be perfect! Although the language is very consistent, there are occasional
lapses, such as optional subprogram names after their final **end**, whereas
named loops and blocks have to be named at their termination. I have
already complained about the overloading of reserved words, in particular
select and **delay**.

Given the circumstances that led to the development of Ada, it was
almost inevitable that the language would be large. A large set of reserved
words and syntactic structures does impede learning. A more serious
consequence of a large language is the complexity required of a compiler
in order to implement it. I have remarked that the LRM is not always the
source of enlightenment that you might like. A would-be compiler writer
needs the additional support and clarification of a compiler writer's guide.
(Consequently, the LRM is not the ultimate arbiter, the compiler is!) It is
virtually impossible, at the present time, to produce a compiler for Ada
that is free of bugs. A validation certificate asserts that a compiler has
passed the tests of the ACVC, it does not guarantee correct compilation
and execution of all Ada programs. This has been substantiated by my
own experience of Ada compilers, which, when all else fails, come up
with such gems as:

> "Illegal instruction. Core dumped."(run time.) or:
> "Stack overflow." (Compile time and run time!)

One major producer of Ada compilers obviously shares these views,
when its literature proclaims:

> "... and the inevitable existence of compiler bugs."

For an interesting article by an Ada detractor, see Hoares' Turing Award
lecture, published in [3].

A language with which Ada is frequently compared is Modula-2, from
the same author as Pascal. Modula-2 also supports many of the requirements of software engineering. For example, it is possible to control what
a module exports, and it is also possible to control what it *imports*. This
adds a logical symmetry to information hiding. I do not intend to reduce
this to a blow by blow comparison of the two languages. Each has its
(considerable) merits. Ada, however, is applicable to a wider range of
problems, which accounts in part for its size.

It is surprising, perhaps, to discover that in the one area where you would expect Ada to excel, namely tasking, this is not the case. Experience with compilers so far has shown just how expensive the rendezvous is. This is attributable partly to the rendezvous scheme itself and partly to its implementation. Before you implement a real-time nuclear power station controller using Ada read a more specific text, such as [1]!

Devotees of other languages curse the designers of Ada for omitting their particular favourite feature. Personally, I will not rue the omission of the **class** of SIMULA, which I find attractive, if, at the same time, it means that FORTRAN and the indiscipline it encourages are finally laid to rest.

One criticism levelled at *all* procedural language, is the difficulty of proving correct behaviour. Declarative languages, on the other hand, are usually based on some mathematical formalism, which enables correctness to be demonstrated (at least by those who can understand and apply that formalism).

Conclusions

I seem to have taken more space to discuss some of Ada's faults than I used to talk about its advantages. I would hope, however, that the many good features of Ada will have spoken for themselves, as you discovered and used them.

There are problems with Ada, it is true. However, if you look closely at the criticisms of the last section, it is clear that most of them are not insuperable. The Ada standard is not yet four years old (at the time of writing). Writing an Ada compiler *is* a very complex undertaking: not only are there tasking and generics to implement, but some library for compiled program units has to be established and maintained. I look forward to the advent of third generation Ada compilers, which will benefit from the experience accrued during previous implementations. The maxim, that you have to do the job once before you know what it entails, is certainly applicable here.

Educating and training Ada users also involves a learning process on the part of the educators. It is possible to teach Ada effectively, without overwhelming the student, but it takes time. Even with a 'small' language like Pascal, it is now being recognized that it is better to teach the language slowly, with an emphasis on good practice. Using Ada instead of Pascal would enable many more aspects of good software engineering methodology to be demonstrated *practically*.

With rapid advances in VLSI technology, chips that directly support the Ada tasking model are a possibility. The trend towards true parallelism might make us more tolerant of a relatively slow rendezvous.

Because of human inertia (and ignorance) and a lack of compilers, the adoption of Ada has been slow. Interest is now growing fast in the commercial world as well as the military one. Increasingly, Ada is being used as a program design language (PDL), which enables its modularity and data abstraction to be utilized. This can be of inestimable value, even if the target program is to be coded in another language.

No mention has been made in the book of the Ada Programming Support Environment (APSE), which was the subject of another series of design requirements, culminating in STONEMAN (1980). APSE development stalled for a while but is now under way again. The intention is that there will eventually be a standard environment in which Ada can be run, thereby adding another aspect of portability to the equation — user portability. Even without an APSE, some of the Ada implementations, which are more than just a language translator, are a pleasure to use, with good library management, language orientated debugging and so on.

Ada has so many good features that any serious programmer should get to know it and use it in a production environment. Don't pass judgement until you are well versed in its use — while you are learning, enjoy the experience!

Appendix A

The implementation of real numbers

This is an attempt to describe, in more detail, how real numbers are represented in Ada implementations. Of course, any computer representation of a real number can only represent a finite set of approximations to the real numbers. A real number may possess an infinite number of digits, as is the case with the reciprocal of 3.0, but only a finite (and small) number of digits can be allocated for its representation. This truncation leads to a loss of precision, such that the accuracy of a value of a real type is bounded by plus or minus half the value of the least significant digit.

The LRM [3.5.6] does not dictate one, and only one, representation for a particular real type, which must hold across all implementations. Instead, it specifies the *minimum* requirements consistent with the requested range and precision. For each real type, there is an associated set of numbers, called *model numbers*, which must be represented exactly in all implementations. This is the minimum requirement and not how the numbers are necessarily implemented. To illustrate this distinction and its significance, the discussion will concentrate on floating point numbers.

Floating point model numbers [LRM 3.5.7, 3.5.8]

You have seen how a floating point type is defined, by specifying the number of digits of precision required. Usually, the base of this specification is decimal, but any radix from two to sixteen may be used (if appropriate).

Floating point numbers are usually held in the form:

±1.0 * mantissa * 2 ** exponent

The mantissa is a binary fraction, which is less than one and greater than or equal to 0.5. In other words, the first digit of the mantissa is always one, unless the number itself is zero.

Given the type declaration:

type MY_REAL is digits D;

the model numbers for MY_REAL are defined by two parameters:

(i) The number of binary digits (B) required in the mantissa in order to ensure an accuracy of at least D (decimal) digits
(ii) an exponent range.
B is defined to be the integer immediately above the value of:

D * 3.32 + 1

(3.32 is an approximation to log(10)/log(2)). The exponent range of the model numbers is deemed to be:

−4 * B .. +4 * B

The set of model numbers of a floating point type also includes zero.

Some of the attributes of the floating point types have already been met. They will be explained again here, along with additional attributes. Three of the attributes are of topical significance. Each of them may be applied to a floating point type or subtype identifier (here represented by FLTS) and each yields a universal_integer result.

FLTS'DIGITS
yields the number of decimal digits for the mantissa of the model numbers of the (sub)type FLTS.

FLTS'MANTISSA
yields the binary equivalent of FLTS'DIGITS (i.e. B of the discussion above).

FLTS'EMAX
yields the largest exponent value of the model numbers of the (sub)type, (i.e. 4*B).

The attributes FLTS'LARGE and FLTS'SMALL represent, respectively the largest and smallest (non zero) positive model numbers of the given (sub)type. Both attributes yield a universal_real result. If we use B to represent FLTS'MANTISSA, then the values of LARGE and SMALL are derivable from B thus:

FLTS'LARGE = 2.0**(4*B) * (1.0 −2.0**(−B))
           = 2.0**(4*B) −2.0**(3*B)

FLTS'SMALL = 2.0**(−(4*B+1))

(Do not confuse these attributes with FIRST and LAST, which were mentioned in Chapter 8.)

To show the significance and application of the model number concept, take a rather simple (but workable) floating point example:

type TWO_DITS is digits 2;

Verify that the model number parameter attributes will be:

TWO_DITS'MANTISSA = 8
TWO_DITS'EMAX   =32

The mantissa can have 128 (2**7) possible values, given that the most significant bit must always be 1. The least significant bit will be 2**(−8) or the reciprocal of 256. So, the mantissa value range is:

$$\frac{128}{256}, \frac{129}{256} \text{ and so on up to } \frac{255}{256}$$

The largest positive model number is therefore:

$$\frac{255}{256} * 2**32$$

and the smallest positive non zero model number is:

$$\frac{128}{256} * 2**-32$$

The model numbers, then, relate to the more general discussion of real numbers given in Chapter 8. If we were to list some of the model numbers from the set of such numbers for TWO_DITS, we can see from the difference between adjacent numbers how the precision is relative to the exponent. Rather than list cumbersome fractions, the mantissa is represented in binary form.

Model number	Difference (absolute)	
2#0.1111_1111# * 2**32		TWO_DITS'LARGE
	2**24	
2#0.1111_1110# * 2**32		

2#0.1000_0001# * 2**32		
	2**24	
2#0.1000_0000# * 2**32		
	2**23	
2#0.1111_1111# * 2**31		
	2**23	
2#0.1111_1110# * 2**31		

2#0.1000_0001# * 2**(−32)		
	2**(−40)	
2#0.1000_0000# * 2**(−32)		TWO_DITS'SMALL
	2**(−33)	
0.0		
	2**(−33)	
−2#0.1000_0000# * 2**(−32)		−TWO_DITS'SMALL
	2**(−40)	
−2#0.1000_0001# * 2**(−32)		

−2#0.1111_1110# * 2**32		
	2**(24)	
−2#0.1111_1111# * 2**32		−TWO_DITS'LARGE

Note how the precision deteriorates around zero. This results from the fact that the most significant bit of the mantissa (for a non-zero number) must be 1.

In 8.6, the use of the attribute EPSILON was demonstrated. The universal_real value returned represents the (absolute) difference between the model number 1.0 (a model number of all floating point types) and the model number immediately above it. So, using B again, we have:

FLTS'EPSILON = 2**(1−B)

EPSILON is a measure of the precision of the model numbers, and can be used as a relative precision metric as illustrated in 8.6, by multiplying by the number in question.

Floating point safe numbers

Now, it is time to think about how floating point numbers will actually be held. It was explained in Chapter 8 that a definition like:

type TWO_DITS is digits 2;

is equivalent to:

        type ANON is new pre-defined type;
        subtype TWO_DITS is ANON digits 2;

So, all floating point types are, in fact, derived from pre-defined floating point types. (There are usually several pre-defined floating point types provided by an implementation, although only one *has* to be provided and it must be called FLOAT.) If there is not a pre-defined type with sufficient accuracy to support that requested, the type declaration will be rejected by the compiler. (SYSTEM.MAX_DIGITS represents the implementation limit.)

Now, let us assume that FLOAT is pre-defined with FLOAT'DIGITS being 6. TWO_DITS might then be derived from FLOAT. The *safe numbers* of a floating point type *for a particular implementation* are defined to be those numbers with the same precision as the *base type* of its model numbers, but with a range determined by the implementation (the range of FLOAT for example). The range of safe numbers must be at least that of the model numbers of the same type, so that the model numbers form an improper subset of the safe numbers. Attributes are provided for ascertaining the properties of safe numbers. These attributes, SAFE_MAX, SAFE_SMALL and SAFE_LARGE, yield properties that relate to the base type of the given (sub)type, so that, if we had:

        subtype ONE_DIT is TWO_DITS digits 1;

then ONE_DIT and TWO_DITS would have the same values for the safe number attributes.

As we have seen, TWO_DITS is a subtype of some anonymous type, which was derived from some pre-defined type. If we assume that FLOAT is that pre-defined type, then ONE_DIT, TWO_DITS and FLOAT all have the same safe numbers. Model numbers, however, relate to the subtypes themselves, so each subtype will have its own set of model numbers.

If a floating point (sub)type is given a range constraint, this has no effect on the model numbers and safe numbers — it simply provides the ability to raise CONSTRAINT_ERROR in the event of a violation.

Floating point operations [LRM 4.5.7]

We must now think about what all this implies in relation to operations on floating point types.

The expected accuracy of any pre-defined operation on a floating point (sub)type is determined by the *model* numbers of that (sub)type. A *model interval* is an indication of the upper and lower bounds (both of which are model numbers of the (sub)type) of some value in the (sub)type. If the value *is* a model number, then the model interval is that single number.

The model interval of the result of some floating point operation is the smallest interval in the (sub)type of the result that includes the range of values possible from the application of the operation to all combinations of model interval values for its operands. So, we can use model intervals to analyse the behaviour of floating point algorithms that can be guaranteed over all implementations.

Continuing to use TWO_DITS, we look at what model numbers would tell us about the following program.

        with TEXT_IO;
        procedure MODEL is
            type TWO_DITS is digits 2;

```
    A:TWO_DITS:=1.0;                              -- i)
    A:TWO_DITS:=1.5;                              -- ii)
    C:TWO_DITS:=1.3;                              -- iii)
    D:TWO_DITS;
    TF:BOOLEAN;
    package TWO_DITS_IO is new TEXT_IO.FLOAT_IO(TWO_DITS);
    use TWO_DITS_IO;
  begin
    D:=A + B;                                     -- iv)
    D:=A * B;                                     -- v)
    D:=C + C;                                     -- vi)
    TF:=D=2*C;                                    -- vii)
    TF:=abs(D-2*C) <= TWO_DITS'EPSILON*D;         -- viii)
    C:=4.25;                                      -- ix)
    D:=C * C;                                     -- x)
    PUT(D);                                       -- xi)
    A:=A * 2.0**20;                               -- xii)
    B:=B * 2.0**20;                               -- xiii)
    C:=C * 2.0**20;                               -- xiv)
    D:=B*C / A;                                   -- xv)
  and MODEL;
```

The whole point of the model number concept, remember, is to be able to predict some aspects of the behaviour of floating point operations on any implementation. Working through the above program in sequence, we will examine the effect of each assignment and operation, using the same notation for mantissa and exponent as before.

1.0 and 1.5 will be model numbers of any floating point type. For TWO_DITS, they will be:

(i) 2#0.1000_0000#   2**1
(ii) 2#0.1100_0000#   2**1

1.3 cannot be represented exactly by a model number, therefore the only thing that we can assume is that it will be represented by one of the model numbers given by the model interval:

(iii) 2#0.1010_0110#   2**1
      2#0.1010_0111#   2**1

The addition and multiplication of A and B operate on two model numbers, and each operation produces a model number as a result. (An operation on model numbers does not necessarily produce a model number as a result — satisfy yourself about this before going on.)

(iv) 2#0.1010_0000#   2**2
 (v) 2#0.1100_0000#   2**1

The only assumption we can make about the operand, C, is that it is bounded by the model interval ii) above. The result of the addition in vi) will therefore be bounded by the largest model interval that could result from the addition, giving:

(vi) 2#0.1010_0110#   2**2
     2#0.1010_0111#   2**2

Note that, in absolute terms, the model interval is now twice as wide as it was before.

One thing that is explained by looking at model numbers, is why you have to be careful with the application of relational operators to real types. The Boolean expression in (vii) looks innocuous enough — it will be evaluated and will produce a result on every implementation. The trouble is, that we cannot predict what that result will be — it might be TRUE on some implementations and FALSE on others. The model interval for the expression 2*C will be the same as that for D. However, that is all we do know. We cannot assume that their representation will be the same. If it is the same, then TRUE would result, otherwise we will get FALSE. Hence our conclusion for (vii) is:

    (vii) TRUE or FALSE (effect undefined)

The second Boolean expression is a formulation to test whether or not the values of D and 2*C are no more than one model interval apart. Work through this and confirm that the model interval for $D - 2*C$ is bounded by $\pm 2^{**}(-6)$ and 0.0, and that the model interval for TWO_DITS'EPSILON*D is:

    2#0.1010_0110# $2^{**}(-5)$
    2#0.1010_0111# $2^{**}(-5)$

both extremes of which are *always* greater than the absolute value of the model interval for $D - 2*C$. Consequently, the Boolean result is always defined as:

(viii) TRUE

Be careful not to assume that this result will apply in different circumstances. If C had been derived by multiplication, for example, its model interval would have been wider — prove it!

    The next assignment is straightforward:

(ix) 2#0.1000_1000# $2^{**}3$

The multiplication of C by itself, although involving model numbers, results in a loss of accuracy, as the result requires more bits than the mantissa provides. Show that the model interval is

(x) 2#0.1001_0000# $2^{**}5$
    2#0.1001_0001# $2^{**}5$

The next statement, a call of PUT, is very interesting, because its result is implementation dependent. The model numbers are only used for predicting the behaviour of operations. However, this output request serves a useful purpose. We know from the calculation of the model interval for D, that only one bit of precision was lacking in the model number. We also know that some pre-defined type, probably with six decimal digits of precision, will be used for TWO_DITS values. Therefore, the exact value of D will be in the range of *safe* numbers. Consequently, we will have an output of:

(xi) 1.80625E+01

The remaining statements of the program provide no real challenge by way of model interval calculation — they are all model numbers. The interesting part is the evaluation of the expression in xiv) — in particular, the multiplication of B and C. There are no problems with precision here. However, the partial result goes outside the *range* of the *model* numbers. As long as the result is in the range of the *safe* numbers, all will be well.

    In general, NUMERIC_ERROR may only be raised, if a result is within the range of safe numbers. An implementation is not obliged to raise NUMERIC_ERROR, even if the range of safe numbers is violated; some machines do not facilitate the detection of overflow and, as we are about to discover, the hardware realization of real numbers may even be different from the set of safe numbers!

Physical representation of floating point numbers

In reality, there are three levels of representation of real numbers. The model numbers provide an implementation-independent set of numbers with the specified precision. As we have seen, this is derived from some pre-defined type, which may have greater accuracy and range, in which case the safe numbers will be a superset of the model numbers.

If the pre-defined type, FLOAT, is defined as having 6 decimal digits of precision, then the safe numbers for all (sub)types derived from it will have a 21 bit mantissa and an exponent range of ±84. Working out how many bits would be required for a FLOAT value, we need 1 for the sign of the mantissa, 21 for the mantissa itself, and 8 for the exponent, which gives a total of 30. It is almost certain that the hardware will have some 32 bit representation of floating point numbers — in other words there are two bits to spare! So, the actual hardware representation may use a 23 bit mantissa, and utilize the full exponent range possible with 8 bits, i.e. ±127. (You may find a 'bonus' bit for the mantissa in systems, which do not require the most significant bit to be explicitly stored — why bother, when it is always 1, except for 0.0?)

There is a set of machine-dependent attributes that reveals the nature of the underlying physical representation of a pre-defined floating point type. So, from the above discussion, we might find the following:

```
FLOAT'MACHINE_MANTISSA  =    24
FLOAT'MACHINE_EMAX      =   127
FLOAT'MACHINE_EMIN      = -127
```

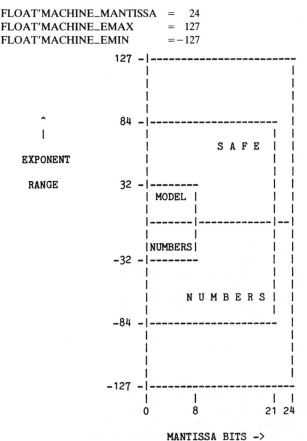

Fig. A.1 Floating point number representation.

Consequently, values may be representable, which are not safe numbers (they have greater precision), while others may be outside the range of safe numbers for the pre-defined type.

Figure A.1 summarizes the floating point hierarchy for TWO_DITS, FLOAT and the implementation assumed above.

Implementation of Fixed Point Types [LRM 3.5.9, 3.5.10]

The model numbers of fixed point types are determined by the value of the increment (referred to as SMALL) chosen by the implementation. Given the fixed point declaration:

> type MY_FIXED is delta D range LO..HI;

this is equivalent to:

> type ANON is new pre-defined fixed point type;
> subtype MY_FIXED is ANON range ANON(LO)..ANON(HI);

The pre-defined fixed point type from which MY_FIXED is derived, is selected such that its model numbers include the model numbers of MY_FIXED. These model numbers are determined from the specification parameters, D, LO and HI. The value of D, which specifies the required accuracy, is used to determine the corresponding (binary) value of SMALL, which is defined as the largest power of two that is not greater than D.

The form of all fixed point numbers, other than 0.0, is:

> ±1.0 * mantissa * SMALL

where the mantissa is a positive integer. The effect of the range constraint is to impose a limit on the size of the mantissa. For CONSTRAINT_ERROR purposes, the limit is taken to be the model number that is the limit itself, or a model number that is within that limit, but by a value no larger than SMALL. For example:

> type COARSE is delta 0.2 range 0.0..99.9;

will have model numbers with a SMALL of 0.0625, thus the mantissa will require 11 bits. The actual mantissa value for the largest model number that does not violate the range constraint, will be 1598, which corresponds to the model number 99.875. As with floating point types, the implementation may select the pre-defined type to represent a fixed point type. Consequently, fixed point types have a set of safe numbers, which include the model numbers.

The attributes of fixed point types are as listed below, where FXTS represents a fixed point type or subtype. All of them yield universal_real results, unless otherwise indicated.

> FXTS'DELTA
> yields the specified accuracy for (sub)type FXTS

> FXTS'MANTISSA
> yields the number of bits (universal_integer) in the mantissa for the model numbers of the (sub)type FXTS

> FXTS'SMALL
> yields the smallest positive non-zero value of the (sub)type — the difference between any two adjacent model numbers

> FXTS'LARGE
> yields the largest positive model number of FXTS

FXTS'FORE and FXTS'AFT yield universal_integer results, which represent, respectively: the number of characters required for the integer part of any value in FXTS (including a space for a positive number, or a minus sign for a negative one); the number of decimal digits in the fractional part required to represent the precision requested for FXTS.

In addition, FXTS'SAFE_SMALL and FXTS'SAFE_LARGE yield the corresponding SMALL and LARGE values of the safe numbers of the base type of FXTS.

In the type of environment in which fixed point numbers are frequently used, predictable and controlled behaviour is essential. An implementation is free to select the most appropriate pre-defined fixed point type to represent a user-defined type. The type used will obviously vary from implementation to implementation. In order to obtain the same *underlying* precision across all implementations, it is possible to use a *length clause* [LRM 13.2] to specify the actual value to be used, as in:

    for MY_FIXED'SMALL use 0.0625;

This specifies the value to be used, rather than leaving it to chance. The value specified after **use** must obviously not exceed the precision implied by the value specified after **delta** in the type definition.

The accuracy of operations on fixed point types can be understood by analogy with floating point operations. The relationship between model numbers and safe numbers is the same.

Appendix B

Predefined language environment

This annex outlines the specification of the package STANDARD containing all predefined identifiers in the language. The corresponding package body is implementation-defined and is not shown.

The operators that are predefined for the types declared in the package STANDARD are given in comments since they are implicitly declared. Italics are used for pseudo-names of anonymous types (such as *universal_real*) and for undefined information (such as *implementation_defined* and *any_fixed_point_type*).

package STANDARD **is**

    type BOOLEAN **is** (FALSE, TRUE);

    -- The predefined relational operators for this type are as follows:

```
--  function "="    (LEFT, RIGHT : BOOLEAN) return BOOLEAN;
--  function "/="   (LEFT, RIGHT : BOOLEAN) return BOOLEAN;
--  function "<"    (LEFT, RIGHT : BOOLEAN) return BOOLEAN;
--  function "<="   (LEFT, RIGHT : BOOLEAN) return BOOLEAN;
--  function ">"    (LEFT, RIGHT : BOOLEAN) return BOOLEAN;
--  function ">="   (LEFT, RIGHT : BOOLEAN) return BOOLEAN;
```

    -- The predefined logical operators and the predefined logical negation operator are as follows:

```
--  function "and"  (LEFT, RIGHT : BOOLEAN) return BOOLEAN;
--  function "or"   (LEFT, RIGHT : BOOLEAN) return BOOLEAN;
--  function "xor"  (LEFT, RIGHT : BOOLEAN) return BOOLEAN;

--  function "not"  (RIGHT : BOOLEAN) return BOOLEAN;
```

    -- The universal type *universal_integer* is predefined.

    type INTEGER **is** *implementation_defined*;

    -- The predefined operators for this type are as follows:

```
--  function "="    (LEFT, RIGHT : INTEGER) return BOOLEAN;
--  function "/="   (LEFT, RIGHT : INTEGER) return BOOLEAN;
--  function "<"    (LEFT, RIGHT : INTEGER) return BOOLEAN;
--  function "<="   (LEFT, RIGHT : INTEGER) return BOOLEAN;
--  function ">"    (LEFT, RIGHT : INTEGER) return BOOLEAN;
--  function ">="   (LEFT, RIGHT : INTEGER) return BOOLEAN;
--  function "+"    (RIGHT : INTEGER) return INTEGER;
--  function "-"    (RIGHT : INTEGER) return INTEGER;
--  function "abs"  (RIGHT : INTEGER) return INTEGER;

--  function "+"    (LEFT, RIGHT : INTEGER) return INTEGER;
--  function "-"    (LEFT, RIGHT : INTEGER) return INTEGER;
--  function "*"    (LEFT, RIGHT : INTEGER) return INTEGER;
--  function "/"    (LEFT, RIGHT : INTEGER) return INTEGER;
--  function "rem"  (LEFT, RIGHT : INTEGER) return INTEGER;
--  function "mod"  (LEFT, RIGHT : INTEGER) return INTEGER;

--  function "**"   (LEFT : INTEGER; RIGHT : INTEGER) return INTEGER;
```

310

-- An implementation may provide additional predefined integer types. It is recommended that the
-- names of such additional types end with INTEGER as in SHORT_INTEGER or LONG_INTEGER.
-- The specification of each operator for the type *universal_integer*, or for any additional
-- predefined integer type, is obtained by replacing INTEGER by the name of the type in the
-- specification of the corresponding operator of the type INTEGER, except for the right operand
-- of the exponentiating operator.

8

-- The universal type *universal_real* is predefined.

9

type FLOAT **is** *implementation_defined*;

-- The predefined operators for this type are as follows:

```
-- function "="   (LEFT, RIGHT : FLOAT) return BOOLEAN;
-- function "/="  (LEFT, RIGHT : FLOAT) return BOOLEAN;
-- function "<"   (LEFT, RIGHT : FLOAT) return BOOLEAN;
-- function "<="  (LEFT, RIGHT : FLOAT) return BOOLEAN;
-- function ">"   (LEFT, RIGHT : FLOAT) return BOOLEAN;
-- function ">="  (LEFT, RIGHT : FLOAT) return BOOLEAN;

-- function "+"   (RIGHT : FLOAT) return FLOAT;
-- function "-"   (RIGHT : FLOAT) return FLOAT;
-- function "abs" (RIGHT : FLOAT) return FLOAT;

-- function "+"   (LEFT, RIGHT : FLOAT) return FLOAT;
-- function "-"   (LEFT, RIGHT : FLOAT) return FLOAT;
-- function "*"   (LEFT, RIGHT : FLOAT) return FLOAT;
-- function "/"   (LEFT, RIGHT : FLOAT) return FLOAT;

-- function "**"  (LEFT : FLOAT; RIGHT : INTEGER) return FLOAT;
```

10

-- An implementation may provide additional predefined floating point types. It is recom-
-- mended that the names of such additional types end with FLOAT as in SHORT_FLOAT or
-- LONG_FLOAT. The specification of each operator for the type *universal_real*, or for any
-- additional predefined floating point type, is obtained by replacing FLOAT by the name of the
-- type in the specification of the corresponding operator of the type FLOAT.
-- In addition, the following operators are predefined for universal types:

11

```
-- function "*"  (LEFT : universal_integer;  RIGHT : universal_real)     return universal_real;
-- function "*"  (LEFT : universal_real;      RIGHT : universal_integer)  return universal_real;
-- function "/"  (LEFT : universal_real;      RIGHT : universal_integer)  return universal_real;
```

-- The type *universal_fixed* is predefined. The only operators declared for this type are

```
-- function "*"  (LEFT : any_fixed_point_type; RIGHT : any_fixed_point_type) return universal_fixed;
-- function "/"  (LEFT : any_fixed_point_type; RIGHT : any_fixed_point_type) return universal_fixed;
```

-- The following characters form the standard ASCII character set. Character literals cor-   12
-- responding to control characters are not identifiers; they are indicated in italics in this definition.

type CHARACTER **is**   13

(*nul*,	*soh*,	*stx*,	*etx*,	*eot*,	*enq*,	*ack*,	*bel*,
bs,	*ht*,	*lf*,	*vt*,	*ff*,	*cr*,	*so*,	*si*,
dle,	*dc1*,	*dc2*,	*dc3*,	*dc4*,	*nak*,	*syn*,	*etb*,
can,	*em*,	*sub*,	*esc*,	*fs*,	*gs*,	*rs*,	*us*,
' ',	'!',	'"',	'#',	'$',	'%',	'&',	''',
'(',	')',	'*',	'+',	',',	'-',	'.',	'/',
'0',	'1',	'2',	'3',	'4',	'5',	'6',	'7',
'8',	'9',	':',	';',	'<',	'=',	'>',	'?',
'@',	'A',	'B',	'C',	'D',	'E',	'F',	'G',
'H',	'I',	'J',	'K',	'L',	'M',	'N',	'O',

```
'P',   'Q',   'R',   'S',      'T',   'U',   'V',   'W',
'X',   'Y',   'Z',   '[',      '\',   ']',   '^',   '_',

'`',   'a',   'b',   'c',      'd',   'e',   'f',   'g',
'h',   'i',   'j',   'k',      'l',   'm',   'n',   'o',
'p',   'q',   'r',   's',      't',   'u',   'v',   'w',
'x',   'y',   'z',   '{',      '|',   '}',   '~',   del );
```

for CHARACTER **use**   --   128 ASCII character set without holes
     (0, 1, 2, 3, 4, 5, ..., 125, 126, 127);

-- The predefined operators for the type CHARACTER are the same as for any enumeration type. 14

15   **package** ASCII **is**

   —   Control characters:

```
NUL        : constant CHARACTER := nul;   SOH        : constant CHARACTER := soh;
STX        : constant CHARACTER := stx;   ETX        : constant CHARACTER := etx;
EOT        : constant CHARACTER := eot;   ENQ        : constant CHARACTER := enq;
ACK        : constant CHARACTER := ack;   BEL        : constant CHARACTER := bel;
BS         : constant CHARACTER := bs;    HT         : constant CHARACTER := ht;
LF         : constant CHARACTER := lf;    VT         : constant CHARACTER := vt;
FF         : constant CHARACTER := ff;    CR         : constant CHARACTER := cr;
SO         : constant CHARACTER := so;    SI         : constant CHARACTER := si;
DLE        : constant CHARACTER := dle;   DC1        : constant CHARACTER := dc1;
DC2        : constant CHARACTER := dc2;   DC3        : constant CHARACTER := dc3;
DC4        : constant CHARACTER := dc4;   NAK        : constant CHARACTER := nak;
SYN        : constant CHARACTER := syn;   ETB        : constant CHARACTER := etb;
CAN        : constant CHARACTER := can;   EM         : constant CHARACTER := em;
SUB        : constant CHARACTER := sub;   ESC        : constant CHARACTER := esc;
FS         : constant CHARACTER := fs;    GS         : constant CHARACTER := gs;
RS         : constant CHARACTER := rs;    US         : constant CHARACTER := us;
DEL        : constant CHARACTER := del;
```

   -- Other characters:

```
EXCLAM     : constant CHARACTER := '!';   QUOTATION  : constant CHARACTER := '"';
SHARP      : constant CHARACTER := '#';   DOLLAR     : constant CHARACTER := '$';
PERCENT    : constant CHARACTER := '%';   AMPERSAND  : constant CHARACTER := '&';
COLON      : constant CHARACTER := ':';   SEMICOLON  : constant CHARACTER := ';';
QUERY      : constant CHARACTER := '?';   AT_SIGN    : constant CHARACTER := '@';
L_BRACKET  : constant CHARACTER := '[';   BACK_SLASH : constant CHARACTER := '\';
R_BRACKET  : constant CHARACTER := ']';   CIRCUMFLEX : constant CHARACTER := '^';
UNDERLINE  : constant CHARACTER := '_';   GRAVE      : constant CHARACTER := '`';
L_BRACE    : constant CHARACTER := '{';   BAR        : constant CHARACTER := '|';
R_BRACE    : constant CHARACTER := '}';   TILDE      : constant CHARACTER := '~';
```

   -- Lower case letters:

```
LC_A : constant CHARACTER := 'a';
...
LC_Z : constant CHARACTER := 'z';
```

end ASCII;

16   -- Predefined subtypes:

```
subtype NATURAL  is INTEGER range 0 .. INTEGER'LAST;
subtype POSITIVE is INTEGER range 1 .. INTEGER'LAST;
```

   -- Predefined string type: 17

```
type STRING is array(POSITIVE range <>) of CHARACTER;

pragma PACK(STRING);
```

-- The predefined operators for this type are as follows: 18

```
-- function "="   (LEFT, RIGHT : STRING) return BOOLEAN;
-- function "/="  (LEFT, RIGHT : STRING) return BOOLEAN;
-- function "<"   (LEFT, RIGHT : STRING) return BOOLEAN;
-- function "<="  (LEFT, RIGHT : STRING) return BOOLEAN;
-- function ">"   (LEFT, RIGHT : STRING) return BOOLEAN;
-- function ">="  (LEFT, RIGHT : STRING) return BOOLEAN;
```

```
-- function "&" (LEFT : STRING;     RIGHT : STRING)    return STRING;
-- function "&" (LEFT : CHARACTER;  RIGHT : STRING)    return STRING;
-- function "&" (LEFT : STRING;     RIGHT : CHARACTER) return STRING;
-- function "&" (LEFT : CHARACTER;  RIGHT : CHARACTER) return STRING;
```

type DURATION **is delta** *implementation_defined* **range** *implementation_defined*;   19

-- The predefined operators for the type DURATION are the same as for any fixed point type.

-- The predefined exceptions: 20

```
CONSTRAINT_ERROR  : exception;
NUMERIC_ERROR     : exception;
PROGRAM_ERROR     : exception;
STORAGE_ERROR     : exception;
TASKING_ERROR     : exception;
```

end STANDARD;

Certain aspects of the predefined entities cannot be completely described in the language itself.   21
For example, although the enumeration type BOOLEAN can be written showing the two
enumeration literals FALSE and TRUE, the short-circuit control forms cannot be expressed in the
language.

Note:

The language definition predefines the following library units: 22

- The package CALENDAR	(see 9.6)
- The package SYSTEM	(see 13.7)
- The package MACHINE_CODE (if provided)	(see 13.8)
- The generic procedure UNCHECKED_DEALLOCATION	(see 13.10.1)
- The generic function UNCHECKED_CONVERSION	(see 13.10.2)
- The generic package SEQUENTIAL_IO	(see 14.2.3)
- The generic package DIRECT_IO	(see 14.2.5)
- The package TEXT_IO	(see 14.3.10)
- The package IO_EXCEPTIONS	(see 14.5)
- The package LOW_LEVEL_IO	(see 14.6)

References

1 Burns, A. (1985) *Concurrent Programming in Ada*, Cambridge University Press, Cambridge, UK.
2 Downes, V.A. and Goldsack, S.J. (1982) *Programming Embedded Systems with Ada*, Prentice-Hall, New York, USA.
3 Hoare, C.A.R. (1981) The Emperor's Old Clothes, *Communications of the ACM*, **24** (2), 75–83.
4 Ichbiah, J.D. *et al.* (1983) *Reference Manual for the Ada Programming Language*, ANSI/ MIL-STD-1815A-1983, US Department of Defense. Published, with permission, by various publishers. Also available in: Rogers, M.W. (1984) *Ada: Language, Compilers and Bibliography*, Cambridge University Press, Cambridge, UK.
5 Lieblein, E. (1986) The Department of Defense Software Initiative — a status report, *Communications of the ACM*, **29** (8), 734–44.
6 Nissen, J. and Wallis, P. (1984) *Portability and Style in Ada*, Cambridge University Press, Cambridge, UK.
7 Sammet, J.E. (1986) Why Ada is not Just Another Programming Language, *Communications of the ACM*, **29** (8), 722–32.
8 Woodger, M. (1987) Origins of Ada Features, *Ada Letters (SIGAda)*, **VII** (1), 59–70.
9 Various publications of INMOS Ltd, PO Box 424, Bristol, BS99 7DD (or INMOS Corporation, PO Box 16000, Colorado Springs, CO 80935, USA).

314

Useful addresses

Ada UK, H Byard, Computer Science Department, University of York, Heslington, York, Y01 5DD.

SIGAda, Association for Computing Machinery, 11 West 42nd Street, New York, NY 10036, USA.

Ada Information Clearinghouse, 3D139 (Fern ST., C-107), The Pentagon, Washington DC, 20301-3081, USA.

Index

317